1900-1945

A CRITICAL HISTORY

TWAYNE'S CRITICAL HISTORY
OF THE SHORT STORY

William Peden, General Editor
University of Missouri-Columbia

The American Short Story, 1850—1900
Donald Crowley, University of Missouri-Columbia

The American Short Story, 1900—1945
Philip Stevick, Temple University

The American Short Story, 1945—1980
Gordon Weaver, Oklahoma State University

The British Short Story, 1890—1945
Joseph M. Flora, University of North Carolina-Chapel Hill

The British Short Story, 1945—1980
Dennis Vannatta, University of Arkansas-Little Rock

The Irish Short Story
James Kilroy, Vanderbilt University

The Latin American Short Story
Margaret Sayers Peden, University of Missouri-Columbia

THE
AMERICAN
Short Story

1900 - 1945

A CRITICAL HISTORY

Philip Stevick, Editor
Temple University

Twayne Publishers

The American Short Story
1900–1945:
A Critical History

Published in 1984 by Twayne Publishers
A Division of G. K. Hall & Company
70 Lincoln Street, Boston, Massachusetts 02111

Printed on permanent/durable
acid-free paper and bound in
the United States of America

First Printing

Book production by Marne Sultz
Book design by Barbara Anderson

Typeset in 11 pt. Perpetua
by Compset, Inc. of Beverly, MA

Library of Congress Cataloging in Publication Data

Main entry under title:

The American short story, 1900–1945
(Twayne's critical history of the short story)
Includes bibliographies and index.
1. Short stories, American—History and criticism.
2. American fiction—20th century—History and criticism.
I. Stevick, Philip. II. Series.
PS374.S5A366   1984   813'.01'09   84-641
ISBN 0-8057-9353-4
ISBN 0-8057-9356-9 (pbk)

Contents

Chronology

The numbers in parentheses indicate (1) The Short Story; (2) Other Literary Forms; (3) The General Culture.

1900 (1) Twain: *The Man That Corrupted Hadleyburg and Other Stories;* London: *The Son of the Wolf: Tales of the Far North.* Death of Crane.
(2) Dreiser: *Sister Carrie;* Baum: *The Wonderful Wizard of Oz.*

1901 (1) Wharton: *Crucial Instances.*
(2) Norris: *The Octopus.*
(3) Assassination of McKinley; Theodore Roosevelt's inauguration; first transoceanic wireless message by Marconi.

1902 (2) Henry James: *The Wings of the Dove;* William James: *The Varieties of Religious Experience;* Wister: *The Virginian.*

1903 (1) James: *The Better Sort* (includes "The Beast in the Jungle").
(2) Norris: *The Pit;* James: *The Ambassadors;* London: *The Call of the Wild.*
(3) The Wright Brothers make the first manned, sustained flight.

1904 (1) Wharton: *The Descent of Man and Other Stories.*
(2) James: *The Golden Bowl;* Harris: *Tales by Uncle Remus.*

1905 (1) Cather: *The Troll Garden* (includes "Paul's Case").
(2) Sinclair: *The Jungle.*
(3) Einstein first proposes a revision of classical physics.

1906 (1) O. Henry: *The Four Million* (includes "The Gift of the Magi").
(3) The San Francisco earthquake and fire.

1907 (2) Adams: *The Education of Henry Adams.*

1908 (3) The Model T introduced by Henry Ford.

1909 (2) Stein: *Three Lives.*
(3) Peary reaches North Pole.

1910 (1) James: *The Finer Grain* (includes "The Bench of Desolation"). London: *Lost Face* (includes "To Build a Fire"). Death of Twain.

1911 (2) Wharton: *Ethan Frome*

1912 (3) The sinking of the Titanic.

1913 (3) Brill's translations of Freud begin to appear; the Armory show introduces cubism, futurism, and expressionism to the American public.

1914 (2) Frost: *North of Boston.*
(3) Outbreak of war in Europe; completion of the Panama Canal.

1915 (2) Masters: *A Spoon River Anthology.*

1916 (1) Wharton: *Xingu and Other Stories.* Death of James.

1917 (1) Lardner: *Gullible's Travels.*
(3) The Russian Revolution begins.

1918 (1) Dreiser: *Free and Other Stories.*
(3) Armistice in France.

1919 (1) Anderson: *Winesburg, Ohio.*
(2) Reed: *Ten Days That Shook the World.*

1920 (1) Fitzgerald: *Flappers and Philosophers.* Death of Howells.
(2) Pound: *Hugh Selwyn Mauberley;* Lewis: *Main Street.*
(3) First commercial radio station established in Pittsburgh.

1921 (1) Anderson: *The Triumph of the Egg* (includes "I Want to Know Why").

1922 (1) Fitzgerald: *Tales of the Jazz Age.*

1923 (1) Toomer: *Cane;* Glasgow: *The Shadowy Third and Other Stories.*
(2) Stevens: *Harmonium.*

1924 (1) Lardner: *How to Write Stories* (includes "Some Like Them Cold").
(2) Melville's *Billy Budd* is discovered and published, leading to a Melville revival; O'Neill: *Desire Under the Elms.*

1925 (1) Hemingway: *In Our Time* (includes "Big Two-Hearted River").

(2) Fitzgerald: *The Great Gatsby;* Dreiser: *An American Tragedy;* Pound: *The Cantos.*

1926 (1) Fitzgerald: *All the Sad Young Men* (includes "Winter Dreams"); Lardner: *The Love Nest and Other Stories* (includes "Haircut"); Suckow: *Iowa Interiors.*

(2) Hemingway: *The Sun Also Rises.*

(3) Book-of-the-Month Club founded.

1927 (1) Hemingway: *Men without Women* (includes "The Killers," "In Another Country," "Hills Like White Elephants"); Steele: *The Man Who Saw through Heaven and Other Stories.*

(3) Execution of Sacco and Vanzetti; Lindbergh's flight; *The Jazz Singer,* the first full-length talking picture.

1928 (1) Wescott: *Goodbye, Wisconsin.*

(2) O'Neill: *Strange Interlude.*

1929 (2) Wolfe: *Look Homeward, Angel;* Faulkner: *The Sound and the Fury;* Hemingway: *A Farewell to Arms.*

(3) The Great Depression begins with the collapse of the New York stock market.

1930 (1) Boyle: *Wedding Day and Other Stories.*

(2) Faulkner: *As I Lay Dying;* Hammett: *The Maltese Falcon.*

1931 (1) Faulkner: *These Thirteen* (includes "A Rose for Emily," "That Evening Sun," "Dry September").

(2) O'Neill: *Mourning Becomes Electra.*

(3) The Empire State Building opens.

1932 (1) Cather: *Obscure Destinies* (includes "Neighbor Rossicky").

(2) Eliot: *The Waste Land;* Faulkner: *Light in August;* Caldwell: *Tobacco Road.*

1933 (1) Anderson: *Death in the Woods and Other Stories;* Hemingway: *Winner Take Nothing* (includes "A Clean, Well-Lighted Place"); William March: *Company K.*

(2) Stein: *The Autobiography of Alice B. Toklas;* West: *Miss Lonelyhearts,* Joyce's *Ulysses* first published in the United States.

(3) Prohibition repealed; Franklin Roosevelt inaugurated.

1934 (1) Faulkner: *Doctor Martino;* Farrell: *Calico Shoes;* Aiken: *Among the Lost People* (includes "Mr. Arcularis"); Saroyan: *The Daring Young Man on the Flying Trapeze;* Hughes: *The Ways of White Folks.*

      (2) Fitzgerald: *Tender is the Night;* Miller: *Tropic of Cancer* (published in France); O'Hara: *Appointment in Samara;* Farrell: *The Young Manhood of Studs Lonigan.*

1935 (1) Caldwell: *Kneel to the Rising Sun;* Porter: *Flowering Judas and Other Stores* (includes, besides the title story, "The Jilting of Granny Weatherall"); O'Hara: *The Doctor's Son and Other Stories;* Wolfe: *From Death to Morning* (includes "Only the Dead Know Brooklyn"); Sinclair Lewis: *Selected Short Stories;* Fitzgerald: *Taps at Reveille* (includes "Babylon Revisited").

      (3) The Gershwins' *Porgy and Bess.*

1936 (1) Wharton: *The World Over* (includes "Roman Fever").

      (2) Mitchell: *Gone with the Wind.*

      (3) Chaplin: *Modern Times.*

1937 (2) Eliot: *Collected Poems;* Stevens: *The Man with the Blue Guitar.*

1938 (1) Steinbeck: *The Long Valley* (includes "The Chrysanthemums," "The Snake"); Wright: *Uncle Tom's Children;* Faulkner: *The Unvanquished;* Hemingway: *The Fifth Column and the First Forty-Nine Stories* (includes "The Short, Happy Life of Francis Macomber," "The Snows of Kilimanjaro").

      (2) Dos Passos: *The 42nd Parallel;* Wilder: *Our Town.*

      (3) Walt Disney's *Snow White.*

1939 (1) Porter: *Pale Horse, Pale Rider;* Parker: *Here Lies: The Collected Stories* (includes "Big Blonde").

      (2) Steinbeck: The Grapes of Wrath; Hellman: *The Little Foxes.*

      (3) War begins in Europe.

1940 (1) Death of Fitzgerald.

      (2) Hemingway: *For Whom the Bell Tolls;* McCullers: *The Heart Is a Lonely Hunter;* Wright: *Native Son.*

1941 (1) Welty: *A Curtain of Green and Other Stories* (includes "A Worn Path"); Wolfe: *The Hills Beyond.* Death of Anderson.

      (3) Japanese attack on Pearl Harbor; American entry into the war.

1942 (1) Faulkner: *Go Down, Moses* (includes "Delta Autumn," "The Bear"). Thurber: *My Life and Welcome to It* (includes "The Secret Life of Walter Mitty").

1943 (1) Cheever: *The Way Some People Live;* Brooks and Warren's *Understanding Fiction* profoundly alters the teaching and reading of the short story; Hammett: *The Adventures of Sam Spade and Other Stories.*
  (2) Eliot: *Four Quartets.*

1944 (1) Porter: *The Leaning Tower and Other Stories* (includes, besides the title story, "The Downward Path to Wisdom"); Raymond Chandler: *Five Murderers.*
  (2) Bellow: *Dangling Man.*
  (3) Allied invasion of Europe.

1945 (3) Death of Roosevelt; atomic bomb exploded over Hiroshima and Nagasaki; the war ends.

Introduction

If we take the measure of works of enduring value published within a few years of 1900—Crane's "The Open Boat" (1897), James's "The Beast in the Jungle" (1903), Dreiser's *Sister Carrie* (1900), or Veblen's *The Theory of the Leisure Class* (1899)—it can be seen that they display qualities of irony and wit, toughness of mind, and a curiously intricate, energetic, and highly individual style that make them seem very much of our time. The nature of the lived experience that such works reflect we fully understand. We respond to Carrie's desires and constraints without much sense of historical strain. Veblen's "conspicuous consumption" is no less central now than when he wrote the phrase. And we are all contemporaries of the unlucky occupants of Crane's absurd boat and James's John Marcher, master of the unlived life. It is our literature, more than anything else, that establishes our common humanity with those who were alive in 1900.

It is necessary, however, to reflect on the enormous gulf between our time and that one. At the risk of banality, it is useful to begin not with the death of Queen Victoria abroad and the presidency of McKinley at home but with the data of our dailiness. In 1900, there were 144 miles of paved roads in the United States. The average age at death was forty-seven. One home in seven had a bathtub, far fewer had showers. The population was three-fifths rural. The hamburger, the safety razor, the vacuum cleaner, and the brassiere were about to be invented: none existed in 1900. That year, Eastman Kodak introduced the Brownie box camera, which sold for one dollar. Other staples of our national culture were far in the future: commercial radio, for example, was two decades away. Although New York was a massive city of 3.5 million, one reflects on its skyline. What would be the country's tallest building, the legendary Flatiron Building, completed in 1902, was all of twenty stories high. If our literature links us easily with the turn of the century, the raw facts tell us, on the contrary, that 1900 was a long time ago.

It is touching, in retrospect, to recall that the new century was celebrated twice: on New Year's Eve of 1899 and on New Year's Eve of 1900. At our

1

distance, the expectations of those celebrations can be seen to have been unfulfilled. Conventional histories of the first fifteen years of the century, to be sure, are filled with issues and events: tariff legislation, tentative efforts to restrict child labor, the beginnings of a massive federal involvement in con- servation, the creation of the Panama Canal. Yet those events, recorded by the historians, altered very little the perception of the culture by those who lived then. Everyone is affected by tariff legislation; but the effect is gradual and diffuse and the perception of the effect depends upon an expertise pos- sessed by few. Anyone might have felt a flush of pride at the accomplishment of the building of the Panama Canal, but its effect upon the general culture was minimal.

In fact, a sensitive observer in the early twentieth century might well have recorded a perception that the rich were very rich, the poor very poor, and the gap between them immense, and widening—which was perfectly ob- vious in the last quarter of the nineteenth century. A sensitive observer then would have recorded the perception that the open spaces of the continent were appealing, challenging, and intimidating—which was perfectly obvious in the last quarter of the nineteenth century. And he would have noted that the United States, never the melting pot of popular conception, was filled with the nuances and tensions of different regions and different national origins—which is what the most enterprising writers of the late nineteenth century had been saying all along. In short, the years before the war express a continuation of both the social order and the cultural conventions of the late nineteenth century, with a minimum of discernible change and a maxi- mum of complacency.

There are writers who opted out of that culture altogether, choosing an aestheticism and a preciosity that has long since worn thin. The best writers of that period are aliens and survivors, Edith Wharton and Willa Cather, for example, James in late career, late Twain, Dreiser, Henry Adams, all of them in some way marginal figures in that complacent culture, central figures in the life of the imagination. A now-forgotten man of letters, Burton Rascoe, speaks melodramatically but effectively of that period of gentility and conti- nuity, punctuated by a handful of writers so penetrating that we read them now. "There were two things for an artist in America to do in those days," he writes, "—stay drunk or commit suicide."

The war, of course, changed everything. "Never such innocence again," writes Paul Fussell in his magisterial *The Great War and Modern Memory*, quot- ing a line from the poet Philip Larkin, whose speaker is contemplating a photograph of sweet, smiling, patient faces lined up outside a British recruit- ing station. Fussell records the illusion with which the war was begun, at least in Great Britain, the sense that it was being fought in a world in which the abstractions—honor and glory—were stable and real. The reaction to that war is one of the great changes in Western consciousness. And it all took not a century, as with the Renaissance or the Enlightenment, but five appalling years.

The reaction in the United States seems muted by comparison to that in Great Britain: American involvement, of course, was briefer, the casualties less overwhelming, and the action far away. Yet the changes were immense all the same. Fussell notes the beginnings of binary consciousness, splitting the world into "us" and "them," which he sees as deriving from the war. It is a habit of thought that runs through all the years since, both in Great Britain and the United States: there is high art and low, the literate and the philistines, and rarely does a serious writer function without a sense of cultural allies and cultural enemies. There are, of course, the great myths and images that undergird Western literature since 1918, images of darkness and the abyss, apocalypse, the waste land, and the valley of ashes. There is a much crueler sense of irony than anyone, excepting Hardy, was prepared to imagine in the years before the war, in which the nature of the world meets noble intentions head-on and leaves them not only defeated but debased and dehumanized. And finally, there is an altered sense of language. The gentilities, euphemisms, and abstractions of the years before the war were now dead, drained of their capacity to mean; and the language of the imagination was obliged to begin afresh, with the data of experience and the irreducible materials of plain and honest English. Hemingway reflects such an altered sensibility most acutely, but others of the postwar period, from Sherwood Anderson to Dorothy Parker, even when they record nothing of the direct experience of the war, demonstrate nonetheless the altered consciousness that was its result.

The twenties presents an unusual contrast: the election of Harding, the return to "normalcy," a bland and incompetent period in our federal administration, coupled with a frightening repression of the radical, the unpopular, and the minority: the Red Scare, the savage resistance to a variety of strikes, the notorious tenure of Attorney General Palmer, and the rise of a particularly virulent bigotry. The official ethics of the decade were unabashedly derived from business. It seems now that it might well have been a time for a holding action among the best writers of the time. Yet it was a brilliant period, one of two successive decades more virtuose and accomplished than any time we have seen before or are likely to see again. And the reason is that the twenties produced not only that historical mystery, a remarkable confluence of talent, but a general, popular culture antithetical to the official culture of Harding, and fiction managed to nourish itself from the energies of that nonofficial culture.

The mood after the war adjusted to the condition of those who had fought it. Americans who had been in the trenches had little use for the manners and morals of the period before the war. The constant prospect of risk and death left no possibility for pleasure in the bland ideals the war had killed. Women, having won the suffrage, began to liberate themselves from the house and to enter occupations unthinkable a few years before. The automobile presented a constant possibility for escape, in an enclosed space, to another arena a few miles down the road. The movies, in those days, seeking to pander to the general taste, in fact transformed taste, evoking a world of sensuous pleasure. And the vulgarization of Freud suggested that the most fully lived life was one lived in response to the libido, not to the heavy and arbitrary demands of the superego.

The new decade would have seemed to present an explosion of potential subject matter: the agony of the war and the difficulties of returning; the incredibly altered meaning of the eternal verities—love, marriage, and home, faith, hope, and charity; the altered styles of high prosperity and middle-class respectability, new styles, too, of poverty and minority oppression; and a multitude of new occupations and stations in life. But it is not so much a revolution in subject matter that the short fiction of the twenties represents, although there is no lack of new subject matter. It is rather a revolution in form.

Time, sequence, cause and effect, motive and act, intention and consequence, the relation of individual to culture and individual to myth—all these seemed different after the war. Take simply that ancient mythic pattern of the rite of passage, which has so often been adaptable to the purposes of short fiction. With the vivid recollection of men not yet twenty dying in the mud of France, no one could imagine that the achievement of maturity and the structure by means of which one arrived there could be presented as it had been before the war. And so the energy of the twenties, as it became available to writers of short fiction, was not simply the release from inhibition celebrated in the popular image of that roaring decade. The energy came from the imperatives the general culture impressed upon writers—that the very form of experience was altered and must be rediscovered by the imagination.

What we have learned to call the epiphany, extending Joyce's original use of the word to a moment of self-awareness at the end of a fiction, comes to seem especially characteristic of fiction in the twenties and consistently after.

It is myopic, of course, to think of the moment of awareness as exclusively modern. When Hawthorne's Robin Molineux laughs, at the end of "My Kinsman, Major Molineux," he understands—what, we are not sure, but the moment is clearly epiphanic. Any number of James's fictions present moments of self-insight that seem continuous with the tradition after the twenties. Still, the epiphany does seem particularly modern, which means, in the present context, post–World War I. It seems so because earlier stories "contain" an epiphany as the climax to a series of overt actions, whereas American stories after the war, often presenting themselves as "plotless," sketches in the manner of Chekhov or Joyce, offer an epiphany as the only justification for the story, its single, low-keyed climax, as in Hemingway's "The Three-Day Blow."

The epiphany is an imaginative response to a loss of religious faith, a secularization of religion, a representation of what would seem to be a moment of mystical transcendence, as, on the contrary, a moment of quite earthbound self-knowledge. Moreover, it is a moment that represents a loss of faith in reason. It is axiomatic that no orderly thought process carries a character to an epiphanic moment; that moment transcends reason altogether. The technique of the epiphany had been in the air for at least a decade before the war was over, from the example of translated Chekhov, early Joyce, early Lawrence, Virginia Woolf. But it took the temper of the postwar period for it to establish itself in American fiction, a period notably deficient in religious faith and a trust in reason, notably congenial to the climactic moment and intuitive transcendence, to a technique that would convert the monstrous world of action into moments of self-awareness.

As with the epiphany, certain formal alterations in the art of the story— the representation of time, the management of transition, and the movement to climax—take their special character from the nature of the postwar period and do not substantially change for forty years. What does change, as the decade ends, is the general culture. American life, at the end of the twenties, absorbs a trauma greater than that of the war, greater because it is more immediate and more widely shared. And that is, of course, the Great Depression. The despair following the war was universal: one altered one's sense of language, human possibilities, and Western ideals. The despair following the crash was local: one altered one's sense of how to get through the day. A hundred voices could testify to that quality of experience. William Saroyan will suffice. In the early thirties, he had made a reputation with tales of the raffish and buoyant life of his Armenian minority in Fresno in the years before. By 1936, he wrote this:

Less tangible, less visible, but not less important, has been the change in sentiment which has developed during the recent years of misery. Hardly anybody is out to make a killing one way or another. Hardly anybody dreams of becoming the owner of an apartment building, a country home, and three expensive automobiles. Hardly anybody is interested in anything much. Hardly anybody *is* at all.[1]

Why we have come to see our history marked off in decades, even now, is a curious question, worth a thoughtful essay in itself. History does not move by ten-year leaps and cluster itself so that decades have a discrete identity. Yet the movement into the twenties, and subsequently into the thirties, *is* one of leaps; and the decades that begin in 1920 and 1930 *do* have a remarkable internal coherence. It is a phenomenon that establishes the pattern we all know, as we talk easily about the fifties and the sixties: that history does seem to cluster itself by decade.

As with the base point with which we began, 1900, it is easy to distance the 1930s. In the imagination, the Great Depression exists in grainy photographs of bread lines, soup kitchens, protest signs, and apple vendors. But again, to assemble a handful of data, the early thirties are not so far away, at least if we measure the details of our dailiness. These things appeared in 1930: the first airline stewardess, the electric phonograph, the electric shaver, the first supermarket, frozen vegetables, and sliced bread. In 1930, Mickey Mouse was two years old.

Curiously, the criticism of that time often registered dismay at the alarming decline in fiction of quality. To us, reading the short fiction of the thirties now, it seems an odd judgment, the thirties being as rich in stories of the first rank as the decade before. It is a judgment that comes, no doubt, from the insufficient recognition of Faulkner in his own time and from the general malaise that was a natural consequence of economic depression. Besides Faulkner, the decade includes some of the best of middle Hemingway, the best of Katherine Anne Porter, early Richard Wright, early Steinbeck, early Caroline Gordon, early Robert Penn Warren.

Frank O'Connor, in *The Lonely Voice,* has characterized the short story by its interest in "a submerged population group." It is a provocative view of the short story that nonetheless applies rather badly, at least unevenly, to classic American stories of the nineteenth century or, for that matter, to the tradition of short fiction as it extends into the twenties. There is no lack of marginality and alienation in Hawthorne's and Poe's stories; yet they hardly center themselves on a "submerged population group." By the thirties, however, the general sense of powerlessness in the face of economic collapse created a kinship, precisely, with submerged population groups. Faulkner settled into the cultivation of an obscure corner of a backward state. And Caldwell's sharecroppers, Farrell's Chicago poor, Steinbeck's various marginal Californians, Wright's southern blacks all fulfill O'Connor's observation; for in the thirties, a remarkable amount of short fiction does focus on alienated groups, not only for their own human drama, but for the capacity of those groups and their elemental struggles to take on an emblematic meaning in the general world of the thirties.

Technically, the short fiction of the thirties hardly excelled the artistic seriousness and the craft of the best of the twenties. It extended certain possibilities—of symbolic compression, the manipulation of point of view, the arrangement of time. What the thirties added was a range of voices, some of which had never been heard in short fiction. The voices of the disinherited in thirties fiction are very far from the regional dialects of turn of the century local color. And Faulkner's involuted interiority, quite far from building upon Hemingway's stylistic austerity, established a polar opposite, so striking that it has influenced, in its way, as many subsequent writers as Hemingway did in his.

One dates easily the ends of the earlier decades: the Armistice and the great crash. The thirties end with the coming of World War II. But it is not so easy to say when the war begins in the American imagination. Surely some time far short of the attack on Pearl Harbor in 1941, it seemed that the domestic crisis had at last leveled out and that the escalating crisis in Europe had become the center of American concern. Yet in those years from the late thirties to the end of the war, American short fiction reflected the new decade only slightly. In due course, the experience of the war would alter the American sensibility almost as profoundly as the experience of World War I. But that feeling of having looked again into the abyss would have to wait until the revelations of Auschwitz and Buchenwald and the knowledge of the bomb.

Excepting perhaps the years of the American Revolution and the establishment of the Republic, no other period has been more filled with events and transformations. The Civil War was the great crisis of the American nineteenth century. Yet neither period transformed our collective inner life and the texture of our surroundings so profoundly as the years from the beginning of World War I to the end of the second. Responding, in that period, both to the transformations of the culture and to its own currents of energy and development, short fiction moves from a largely stereotypical craft, genteel and predictable in the hands of all but a few, to an art form that can stand with the finest examples of modern fiction.

• • •

In the nineteenth century, American stories appeared in an amazing variety of periodicals, many of them limited in their circulations, parochial in their interests, and regional in their appeal. By the early years of the twentieth century, the diverse and amorphous group of magazines that had published Hawthorne, Poe, and a legion of lesser writers of "tales" and "sketches" had largely disappeared, leaving the three-part structure that we know now: the mass circulation magazines such as the *Saturday Evening Post, Everybody's Magazine, Red Book, Blue Book, Popular Magazine,* and *Collier's;* the little magazines, including *Partisan Review* and *Transatlantic Review* and others with names like *Gently, Brother,* and *Gyroscope,* deliberately minuscule in their circulation, yet with an informed and passionate purpose; and the literate, middle-range magazines, including the *Century,* which was to die, and *Harper's,* which was to live, comparatively small in circulation but large in influence.

The mass magazines are the easiest to dispense with although they are in some ways the most problematic. The phenomenon, in any case, is a new one—the instantly recognizable magazine with a massive national circulation. A publisher before the end of the nineteenth century would have been proud of a circulation of between 100,000 and 200,000. But by 1900, *Ladies Home Journal* had approached a circulation of 1 million. The price of the new magazines was remarkably low by nineteenth-century standards—five or ten cents. And the editorial policies had become attuned to an audience that was, if not "mass," at least national and very large. It is, above all, the *Saturday Evening Post* that best exemplifies the new magazine.

Its editorial policy was oriented toward business and the ethics of success, its politics conservative. And a cultural observer now, reflecting on the limitations of the *Post,* is entitled to condescension. Yet, in its prime, it published, to name only the best of them, Faulkner, Hemingway, and Fitzgerald. The case is clearly not closed. In fact, the *Saturday Evening Post* cultivated a breadth of taste in its readers rather wider than may seem in retrospect. It published nearly seventy stories by Fitzgerald, and although some of them represent Fitzgerald at his most facile, some of them are among his best, "Babylon Revisited," for example. And surprisingly, it published Faulkner. Even more surprising, there was a demonstrable audience for Faulkner, and devotees would write to the *Post,* inquiring why it had been so long since the last Faulkner story had appeared. Yet there was a price to be paid. Joseph Blotner, in his life of Faulkner, records episodes in which Faulkner revised a rejected story, modifying the baroque intricacies of his prose and muting his idiosyncratic voice. It seems clear that, like Faulkner, the best writers of the period sometimes wrote down, either by crafting deliberately direct and nonproblematic stories for the mass market or by revising so as to meet the demands of that clientele.

The middle range of magazines offered a consistent outlet for established writers of quality. And there is scarcely a writer of enduring reputation who did not, sooner or later, appear in the pages of *Forum* or the *Atlantic*. Responsive, largely, to established reputations and a fairly conventional range of techniques, they provided, all the same, an earnest, literate audience. Yet, as with the mass magazines, the whole is more complex than the dominant trend. Faulkner's "A Rose for Emily" was first published in *Forum* when Faulkner was unknown, and neither its technique nor its subject matter could have seemed altogether comfortable to the readers of that magazine. It is the periodicals on the fringe of that middle range that actually did seek to alter taste and sometimes did. Mencken's *Mercury,* in the late twenties, offered a crusty, iconoclastic context for fiction. And writers such as Dreiser, Sinclair Lewis, and Fitzgerald could be sure that, no matter how savage their view of American institutions, Mencken and his readers would listen. The *New Yorker,* begun in 1925, took several years to find its own voice. But when it did, it was an Eastern, metropolitan voice, ironic and sophisticated, with no concessions, as its editor Harold Ross put it in his legendary statement of purpose, to "the little old lady from Dubuque." Ultimately it provided a home for a brilliant body of short fiction, knowing, arch, indirect, and very well written, a body of fiction that few large-circulation magazines would have touched and one that has profoundly altered our sense of what a story can do.

The little magazines, finally, provided an outlet of extraordinary virtuosity. The first two decades were not a fertile ground for them. But from 1920 through the rest of the period, the impulse was irresistible to make a manifesto, at least to stake out a territory implicitly, to assume an adversary stance toward the official culture, to gather the work of one's friends and others who liked their company, to find a press that would print cheaply, and to seek a small circulation that would actually *read* the work that was printed, and *care.* The result of that impulse is a body of small-press publications extraordinary in its breadth—magazines some of which lasted a year, some for an issue, some of which survived long enough to publish the best and contribute to the transformation of the art of the story, some of which exist now as vital forces in the life of our culture.

No one would make extravagant claims for the whole of the work published in the little magazines. A fair amount of it was fatuous and self-congratulatory, or sophomoric, or simply third rate and forgettable. But a remarkable amount was none of these. To begin with the more easily forgotten little magazines, *Broom,* which ran for less than two and a half years, was published in the early twenties in Rome, Berlin, and New York. At its best, it could never have reached more than a few hundred readers. Yet it published criticism by Conrad Aiken and Jean Toomer, short fiction by Sherwood Anderson and James Stephens. *The Double Dealer,* published for three and a half years in New Orleans, was as uneven as *Broom,* yet it published short fiction by Faulkner, Carl Van Vechten, and Thornton Wilder. *Hound and Horn,* beginning exclusively with material having "a general Harvard interest," moved to New York, found a new editor, and published fiction by Katherine Anne Porter, Kay Boyle, and Erskine Caldwell. And *Story,* first published in 1931 and continued serially through 1948, devoted itself, with passion and intelligence, to the publication of short narrative without restrictions upon technique or size, ultimately publishing nearly every figure of consequence in the period.

Few writers of short stories have ever been content with the marketplace. It was very hard in the first half of the century, as it is now, to publish, in book form, a collection of short fiction for which an audience had not been already created by a reputation made in the periodicals. And the periodicals presented compromises at every hand. For writers of the first half of the century, the mass magazines paid well and presented the possibility of an immense readership while also muting the proper excesses of the imagination. The middle-range magazines presented an official context and a fairly unadventurous editorial policy while offering the possibility of reaching a responsive, influential readership. The little magazines offered no money at all and a minuscule audience while offering publication, a community of values, and a passion for art, along with the guarantee of an audience that would be committed to what it read. Still, however compromising to the writers themselves, that three-part structure, the product of mere commerce and historical accident, really did serve the art of short fiction.

• • •

For a long time, literary history that describes the period from some time after the Civil War to roughly 1920 was badly incapacitated by the amazing persistence of the word *realism.* It is scarcely possible to pick up a history of the period without encountering the word, centrally placed and ritually invoked, usually in an agonistic or militaristic context—"the struggle of realism," "the rise of realism," "the triumph of realism"—as if realism were a combatant in a cultural wrestling match. The word loomed as large as it did partly because it was a programmatic word for such writers as Howells,

Garland, and Crane: *they* used the word with a considerable charge of intent. In those older histories, the word surely meant to point to the genuine problem for writers of that time in overcoming a facile gentility and in discovering new means for the representation of experience. More recently, however, we have come to agree that if *Pride and Prejudice, Bleak House, Huckleberry Finn,* and *The Sound and the Fury* are all "realistic," then the word means very little since each writer sees a different version of what is "out there" and each finds a different set of presentational conventions for laying out that sense of reality on the page. To put the matter in a different way, Erich Auerbach's great *Mimesis* inquires into the presentation of reality in writers from Homer and the biblical scribes to Virginia Woolf. All of them are "realists," which is to say that all of them wish to present a richly responsive version of the visible world, along with its implicit coherence. If that is the case with so varied a group of writers, then *realist* is a more elusive word than those literary historians ever thought.

The trouble is that *realism,* all those years, was taken as a positive term, whereas it is, in fact, a dialectical term. I take the dichotomy from Kenneth Burke. *Freedom,* he points out, is a dialectical term. It means nothing until it is contrasted with a particular sense of constraint, or antifreedom. *Apple,* on the other hand, is a positive term. It needs, for our comprehension, no sense of antiapple. It is true that a fair amount of American literary history does take *realism* in a rather special dialectical way, finding a consistent contrast between realism and romance. Still, that contrast does not undermine my contention that the word is often used naively and that it is time to inquire both into what those presentational conventions were that allowed their practitioners to lay claim to the real and also what those conventions were that seemed then, presumably seem now, antireal.

Thinking of that body of short fiction around the turn of the century that seemed antithetical to a persuasive representation of experience, several qualities of antirealism are especially obvious. The first of these is language, not so much style in the larger sense as language qua language. There is an obsessive adverbial quality in that magazine fiction. In the fiction that endures, from that period and later, the nouns and the verbs carry the burden. Reading that magazine fiction, the adverbs give us a directed attention to manner in a facile and undramatized way. And that adverbial quality is likely to seem false to experience. I quote from a single story from *Harper's* of 1901: "said Siddons to the other, with rather sudden eagerness"; "as often happened when he was thinking intently"; "he said, indolently"; "nodding his head sagaciously"; "said Jerrold, grimly"; "he answered, gravely"; "when she again spoke it was very coldly"; "Siddons drove over it neatly"; "replied

Braithwait, snappishly"; "he continued, ecstatically"; "he said, wearily"; "she cried, gently"; "read the chairman, on the veranda, slowly." Consistent with the pattern, characters not only say; they break out, purr, call, yell, remonstrate (a great favorite of the period), continue, reiterate, cry, muse, exclaim, and (consistent with the sexual innocence of the period) ejaculate.

Descriptions of characters tend toward antithesis: his features "were too strongly marked and immobile, but they had a certain aloofness of expression not without its charm." (I quote more widely from the magazine fiction of the period, assuming that the particular stories from which I quote are by now irrelevant.) There is a fondness for the pathetic fallacy, or at least a metaphorical correspondence between the human and the nonhuman; both people and vines "cling" and there is a persistent fondness for metaphors of weather and floral background. The energy of the fiction is sometimes carried by rhetorical questions: "Was it possible that here, too, his shortage had been somehow answerable? Was the failure his—not hers?" And sometimes the energy is carried by an intensifying series: "He knew, as a strong man knows himself, that there was no lack of power, of grasp, of brain, of will."

Although such fiction seeks to present moments of great passion, its linguistic resources are not equal to it. Characters are often "desirous of." Faces are prominent in the verbal texture of the fiction, being alternately flushed and pale, red and white. What is perhaps most central is that the language often represents a literature out of its class. The writers, all of them middle class, attempt the leisure class with an arch and specious falsity; or they attempt the underclass with a heavy and unconvincing colloquialism.

"One would pity the modern hostess, were it not that, like the criminal, she originates her own troubles."

"And enjoys them," laughed the girl.

"Presumptively. I can't help hoping, Miss Remson, that you are on your way to Steepside now?"

"Yes. Are you?"

The passage reads like bad Henry James, which is precisely the point. James knew the speech and the nuances of the international aristocracy; the writer from whom I quote knew neither.

Secondly, there is the emotional predisposition within which experience is sought. It is surely fallacious to think, as all of us sometimes do, that there is something more real and commendable about hard, spare, even cynical writing. Life does have some happy endings and an author who writes of one in a generous, affectionate prose is not necessarily a fool. Nevertheless, the prevailing tone of a vast amount of American short fiction of the period is cheerful, optimistic, pervasively sweet. I quote from the conclusion to a story by Thomas Bailey Aldrich (never mind the plot that brings us to this point):

This idea was passing through Helen's brain when she saw her husband come swinging down the street with an elasticity of gait that had been a lost art for the last twelve or fourteen hours. He came smiling along the shell-paved walk, and stood in front of her. Then Helen's malicious plan instantly fell to pieces, for she saw by his face that he knew, and he saw that she knew, and with a great laugh, to which Helen added a merry contralto, Edward sprang up the piazza steps and took her in his arms.

Any one passing the cottage at that moment would have been dead certain that it was a honey-moon.

Beyond the banal language and the happy plots is a system of taboos that inhibited the representation both of action and of speech. Noel Perrin, in *Dr. Bowdler's Legacy*, shows how the expurgations and "purifications" of literature through the late eighteenth and nineteenth centuries finally began to break up in the early twentieth century. But they were a long time breaking. It was only at the end of the fifties and the early sixties that such works as *Tropic of Cancer* and *Lady Chatterley's Lover* were finally published in the United States. And in the meantime, the language of short fiction struggled against the constraint that certain words may not be printed and certain actions not depicted. The reader of Hemingway's letters is aware that, however direct and uncompromising the dialogue of the stories may seem, it is compromising nonetheless. In his letters, Hemingway writes with an authentic coarseness that none of his characters can fully express.

Taking the question of language several degrees further, Richard Bridgman, in *The Colloquial Style in America,* describes the changes in American prose from 1825 to 1925, recording the various abortive attempts at the achievement of an "American" style, describing the achievement of a speech-based, antiliterary style in some ways rather like the movement away from the magazine tales I have pointed to: a reaction against "big words" and complexity of syntax, a "stress on the individual verbal unit, a resulting fragmentation of syntax, and the use of repetition to bind and unify." What Bridgman describes is a difficult movement toward the rendering of the way people really do speak, anticonventional and "real".

Recently, cultural historians have come to refine more precisely what nineteenth-centry gentility consisted of. Perhaps the best of them is Ann Douglas. In *The Feminization of American Culture,* she finds that the dominant pattern of the whole of the nineteenth century resulted from an alliance of a bland and secularized clergy with the conspicuous spokesmen for women, the consequence being a domesticated, sentimental official culture. Conversely, there is, by the end of the century, as a reaction to that feminization, an exaggerated sense of male role. It is a dehumanizing bifurcation, the sentimentalized wife, mother, and homemaker in a polar opposition to the muscular, ostentatiously virile male. And so it is that every writer of consequence in the first half of the twentieth century is obliged to find offensive and "unreal" both the feminization of the century before and the sexual polarization that was its result: Wharton and Cather, with their vital, passional, heroic women; Anderson, with his satiric view of George Willard's swaggering father and his boundlessly compassionate view of his sensitive, ambitious, troubled mother; Dreiser, with his anxious, insecure men; the distribution of courage and baseness in Faulkner's people without regard to gender; even Hemingway's virile males, presented with a problematic irony.

As useful in a different way in laying out that sense of the antireal that fiction of quality implicitly opposes is the body of attitudes described in Richard Hofstadter's *Anti-Intellectualism in American Life.* He traces a pervasively Manichean tendency in popular American religious thought, considering the world as an arena for the conflict of good and evil, an ideology that can support a facile melodrama but must have seemed, to writers of quality then as now, unreal; the fascination of American culture with self-help and spiritual uplift; the distrust of the schoolroom, education, and the visible evidence of the cultivated person; the promotion of practicality; the distrust, finally, of mind itself. Hofstadter considers those writers around the turn of the century, still seeking to make a national literature and achieve an authentic voice, finding sources of energy in the American landscape, American people, and American possibilities, yet unable to accept that broad, easy, widely shared contempt for books, words, nuance, style, and the life of the mind. It was all necessarily antireal to the writer, and to write with conviction was inevitably to draw away from what we now call, in perspective, "anti-intellectualism in American life."

For another viewpoint, there is Leo Marx's brilliant *The Machine in the Garden,* which traces the permutations, through the nineteenth century, of the tension between a bucolic, idyllic, pastoral ideal and the intrusion of the culture of the machine, variously embraced and deplored. It is a tension by no means resolved by the twentieth century, and it suggests the dialectical pattern I have been attempting to describe. Short fiction had had, for a hundred years, a special affinity for the portrayal of a place that is at once the landscape of the mind and the landscape of fact. But in that body of fiction I have sought to portray as counterrealistic, the idyllic is embraced, with sentiment and without reservation. And in that body of fiction we call realistic, the bucolic place is understood, perhaps even loved—frontier farm, wilderness, midwestern town—but not embraced, because no one, writing realistically in the twentieth century, can imagine the happy village, circumscribed, devoid of railroad tracks, factories, and the intrusion of an often meretricious technology.

But finally to return to literary conventions, it is plot, more than anything else, that came to seem antireal. Anderson says it best, and once he has said it and acted upon it, it does not need to be said again, even though there is no writer of significance after him who does not feel it. No segment of life can be said to begin, or end, or resolve itself. Life does not contain plots. The history of short fiction in the first half of the century can be traced, as I have suggested, as a revolt against certain prohibitions and vacuous values; but most of all, it can be traced as a revolt against plot. For the writer seeking to be a realist, the primary imperative, for fifty years, was to avoid making a story look like Maupassant's "The Necklace" or O. Henry's "The Gift of the Magi." For plot, more than anything else, was antireal. It should be said, of course, that we have come to understand plot in a more fluid and comprehensive way, and those stories that must have seemed devoid of plot when they appeared—Hemingway's "Hills Like White Elephants" for example—seem now to be flawlessly plotted in an unobtrusive and subtle way. Still, it is easy enough to understand what the early writers of the century mean by plot. It is linear and overt, with a crisp beginning, middle, and end, and we recognize the end because it contains an element of surprise.

Here is Anderson:

> Would the common words of our daily speech, in shops and offices, do the trick? Surely the Americans, among whom one sat talking, had felt everything the Greeks had felt, everything the English felt? Deaths came to them, the tricks of fate assailed their lives. I was certain none of them lived, felt or talked as the average American novel made them feel and talk, and as for the plot short stories of the magazines—those bastard children of De Maupassant, Poe and O. Henry—it was certain there were no plot short stories ever lived in any life I had known anything about.[2]

Surely other writers had come to comparable conclusions by different routes. But nobody finally says it more magisterially. To make a serious, realistic story in the twentieth century is to avoid the nineteenth-century plot.

To place the matter once again in a wider context, Emerson's "Nature" would have been read by few, if any, writers of the early twentieth century. And had some writer of short fiction happened upon it, it would have seemed a relic, a fragment from an odd and distant cultural past. But there is a sentence of Emerson's that says, better than any of the practitioners of realistic fiction could have said, what the imperatives really were. "But wise men pierce this rotten diction and fasten words again to visible things."

• • •

Discussions of the short story, insofar as they are historical, tend to assume that the story in any given period derives its conventions and its possibilities from other stories. Katherine Mansfield, for example, is customarily spoken of as a disciple of Chekhov, Maugham as a disciple of Maupassant, Edith Wharton of Henry James, and a dozen writers of southern American gothic of Faulkner. It is a particularly insular assumption which is partly true and partly quite false. How true it is we will see in a moment. How false it is has to do with the fact that the short story, for all its economy and singleness of purpose, is remarkably eclectic and derivative, drawing its energy from areas of the general culture that have no obvious connection with it.

It seems banal perhaps to begin with journalism. (In a curious linkage of diction, what a reporter writes is a "story.") But it does happen to be true that some of the distant precursors of the short story are journalistic, the more fictive essays of Addison and Steele or of Samuel Johnson; and it is also true that some of the most distinguished figures of the nineteenth century combined the writing of memorable short fiction with careers as working journalists: Poe, Bret Harte, Howells, Bierce, Twain, and especially Crane. Recalling the work of that group, one senses that, ephemeral and utilitarian though journalism may be, it imposed a certain discipline upon the imagination. At the turn of the century, it was not fiction of enduring quality that influenced Dreiser to become a writer (although ultimately the turning point in his career was his passion for Balzac) but the columnist Eugene Field in the *Chicago Daily News*. And it was in the editorial office of the *Chicago Globe* that Dreiser received his most essential training, as the editor demanded of him precision of information, cutting and blue-penciling his copy.

Significantly, George Willard, the central figure of *Winesburg, Ohio*, is a journalist. Anderson deeply admired journalism, and he became, at a later stage of his career, the proprietor of a country newspaper. It needs to be stressed, however, that the journalism that stands in relation to the art of the story is not much like the newspaper that we know now, in which sober and responsible wire service dispatches are gathered together with columns, features, and editorial matter. It was a more flamboyant trade, as Anderson makes clear in passages in which he expresses his admiration for those reporters and editors whose voices and manners were distinctive and whose names were recognizable to the man on the street. His own country news-paper was full of color, bias, and stylized columns in which he projected an eccentric view of events through the mouth of an invented reporter with a comic name. From Crane to Hemingway, the journalism that affects the na-ture of the short story is both economical and precise so as to serve the wishes of the editor and the busy reader, and highly personal so that the distinctive voice is never lost.

Still photography enters the imagination of short fiction in the latter nine-teenth century and never leaves in a way that is difficult to demonstrate but impossible to deny. The daguerreotype, made publicly available in 1839, had been succeeded by a variety of technical refinements; yet Mathew Brady recorded his remarkable scenes of the Civil War with equipment that seems now incredibly cumbersome: a horse-drawn cart filled with apparatus, a portable darkroom, glass plates on which images were reproduced. By the end of the century, however, the technology was sufficiently advanced and inexpensive that every small town had its portrait photographer. And in the late 1880s, George Eastman perfected the snapshot camera: "You push the button and we do the rest." Photography was, by century's end, not simply something that could be done but something one could do oneself.

So it is that figures in the short fiction of Dreiser, Anderson, and Lewis often "pose" stiffly as they are introduced, as if for a local photographer, with a photographic mixture of their frozen dignity along with their warts and oddities of shape. Anderson especially is attracted to the framed and fixed moment, presented without depth, in which the inner life of the sub-ject is implicit in his visual stance. With a photographer's imagination, Faulkner's narrator in "A Rose for Emily" says, "We had long thought of them as a tableau; Miss Emily a slender figure in white in the background, her father a spraddled silhouette in the foreground, his back to her and clutching a horse-whip, the two of them framed by the back-flung front door." Moreover, the extraordinary development of documentary photog-raphy in the late nineteenth and early twentieth centuries provided a model for short fiction. Stories have often shown an affinity for marginal groups, and photography demonstrated, by century's end, what no one had seen before who had not lived there, what the rural and urban poor, the immi-grant culture of Ellis Island and the lower East Side, and the vanishing tribal life of the Southwest really looked like. There is not much doubt that, as the century proceeds, Farrell, rendering the urban poor, Caldwell, the rural poor, and Richard Wright, *Uncle Tom's Children*, all have one eye on expe-rience and the other eye on the visual specificity of the documentary pho-tography that, by their time, had established the look of those cultures.

In fact, the very nature of the visual imagination changes as a result of the awareness of the camera. Walter Benjamin has written of the "unconscious optics" introduced into our general awareness by photography. We all know how a person walks or picks up a spoon, but we hardly know what a frozen second of that walk looks like or exactly what happens when hand meets spoon, until that moment is fixed on film. There is scarcely a writer of consequence in the twentieth century who does not reflect that peculiar optical acuity that comes not so much from observing as from knowing what the camera can do. In Kay Boyle's early story "Wedding Day," two characters row out into the middle of a pond.

She sat buttoned very tightly in her white furs. The brisk little wind was spanking the waters back and forth and the end of her nose was turning pink. But he, on the contrary, had thrown off his coat, thrown it to the bottom of the boat with his feet on it, and as he rowed he pressed the fresh mud of the spring that had clustered on his soles into every seam and pocket of it. Back and forth went his arms, back and forth, with the little yellow hairs on them standing up in the wind.

It is a photographic imagination, in which the mud in the coat is as distinct as the shape of the boat, and the hairs on the arm are as clear as the figure rowing. In Willa Cather's "Paul's Case," it is a photographic imagination of New York that draws Paul there. And ultimately, when he dies, it is the "picture making mechanism" that is crushed.

Especially after the beginning of World War I, with the broad dissemination of photojournalism, there is an intimate involvement of fiction and the photograph. Alan Spiegel writes of the prevalence in photojournalism for pictures of "wartime violence and disaster where the victim always seems to have the wrong look on his face: boredom, blankness, irritation, surprise, confusion—momentary phenomenal appearances fixed forever by the camera and nothing at all like the ones we expect."[3] It is a technique of vision which he compares to one of the "interchapters" of Hemingway's *In Our Time,* in which one of the cabinet ministers who is about to be executed by a firing squad sits down. In its horrible and quite photographic incongruity, it is absolutely convincing. "One sits down to write a letter," writes Spiegel, "or one sits down to butter a slice of toast, but one does not sit down to die"—except in news photographs, the pages of Hemingway, and, one is persuaded, experience.

If still photography is significant to the art of short fiction, film is even more significant. Gertrude Stein was among the first to acknowledge the significance of the motion picture in her own art. Writing of the composition of *The Making of Americans,* she says:

I was doing what the cinema was doing, I was making a continuous succession of the statement of what that person was until I had not many things but one thing. As I read you some of the portraits of that period you will see what I mean.

I of course did not think of it in terms of the cinema, in fact I doubt whether at that time I had ever seen a cinema but, and I cannot repeat this too often, any one is of one's period and this our period was undoubtedly the period of the cinema and series production. And each of us in our own way are bound to express what the world in which we are living is doing

It is the common technique of incremental repetition in film and fiction of a particular kind that obviously fascinates Stein. What one also needs to note is her feeling for the "period of the cinema." Other writers less eccentric than she have noted the special correspondence between the art of the film and the art of the story, A. E. Coppard and Elizabeth Bowen in England, for example. It is a point that Alan Spiegel makes convincingly. After a particular historical point, it is no longer necessary to ask whether a given writer went to films, admired certain directors or certain cinematic techniques, or wished to emulate the art of the movies.

What being of that period means is complex and diffuse, of course. But surely it means three things: a depersonalization, in which the fiction seems to come not from an involved and caring teller but from a machine; a different sense of eye, focus, vision, and fixity of detail; and a different rhythm, movement, transition, what the filmmaker calls cutting and montage, all three of these tendencies being among the most frequently noted characteristics of the short fiction of the century.

Less clearly, story in the first half of the century draws upon the life of the other arts. All the best writers of short fiction were aware of the movement of painting from impressionism to postimpressionism to cubism, with its gradual undermining of the easel effect of traditional art and its growing fascination with simultaneous, intersecting planes. Perhaps the short fiction of Katherine Anne Porter best suggests that kinship. Curiously, most of southern gothic, despite its obvious wish to render the visceral and direct, displays on every hand an affinity for the cubist. It is, of course, the polarizations of southern art that create that affinity: black and white, old and new, vital and moribund, rich and poor, old wealth and new, bad taste and good, all of it superimposed, within the same fictions, in some bizarre and unresolvable standoff. Working with such materials, the idea of intersecting planes is irresistible, whether or not the writers may have been impressed with Picasso and Matisse.

Intellectual prose suggests a different range of influences and a different set of problems. If we take the four who, by common consent, most clearly shaped the mind of the early twentieth century—Darwin, Marx, Freud, and Frazer—it seems clear that the influence of the first two was general, diffuse, and finally minimal. The ideas of Darwin, to be sure, lie behind the rituals of survival, both social and physical, in London and the later naturalists. But it is not a preoccupation that continues to be central to the major short fiction. As for Marx, the interest in class—in Fitzgerald, O'Hara, and Faulkner, for example—derives from temperament, native observation, and the example of European fiction, not from *Das Kapital*. And the energies of social protest in the thirties found an easier outlet in fiction of novel length than in the story. Even in the best of Richard Wright's short fictions, "The Man Who Lived Underground," the sewer-level view of power and institutions seems only incidentally Marxist, despite the attraction of Wright to Marxian analysis.

But Frazer in particular, early cutural anthropology in general, does alter the nature of short fiction. Frazer focuses the attention of a rather startled public on the continuity of our humanness, the extraordinary coherence of certain mythic patterns, and the implicit, subliminal persistence of those modes of the imagination that are identifiable as ancient and primitive yet are indisputably present in the structure of modern life. Earlier fiction, to be sure, sometimes presents a densely mythic text. Frazer and the early cultural anthropologists, however, gathered, systematized, and made explicit what had been available to the writer all along. And after them, the interpenetration of the primitive and the modern, the literate and the oral, the mythic and the literal became part of the common currency of the Western world. So it is that the continuing fascination of writers of short fiction with the insights of the mind of the child, the instinctual life of the underclass, the ritual confrontations of man and beast or man and man, even the imagination of the death of culture and its regeneration, carry an authority and occupy a centrality that they would not have had, had those early mythographers not written as they did.

The influence of Freud is complex and far more curious. It goes without saying that ideas and images that suggest Freud are as old as human records. Lancelot Law Whyte's *The Unconscious before Freud* traces the presentation of the unconscious from classical antiquity. And Freud himself acknowledged that his most basic ideas were present in literature long before he articulated them. Yet the specific influence of Freud is immense. Its contours run roughly like this.

By 1907, Freud's reputation was confined to the psychological profession; there was some modest publicity when Freud visited the United States in 1909; and in 1913, A. A. Brill's translations of several of the basic works began to appear. By 1915, the vogue of Freud was well under way, with Max

Eastman's popularization in *Everyman's Magazine;* and by the twenties, Greenwich Village and the brightest fringe of American culture had found Freud a tool in the service of a facile revolution, against marriage, repression, moral and social inconvenience, a standard-bearer for the instinctual life. In time, Freud's sense of the mind became more significant and pervasive than that revolutionist's role in which he was speciously cast; and it is that sense of the mind that has been central to the purposes of short fiction.

Freud suggests, for the writer of short fiction, the legitimacy of dreams as an access to the self, along with a language for their understanding. He suggests the centrality of sex, disguised and sublimated in a dozen ways. He suggests the problematics of the self in relation to parents, others, one's own self-image. He suggests a certain discursive linkage, fragmentary and associative, heavily symbolic, derived from his sense of the unconscious. He suggests the agonizing tensions of the self in the modern world, caught between complex constraints and primal needs. And he suggests a duality—the latent and the manifest, what we think we are thinking and what we don't recognize but feel. Short fiction is never the same again after Freud.

As for direct influence, it is Anderson who opens the problem. Today's reader of *Winesburg, Ohio* feels it to be relentlessly Freudian, the Oedipal relation of George Willard and his mother, the sublimations of Kate Swift, the general sense of sexual deprivation, the interest in the latent and the manifest, the feeling for the symbolic import of various overt actions, all of which run through Anderson's accounts of the tortured lives of his villagers. Anderson denied having known Freud by the time of *Winesburg.* And although later scholars may accuse him of dissembling, it still seems useful to accept the verdict of Frederick Hoffman that "Anderson developed his themes quite independently of Freudian influence, but with such a startling likeness of approach that critics fell into the most excusable error of their times; it *seemed* an absolute certainty that Anderson should have been influenced directly by Freud."[4] Indisputable cases of direct influence are not hard to find. Conrad Aiken shows it best: if his reputation as a short story writer has faded, "Silent Snow, Secret Snow" and "Mr. Arcularis" remain as anthology pieces, brilliant renderings of the inner life as charted by Freud. Since the twenties, as with film, it is scarcely necessary to determine that a particular writer has read Freud. It is the age of Freud.

If the influence upon early twentieth-century American short fiction by the art and the intellectual life of its time is considerable, the influence of the European tradition is negligible, although not altogether negligible, to be sure. James had read everybody of consequence and traces of Turgenev and many of the French appear in his work. Every writer of fiction in the twentieth century is influenced, however indirectly, by Flaubert. But when Dreiser speaks of his admiration for Balzac, it is obviously not the stories he admired but the novels, which he found crucial in the determination of his own longer works. If an O. Henry story looks, in certain respects, like a story by Maupassant, it is not that O. Henry learned his craft from Maupassant but that his native talents and the pressures of the marketplace encouraged the development of a form that happens to look like Maupassant at his most facile. (The prudish and highly selective translation of Maupassant through much of the twentieth century was a national disgrace; an American writer who did not read French could have known only a small portion of the stories, many of them Maupassant's worst, badly translated.) If an Anderson story looks, in certain respects, like a story by Chekhov (Paul Rosenfeld, in 1922, called Anderson a "phallic Chekhov"), it is not that Anderson learned his craft from Chekhov but that, reacting against formula and responding to the demands of his subject matter, he developed a form that happens to look like Chekhov's.

Surely any number of writers, Hemingway, for example, were far better read than they ever chose to appear and, covering their tracks, absorbed more of what they had read than we will ever know. And any writer would at least have known the Europeans as their translated stories appeared in the very magazines in which he published. Yet, largely oblivious of the rich and diverse European tradition from Pushkin and Gogol, Kleist and Keller, the Flaubert of *Three Tales* and Maupassant, through the great English practitioners of the turn of the century, Conrad and Kipling, American short fiction tends to make, in Hugh Kenner's phrase, "a homemade world."

In short, then, the stories of the period participate in, and draw upon, the life of their time but not exactly in the ways that the other genres do. Eliot and Pound, the first generation of modernist poets in general, sought to "make it new" while simultaneously drawing upon the whole of the Western tradition. Writers of short fiction, on the contrary, their antennas remarkably attuned to the changes in our general sensibility, still sought to make an art form out of basically native materials.

• • •

Since its beginnings in the United States, with Hawthorne and Poe, writers of and about the short story have responded to what has seemed an insidious split between the "art" story, or the "quality" or "serious" story, and its meretricious counterpart: "slick" (or "pulp"), "commercial," and "popular." There is scarcely a writer of consequence from mid-nineteenth century to mid-twentieth century who does not, sooner or later, register his dismay at the debasement of taste in the mass public and the difficulty, for the serious writer, in finding an audience. Nobody records this feeling more powerfully than Dreiser. In the nineties, after an extraordinarily varied period as a working journalist, he writes, in the autobiographical *A Book about Myself,* of the official culture as he begins, finally, to turn to the writing of fiction.

I set to examining the current magazines and the fiction and articles to be found therein: *Century, Scribner's, Harper's.* I was never more confounded than by the discrepancy existing between my own observations and those displayed here, the beauty and peace and charm to be found in everything, the almost complete absence of any reference to the coarse and the vulgar and the cruel and the terrible . . . . Love was almost invariably rewarded in these tales. Almost invariably one's dreams came true, in the magazines. Most of these bits of fiction, delicately phrased, flowed so easily, with such an air of assurance, omniscience and condescension, that I was quite put out by my own lacks and defects. . . . I read and I read, but all I could gather was that I had no such tales to tell, and, however much I tried, I could not think of any.

Those autobiographical reflections represent a decisive point in the American sensibility because *Sister Carrie* followed in 1900, not only expressing Dreiser's wish not to emulate the official culture and the magazine tales, but also changing forever the nature of fiction in the United States.

For all of Dreiser's conviction, the split between the serious and the popular was by no means so stark as he describes it. In only those three magazines he cites, he could have found some considerable and quite tough-minded fictions by Howells, James, Mary Wilkins, and Crane. Still, if Dreiser overstates, he does point to something that is real and deeply felt, an insidiously divided audience.

Historically, the debate concerning the split between elite and mass culture is a very old one, beginning in the English seventeenth century, reaching a high point in the early eighteenth, and remaining with us ever since. Readers of Dryden, Pope, and Swift will remember the splendid conviction with which those three writers respond to the glut of bad writing in their times. The perception of a large, literate, uncritical reading public, ministered to by a facile and mendacious subliterature, has been one of the standard features of Western thought for two centuries. From a historical point of view, it is hard to see why the observation of the split should have struck writers of short fiction at the end of the nineteenth century with such force. Yet there are reasons for writers of short fiction in the twentieth century to have felt the loneliness of their integrity in their own special ways.

Nobody can write symphonic music without training, and even writing a bad novel requires a sustained and intelligent effort. But third-rate minds have always found a way to duplicate easily the prevailing formulas of short fiction. Moreover, in the century from Poe to television, commercial fiction did not merely offer itself in the manner of a painting in a gallery or a play in a theater; it came into the home. It was on the nightstand, in the bathroom, on the coffee table. Its sheer volume was immense, and its quality was regulated by editors with an eye to circulation. Always, in the nineteenth century, an easy vehicle for the perpetuation of a stereotypical set of official myths, the short story became, in the twentieth century, a stereotypical method. The genre, a decade or so into the century, takes a turn that even the despair of Dreiser could not have foreseen. And it is O. Henry, more than anyone else, who provided the model for the method and the cause for that anxiety that writers of quality felt toward what seemed to be a Gresham's law of short fiction, that the bad really does drive out the good.

The first thing to be said about O. Henry is that he is exceptionally good at what he does. It takes broad experience in art fiction, sophistication, a willing resistance, cynicism perhaps, not to submit to his voice and his manner. Take a typical story.

"The Enchanted Profile" projects an uncommonly intricate voice, mixing the literary and the street colloquial, commenting on itself, shifting, without modulation, from the knowing to the sardonic, to the responsive, to the sentimental. Above all, it draws us into the narrative, both mechanically and empathically. "In New York there is an old, old hotel. You have seen woodcuts of it in the magazines. It was built—let's see—at a time when there was nothing above Fourteenth Street except the old Indian trail to Boston and Hammerstein's office." That strategically placed "let's see" presents the musing, remembering speaker, not detached, clearly one of us. But it is the woodcut that does it. Even if O. Henry had had a particular woodcut in mind, it is unlikely that many of his audience would have known it. How many of them were aficionadoes of urban woodcuts in discarded magazines? But the rhetoric assumes a community of experience, interest, and taste; and the reader, flattered to be included, submits. The story quickly sketches in the profile of a woman of sixty, who dresses and lives at the edge of poverty while being, apparently, extremely wealthy. It is a standard piece of American folklore, the millionaire who lives meanly; that it sometimes does happen simply whets our fascination with the myth.

O. Henry, who is transmuted into the story as "I," a writer of stories, encounters the stenographer of the hotel, a young woman with classic good looks. She tells him a story within a story, of her friendship with the eccentric millionaire. Done with grace and a very light touch, all in stenographer-colloquial, with a keen sense of the class differences implicit in the situation, the story recounts the friendship to its resolution, ending with the problem of the fascination of the millionaire for the stenographer. The reader, understanding the pleasure of the two with each other, yet sensing a latent dimension to the relationship, waits for the last line. It is a newspaper artist, confidant to the writer, who speaks it: "'Isn't Ida's head a dead ringer for the lady's head on the silver dollar?'"

Of course it is a trick ending. Yet to dismiss O. Henry with all of those epithets that have accumulated around his name all these years is a mistake. (H. E. Bates dismisses as well as anybody: "He is a great showman who can talk the hind legs off a donkey and then proceed to sell the public that same donkey as a pedigree race-horse.") None of his characters, to be sure, are apprehended, understood, and deployed upon the page. Yet the story is sharply observed, full of artifice and a splendid range of rhetorical appeals. It is amazing that anybody ever though it possible to imitate O. Henry. Yet people imagined just that, and by early century there were a score of guides advising aspiring writers of ways in which the form and the success of O. Henry could be duplicated. And so when writers of the twentieth century resist the commercial story, they tend to do it not simply in resistance to that bland, genteel, offical fiction that so offended Dreiser but also in resistance to the methodological fixity that the followers of O. Henry seemed to impose upon the genre.

Yet the distinction between art and commercial fiction takes still another turn in the early twentieth century that makes some different problems for the reader intent on sorting out the quality of the period, and that is the development and codification of the popular fictional subtypes. Popular fiction had its subtypes in the nineteenth century, to be sure, formula tales of adventure and moral uplift; but those nineteenth-century subtypes had become nearly obsolete. It is in the early twentieth century that one encounters a detective story pretty much like a detective story written now, an early piece of science fiction that seems to suggest the mind and wit that the form now contains, or a Western fiction that resembles an episode of current television. Those popular subtypes become, in early century, what we still know and have with us. And more than a few of them have a kind of art and power that make us linger a moment before we brush them into a pile of ephemera

Perhaps the best way of discriminating between what legitimately survives and what doesn't is to invoke the idea, from Lionel Trilling, Leslie Fiedler, and a disparate lot of others, of the "adversary culture." Even if magazine fiction is self-imitative and formulaic, it can always find ways of re-energizing those formulas if it finds an angle of observation toward our culture that is sharply defined and, in the best sense, critical. If it tells us that boys in adolescence are impulsive, that unusual places bring out a strenuous element in adventurous men, and that two people, in love, will do their best to overcome obstacles, we will read, at best, with momentary diversion. If it tells us, with a degree of art, that life is more difficult or problematic than we thought it was, we will value it, even if it is formulaic. And that is what an uncommon amount of genre fiction in the first half of the century does.

Western fiction is the easiest to confront and dispose of. Although there had been early stories of the West, including at least two great Western stories by Crane and a variety of dime novels, the popular, mythic West as we know it begins with Owen Wister's *The Virginian,* a full-length novel of 1902. There is no doubt that Wister's invention taps a reservoir central to the American consciousness and thereby gives issue to hundreds of short fictions, not to mention television and movie productions. In fact, Wister not only discovers the mythic center of the Western story; he invents most of the clichés that have pervaded the form ever since. It is startling to turn back to Wister to find that a character really does say, "When you call me that, smile!"

Still, for all its amazing durability, there is no single piece of short fiction within the limits of the formula that seems enduring, despite those hundreds that have passed our way in that half century. Invariably, it seems that when a piece of Western fiction endures, it is because it transcends the formula, even parodies the formula, as is the case with Walter Van Tilburg Clark, for example, or Wallace Stegner, H. L. Davis, A. B. Guthrie. The formula lends itself to narrative energy and the pleasures of the shapely story. But what it finally tells us is what we already know, that the erect posture, the white horse, the clear-eyed gaze, and the steady hand all count for something, that singleness of purpose and courage count for quite a bit, that the old West was filled with innumerable scoundrels, men both devious and malicious, subversive of order and authority, and that a single man, by the force of his character, could transform his immediate world.

Detective fiction is a different matter. For one thing, it enters the literature of early twentieth century as the developed offspring of some very distinguished parents. There is Poe, for whom the detective story exists within that small canon of controlled and artful stories that stand at the very origins of the genre. There is, if one wishes, that group of novels of the first rank—Hugo's *Les Miserables,* Dickens' *Bleak House,* and Dostoevsky's *Crime and Punishment*—that integrate elements of detection into extraordinary imaginative structures; and there is Wilkie Collins's still quite readable *The Moonstone*. But pre-eminently, for short fiction, there is the example of Conan Doyle, perhaps the finest practitioner of a subgenre of short fiction content to stay within its limits. There is something congenial about the presentation of a problem that can be exhausted in twenty pages and the charismatic figure who works it out before our eyes. In addition, detective fiction is ordinarily obliged to work quite closely within the texture of experience, usually urban experience, so that it often carries with its basic problem-solving structure an especially concrete sense of the underside of a particular world, rendered with a vividness that may be the envy of conventional writers of art fiction. (I do not wish, of course, to minimize the triviality of much detective fiction. Howard Haycraft, in *Murder for Pleasure*, effectively demolishes the least considerable variety with a phrase taken from Ogden Nash, the "Had-I-But-Known" school of writing.)

The tale of "pure detection," often with an effete and dilettantish hero derivative of Holmes, runs its course through the first half of the century and devotees will make a case for the value of stories by S. S. Van Dine, Rex Stout, and Eric Ambler. But it is in what we have come to call the "tough-guy" mode of crime fiction that the detective story achieves a voice, a manner, and a form that give it permanent significance. As for the voice, it can still be, some fifty years later, quite arresting. It matters, to be sure, that it has been imitated endlessly, and hearing it now will inevitably remind us of innumerable voice-over narrations and B-grade movies. But the original is crisp and gritty in a way that the imitations can only approximate.

Here is the beginning of "The Gatewood Caper" by Dashiell Hammett.

Harvey Gatewood had issued orders that I was to be admitted as soon as I arrived, so it took me only a little less than fifteen minutes to thread my way past the door-keepers, office boys, and secretaries who filled up most of the space between the Gatewood Lumber Corporation's front door and the president's private office. His office was large, all mahogany and bronze and green plush, with a mahogany desk as big as a bed in the center of the floor.

Gatewood, leaning across the desk, began to bark at me as soon as the obsequious clerk who had bowed me in bowed himself out.

"My daughter was kidnaped last night! I want the gang that did it if it takes every cent I got!"

"Tell me about it," I suggested.

Apparently all business, the passage lingers over color and texture. Apparently toneless, it immediately establishes three ironies, between the urgency of the appointment and the fifteen minutes it takes to work through the labyrinth of functionaries, between the comfort and affluence of the office and the obvious fact that Harvey Gatewood is quite helpless, between the loss of the daughter, which would seem to evoke pathos and anxiety, and the bullish terms of her recovery. Most of all, that beginning thrusts us into a solid institutional world of power and privilege, mahogany and secretaries, into which menace and unreason intrude. And what is needed, in this curious political impasse, is a single man, bright and resourceful, close enough to the underculture that has imperiled Gatewood so that he can find his way to the kidnaped daughter, "the gang," in a way that institutional forces, particularly the police, cannot do.

The contrast with the Western is obvious. The Western speaks to the truisms of our culture. Hammett's work, and the best of the tales that follow in the tough-guy tradition, speak to our anxieties. (It is a contrast reminiscent of the distinction of Rust Hills, that commercial fictions build upon our daydreams, quality fictions upon our night dreams.) And so, true to type though many of such stories may be, the best of them are enduring art by virtue of their vision, at once oblique and central. Raymond Chandler, the best of Hammett's successors, puts it superbly.

Possibly it was the smell of fear which the stories managed to generate. Their characters lived in a world gone wrong, a world in which, long before the atom bomb, civilization had created the machinery for its own destruction and was learning to use it with all the moronic delight of a gangster trying out his first machine gun. The law was something to be manipulated for profit and power. The streets were dark with something more than night.[5]

As with the Western and the fictions of crime, adventure fiction of story length forms its own tradition and now and again rises to the condition of art. Fictions of adventure, to be sure, are as old as classical epic. They flourish in the American nineteenth century in a tradition from Brockton Brown to Cooper. Both Melville and Twain derive much of their energy from their ability to exploit the basic adventure pattern, knowing the nature of "adventure," as it touched the lives of each of them, knowing the verbal means to the representation of that challenge and stress upon the page. But for twentieth-century fiction, Jack London is the great source. By now, only a few will make much claim for the mixture of Marxism, Darwinism, Neitzscheanism, and jingoism that informs London's fiction. But it would be foolish, snobbish, or both to deny the special power of his stories. The merest comparison with most earlier fiction of outdoor adventure reveals a thinness of texture with which London's fiction stands in remarkable contrast—in his ear for the speech rhythms of people at the edge of survival and in his capacity to register the response to fear, fatigue, and pain in the affective mind, the eye, and the very musculature of the body. Even now the Soviets find him one of our three or four finest writers. It is not altogether Soviet perversity that they should judge him so. They know what we all know but suppress, that, given twenty pages in which to pull a reader in, make him care, and make him happy when it is over, nobody is better than London.

Yet one reflects on the durability of the accomplishment and the legacy for others. I happen to think that anyone who has not come under the spell of London at about the age of twelve has had a deprived childhood. Yet not many read him when they are forty. In London's wake, there is a vast amount of ignorable fiction, in the man-versus-bear, man-versus-wolves, man-versus-cold pattern. Also there are some fine fictions by Steinbeck, Paul Horgan, and many more that manage to ironize, energize, and subvert the form, producing adventure fiction of vision and quality. But the real life of London's subgenre lies in its simultaneous acceptance and rejection by the best writers of the period. Both Faulkner and Hemingway implicitly recognize the extraordinary claims of that body of genre fiction that represents the intersection of man and wilderness, mortal danger and the rituals of survival. Yet for both of them, the subgenre is a means to an end, and the end is a body of fiction that pays its obligations to London's mode while achieving a symbolic resonance that London, for all his "philosophy," could not have anticipated. It is a process that critics have sometimes called "rebarbarization," the invigoration of quality literature by the assimilation of the popular. The process is obvious in Conrad and Melville, both of whom knew well the tradition of the sea story, both of whom could write it and did, and both of whom absorbed and moved beyond that limited form to produce enduring fiction. So it is that the real life of London's subgenre lies not so much in its own self-perpetuation, since we are moved less and less by primal tales of survival against great odds as the century proceeds, than by its endless ability to provide a base that writers of quality can absorb and transcend.

As for the science fiction of the period, no one is likely to dispute the general judgment that, at least until the forties, it is crudely written and juvenile in its appeal. European science fiction from the late nineteenth century finds ways to integrate an artful prose and a humane range of interests with a level of speculation designed to move a degree or two beyond the best scientific thought of its time. American science fiction, meanwhile, aims itself at the readership of *Amazing Stories, Astounding Stories of Super-Science,* and

Weird Tales. For all that, a considerable maturity begins to distinguish the form in the forties, with the work of Robert Heinlein, suggesting the capacity of the form to touch areas of politics and eschatology in a way quite unknown in those earlier stories of glittering hardware and intergalactic heroics, in the technological sophistication of Isaac Asimov, and in the stylistic grace of Theodore Sturgeon. The central motifs—utopia and apocalypse, imaginary worlds, and alternative beings—are both ancient and vital. It is hardly surprising that writers of wit and imagination took the form to themselves, discovering, by the forties, a means of making the genre popular and identifiably science fiction and at the same time artful and sophisticated.

Finally, there is that mode of popular fiction which it seems perverse to call popular at all, associated as it is with the *New Yorker,* with its ads for expensive scotch, expensive cars, expensive perfume, its annual cover of Eustace Twilley peering at his cloddish readers through his lorgnette. Yet, for all its courting of an affluent elite and for all its willed and supercilious cultivation of a distant and superior posture, the *New Yorker* generated a body of fictions, "fictions," and "pseudo-fictions" ultimately as popular, as durable, and as influential as any of the rest.

First it is necessary to clear the ground. Histories of short fiction do not deal with S. J. Perelman and the more fictional work of E. B. White, rarely with Thurber, never with that galaxy of lesser *New Yorker* writers such as Frank Sullivan and Woolcott Gibbs. The most obvious reason would seem to be that such work seems trivial and ephemeral in the face of so much short fiction of major rank. It is an objection that is less impressive now than it used to be, when much of our best short fiction is ludic, parodic, highly verbalist, and quite willing to flirt with the possibility of its triviality. We make our own ancestors, as Eliot said, and after him Borges. And in an age of Barthelme, Perelman seems a more plausible ancestor than he did a few years ago. Secondly, such fiction is not taken seriously because it often is a generic hybrid, mixing standard features of the short story and elements of the comic monologue with, especially, features of the light essay, the free and uncircumscribed meditation. Again, that generic hybrid is more likely to intrigue than confound us these days, when a substantial portion of our best short fiction seems not at all like a "story." Used to cross-generic fictions of the most amazing kind, we can hardly be persuaded to value a Perelman piece the less because it does not resemble a classic short story. And so we return to that odd group of *New Yorker* writers now, not merely with a sense of their wit and ingenuity in their own time and place and their glitter in the fashionable pages of the magazine they graced, but with a curious sense of their integrity. For if they never aspired to the seriousness of the great short fiction of their time, they were making superb fictions nonetheless, full of art and grace, wit and nuance, and an exquisite formal shapeliness.

Writing about Liberace, that fatuous, theatrical, fourth-rate pianist, with an affection that is partly feigned, partly quite genuine, Perelman writes, "To equivocate about the phenomenon would be as idle as analyzing a moonbeam." Apply the sentence to his fictions and it fits. A dozen writers now testify to the continuing vitality of his influence. They are not to be found in canonical collections of short fiction but in odd corners, sometimes the brightest and most intelligent corners, of newspapers and magazines. That curious mixture of pseudo-autobiography, the essay, the ordinary news, the rhythms of colloquial speech together with the pomposities of an archaic diction—all of it defies analysis. Yet just as surely, that hybrid mix established a mode, at once popular and sophisticated, still very much alive.

So it is that the first half of the century establishes certain popular forms, the essential nature of which can be endlessly duplicated. Something about their durability suggests a certain mythic authority intrinsic to each of them, even when done in an imitative and vacuous way. Yet each also contains the possibility that writers could employ the form, believe in the form, yet invest their fictions with art and vision.

• • •

The essays that follow trace the major movements of the short story from the beginning of the century to the end of World War II. Yet neither the essays nor this introduction can fully describe the virtuosity of those decades. For in the first forty-five years of the century, writers of short fiction mastered subjects and strategies, learned artifice and craft, sought artistic perfection, all with an industry and passion that is remarkable. It is our richest period.

Philip Stevick

Temple University

THE AMERICAN
SHORT STORY:
1900–1920

In no other period of American literary history (certainly in none of such short duration) is there so clearly demonstrated the versatility of the short story form as in the years between 1900 and 1920. To observe that the period begins with the hugely complex and dilatory works of Henry James's last phase and ends with the bare, anecdotal, and often merely suggestive sketches of Sherwood Anderson in itself makes the point. But while James and Anderson and a whole range of other writers as well were engaged in creating what we now think of as the "art" story or the story that qualifies as literature, the short story in its less elitist form, that is, as a phenomenon of mass culture, had a rather extraordinary life of its own. In the early years of the century, millions of Americans were reading the newly flourishing "family" magazines whose fictional contents were almost exclusivly given over to the short story. The marriage of literary form to contemporary need could not have been more felicitous. The typical magazine story was short, untaxing, amusing; the typical American reader was increasingly hurried and pressured. Escape—a kind of soothing psychic balm—could be found in the quick and entertaining read. But it is in the very nature of its function—providing a release from tension and anxiety— that the magazine story of those earlier years finally fails, and its ultimate demise was, or should have been, predictable.

In stubborn resistance to the fate of the popular short story are the works of O. Henry (1862–1910), whose pieces continue to be selected, collected, anthologized, and, presumably, enjoyed. If O. Henry survives today while other practitioners of the form have achieved only oblivion, it is because he was both very good at what he did and because he did so very much of it. But the limitations of the form—flat characters who emerge as types, a carefully designed plot with a sudden and often bizarre reversal or coincidence

(the surprise or "snapper" ending)—made the O. Henry story easily repro-
ducible by lesser talents whose products were usually banal, didactic, or
slick. In order to hold the reader, they relied on an ingenious contrivance of
events. The problem, of course, is that once the reader is in on the trick,
once he is aware that both he and the material have been manipulated, there
is nothing to return to the story for; its cleverness is its most engaging feature and can only be experienced in the first reading. It is as though one
were to telescope a Dickens novel, purge it of all its psychological penetra-
tion, social astuteness, and symbolic suggestiveness, and leave only theatrical
characters and strange quirks of fate.

Even in the case of a story by O. Henry, whose imaginative plots and sense
of immediacy lend vitality to otherwise fairly sentimental material, the problematics of a second reading are obvious. The most widely known of his
more than six hundred stories, "The Gift of the Magi," is a fine example. In
it, a very poor but blissfully happy young married couple are confronted by
an approaching Christmas holiday with no funds for gift buying. Della's
greatest possession is her long, silken hair; Jim's is his gold watch. The ironic
twist to this story lies in Della's selling her hair to buy Jim a platinum chain
for his watch while at the same time he sells the watch to buy jeweled combs
for her now vanished tresses. Snapper endings of just this kind are the struc-
turing principle in nearly all his stories and thus have become synonymous
with the name, O. Henry. For all his adroitness (he did capture the feel of
the modern American metropolis; he was, doubtless, sympathetic to the
poor and lonely dreamers who were frequently his subjects), the stories tend
to be formulaic, and their immense and ongoing success is directly attributable to their being entertainments whose focus is on surface values rather
than enduring ones.

In her essay "On the Art of Fiction," Willa Cather considers with characteristic astuteness and not a little exasperation the dichotomy between the
commercially motivated story and the esthetically conceived one: "Writing
ought either to be the manufacture of stories for which there is a market
demand—a business as safe and commendable as making soap or breakfast
foods—or it should be an art, which is always a search for something for
which there is no market demand, something new and untried, where the
values are intrinsic and have nothing to do with standardized values." Short
stories that could meet that criterion, that were as richly suggestive as much
of the literature of the past, were in fact being written at the beginning of
the century. The period's most highly esteemed fiction writers—Henry
James, Edith Wharton, Willa Cather, and Theodore Dreiser—as though un-
mindful of the proliferation of meretricious stories with which they had to

compete for inclusion in the magazines of the day, continued to maintain the highest of esthetic standards in their short stories, enlarging their thematic interests, refining their fictional techniques, and thus modulating the form. Although they were writing in the twentieth century, they had been defined by the ethos of the nineteenth and wrote out of that period's sensibility so that, although the value of their work is incontestable, one cannot assign to their stories the labels of "new," "experimental," or "modern." Such terms are to become applicable only at the end of the period with the publication of Sherwood Anderson's *Winesburg, Ohio,* a collection of brief, melancholy tales of small-town life in the Midwest. It is as though the twentieth century, in the modernist sense, does not begin for the short story until 1919.

• • •

Early in his career, Henry James (1843–1916) remarked, "To write a series of good little tales I deem ample work for a lifetime." By the end of his life, he had written 112 short fictions (variously called short stories, tales, and nouvelles); many are indeed good; precious few are little. In his late or major phase, the story functions, as do his longer works, to make yet more subtle his extraordinary prose style, admittedly difficult, but always in the service of an ascertainable moral end. The charges of sententiousness and obscurantism leveled against him—it was said in some quarters that he wrote more and more about less and less—do not bear up under close examination, for although his sentences become increasingly long and even circuitous, their intricacies reflect a probing intelligence pursuing frequently profound themes.

Earlier, James had been drawn to subjects that allowed him a meticulous scrutiny of problems of conduct. In this sense, he had continued in the tradition established by Jane Austen and George Eliot. The question of manners and morals is everywhere evident in all the major novels and in many of the tales of the early and middle periods (e.g., "Daisy Miller," "Washington Square," "The Real Thing"). Whatever their final effect (one finds a creeping skepticism concerning the humanness of human nature), the canvas is broad and sweeping and characters and setting are convincingly realized. By the turn of the century, this richly textured social world and its interest in the subtleties of ethical behavior and the difficulties of interpersonal relations give way to more philosophical considerations, at once more mystical, more meditative, and more somber. Now his stories are relatively unpeopled; often two characters dominate, sometimes only one, in the interest of exploring the problems of the solitary soul, of man removed from a social milieu that, although it provides value and meaning, is also a distraction from the inner life. The atmosphere is often close, airless, oppressive, a metaphor for the interior world whose nature James illuminates.

In "The Great Good Place" (1900), the writer George Dane—clearly a projection of James—is overcome by a sense of world-weariness (a state not unlike the angst that in later decades is to become the hallmark of twentieth-century despair and the posture of existentialism). Surrounded by the paraphernalia of a busy life, the stuff of social and business affairs, of obligations and duties, he is exhausted, oppressed by the physical emblems of his success. He sees encroaching upon him letters, newspapers, journals, and magazines.

[They] made a huddled mound that had been growing for several days and of which he had been wearily, helplessly aware. There were new books . . . books from publishers, books from authors, books from friends, books from enemies, books from his own bookseller. . . . It was the old rising tide, and it rose and rose even under a minute's watching. It had been up to his shoulders last night—it was up to his chin now.

He feels suffocated and seems to have "lost possession of his soul."

If this scene and the larger world of the story are, in one sense, a fictional rendering of Wordsworth's "The World Is Too Much with Us," it is at the same time, a remarkably prophetic enunciation of Eugene Ionesco's plays in which objects proliferate and regenerate everywhere, spilling out into the world, overwhelming and then usurping the human spirit. George Dane knows that, to live, he must be liberated from these accoutrements of his success; he knows, too, that it is impossible to leave them. The only possible salvation is "to be left, to be forgotten." This "being left" is effected by the appearance of a stranger who remains unnamed, undescribed, barely there but for the gentle taking of George Dane's hand, at which moment the writer finds himself in "the great good place." This mystical realm is a kind of paradise of ommissions, a world "without newspapers and letters, without telegrams and photographs, without the dreadful, fatal too much. There he could read and write; there, above all he could do nothing—he could live."

Living, for George Dane, means the recovery of the essential self; and it requires the stripping down, the paring away of the dross of existence. His discovery of timelessness, of perfect peace and quiet order, may be nothing more than a state of consciousness, but it is in any event a means of regaining the soul. That this state of being is not merely an escape from the difficulties of life is evident in Geroge Dane's readiness to return to the quotidian world, refreshed, revitalized, in a sense, reborn. What he has discovered in the great good place, in its "broad deep bath of stillness," is that quintessential self which in the name of fame and achievement he had lost. Now "the inner life woke up again, and it was the inner life . . . that was returning health."

There is, of course, the suggestion in this story of Henry James's own world-weariness, his emotional fatigue in the face of "the modern madness, mere maniacal extension and motion." And there is the peculiarly Jamesian (which is to say, upper-class gentlemanly) nature of the utopia: "an hotel without noise, a club without newspapers." Still its vision is not narrow. The fantasy of a place removed from "the dreadful, fatal too much," the suggestion that there is a means of returning to the true, the solitary self, has perhaps even greater resonance now near the close of the twentieth century than it did at its beginning.

"The Beast in the Jungle" (1903) is usually regarded either as a love story or as a ghost story. In fact, it can with perhaps greater accuracy and a good deal more poignancy be read as James's consummate statement of human isolation, spiritual paralysis, and tragic self-recognition. There is in John Marcher something of Eliot's Prufrock, that later creation who together with *The Waste Land* was to represent for a whole generation of intellectuals the sterility of the modern world. To live is, of course, to take risks, and Marcher's absolute conviction that "something or other lay in wait for him . . . like a crouching jungle beast waiting to spring" is his defense against life, his avoidance of risk taking. His presentiment that something horrific is to happen to him is revealed through his conversations with May Bartram, who, like presumably all else in Marcher's world, is martyred to his obsession.

They meet daily, these two, through the decades, waiting and watching for the catastrophe. That she loves him is indisputable; that they could and indeed should marry is obvious; but Marcher is certain that "a man of feeling didn't cause himself to be accompanied by a lady on a tiger-hunt." And so they wait, their relationship perpetuated solely by the imagined horror, May reaching out to him in understanding and sympathy, Marcher responding ever more analytically about the intricacies of his predicament. May, like so many of James's women, is a principle of affirmation, a representation of fearless human commitment, a suggestion of what might be. Marcher, paralyzed by the terror of relationship (a fear more real than that of the imagined beast), is kept alive by her questions, her insights into his horror, her shy but unwavering support. At last, weary of waiting for him to recognize what she has always known, that his beast is in fact the failure to love, the failure to be, she dies, and his disappearance from his world brings, finally, the truth of his situation to him. The scene of his discovery is as powerful as anything James ever wrote. At May Bartram's graveside, Marcher sees a mourner in an agony of grief at the tombstone opposite:

Marcher knew him at once for one of the truly stricken—a perception so sharp that nothing else in the picture comparatively lived, neither his dress nor his age, nor his presumable character and class; nothing lived but the deep ravage of the features he showed. . . . The stranger passed, but the raw glare of his grief remained, making our friend wonder in pity what wrong, what wound it expressed, what injury not to be healed. What had the man *had,* to make him by the loss of it so bleed and yet live?

Something—and this reached him with a pang—that *he,* John Marcher, hadn't; the proof of which was precisely John Marcher's arid end. No passion had ever touched him, for this was what passion meant; he had survived and maundered and pined but where had been *his* deep ravage? . . . The illumination had begun . . . . it blazed to the zenith, and what he presently stood there gazing at was the sounded void of his life.

Marcher has been unable to immerse himself in experience, intellectualizing rather than living, defending himself against feeling, against both the pleasures and pains of relationship. Like Prufrock, his energy is invested in the shaping of philosophical abstractions, in explanations for delay. Eliot's lines have a chilling applicability: "There will be time yet for a hundred indecisions. . . . and indeed there will be time / To wonder 'Do I dare and Do I dare?' " The suffering of the mourner opposite is the sudden recognition of passions John Marcher had feared and denied; May Bartram's tombstone is a shocking confrontation with mortality. Together, they act to bring him his revelation, his beast: "He had been the man of his time, *the* man, to whom nothing on earth was to have happened." The tale's grand irony is in its representation of the beast in the jungle, not as in Marcher's expectation as some grotesque, unthinkable experience, but as the very absence of experience. Indeed, the moment of understanding is the only real event in his life, and it is rendered with an extraordinary economy and sense of terror:

He saw the Jungle of his life and saw the lurking Beast; then, while he looked, perceived it, as by a stir of the air, rise, huge and hideous, for the leap that was to settle him. His eyes darkened—it was close; and, instinctively turning, in his hallucination, to avoid it, he flung himself, face down, on the tomb.

If "The Beast in the Jungle" has, like "The Great Good Place," autobiographical reverberations (James became increasingly morose about the price he had paid in living the life of the mind), "The Jolly Corner" is even more demonstrably rooted in the facts of his experience. At thirty-three, he left America to reside in England, returning to the country of his birth only for an occasional visit. The last of these was in 1904–5, and when he went back to England, he began work on a whole series of tales and novels whose themes grew out of the American experience. Throughout, one finds a disillusionment with an America James found markedly changed from that of his remembered youth. His biographer, Leon Edel, sees this attitude as a reflection of his defining characteristic: a deep need for "order, composition, restraint, moderation, beauty, duration," in a word, for civilization.

His distress and an accompanying nostalgia for a simpler, more tranquil America are most explicit in a series of travel essays collected as *The American Scene* (1907). But this wistfulness spills over into his fictions as well, frequently shaping those works in which we find his "international theme." We have from James, then, as from no other American writer, a whole constellation of stories on the theme of the returning American as witness to the collapse of values associated, in myth if not in fact, with an earlier era. Among those of his last phase to take up this subject are "Julia Bride" (1908), "Crapy Cornelia" (1910), and "The Round of Visits" (1910). Each is a reworking of his earlier mode of social realism: that is, the worlds they create are of groups of cultivated and leisured people whose interactions allow the close and often ironic analysis of the disparity between social pretensions and moral truths. In each, James emphasizes the vulgarity of new money, the protective cloak of social privilege, and the heartlessness of the American metropolis.

However, "The Jolly Corner" (1909), set like the others in New York, is a tale of a very different order. It is, first of all, a ghost story whose effects as sheer supernatural fiction are considerable. Second, like "A Great Good Place," it is a journey inward, a journey whose ends are both self-revelation and release.

James's ghosts are never gratuitous; which is to say, they never creep or hover only to unsettle or dismay. They appear only to those whose troubled natures make them susceptible to terrifying images and are, beyond their grisly pictorial suggestiveness, technical devices used in the service of psychological analysis. Thus, that which Spencer Brydon finds, indeed, that which he actively seeks in the old house in New York to which he has returned after thirty years, is his "alter ego," the self he might have been had he remained in America, rather than electing, as he had, to live abroad.

Much of the story's fascination derives from the slow bringing to birth of Spencer Brydon's deeply repressed self. The catalyst for the first stage of this slow emergence is Alice Staverton, another in the galaxy of James's perfectly understanding and infinitely patient women, to whom Brydon recounts the history of the old house and his early years within it. As he speaks to her, it becomes clear that the house gives him not only a strong sense of the past but, in fact, an intuition of "ineffable life" behind its walls. Finally, he is moved to wonder what he would have been had he remained: "What," he asks repeatedly, "would it have made of me?"

Curiosity gives way to the conviction that the house on the Jolly Corner contains a different but equally real other self, a self motivated by a purely commercial impulse, a "rank money passion." It is, then, this self that Spencer Brydon had attempted to deny in his long and deliberate expatriation; and it is this self that he pursues and finally faces down in the old house in New York. He becomes a man obsessed, enacting a carefully rehearsed nightly ritual—placing his walking stick in the same corner, lighting candles, slowly traversing first the lower floors, then the top—as though by sacrament and ceremony to hasten the appearance of the "other" he knows to be there.

Finally, in a moment of wonderfully sustained horror, the apparition materializes before him: "Rigid and conscious, spectral yet human, [he saw] a man of his own substance and stature [who] waited there to measure himself with his power to dismay." Brydon recognizes in this specter in evening dress, with dangling eyeglasses, grizzled face, and white hands that show two fingers to be missing, "an opposed projection of himself," odious, aggressive, inexpressibly evil. It is, he sees, a monstrous life, and one even larger, more convincing than his own. Strained beyond the limits of endurance, he collapses.

When he awakens, he finds himself in the comforting cushion of Alice Staverton's lap. "I can only have died," he tells her. "You brought me literally to life." Clearly, Alice Staverton functions here as an agent of salvation—the means by which Brydon can accept all of what he is, potentially and actually. In this sense, "The Jolly Corner" is the story of the regenerative power of love. But its most compelling feature is not in its resolution—Spencer Brydon's spiritual rebirth and the promise of a fruitful relationship—but rather in the awful confrontation with that other self.

That the figure—a phantasmal projection of base capitalism—expresses James's personal revulsion at the disappearance of the old order in America and its usurpation by the vulgar and meretricious is obvious. But this interpretation does not sufficiently account for its disquieting effect on the reader. It is entirely possible that Spencer Brydon's apparition insinuates itself into one's consciousness because it suggests some more universal and sinister truth about the human spirit, suggests perhaps that if we are daylight beings, capable of virtue and principle, we are creatures of the night as well, creatures whose impulses can be, and often are, corrupt, bestial, and malignant.

These tales share, by definition, and certainly in effect, the theme, mood, and atmosphere of supernatural fiction. But taken together, they provide a significant and revealing personal record as well. At the center of each is the suggestion of a world just beyond but unexplored, a road accessible but not taken, an experience fraught with possibilities, but unpotentiated. There is, then, in these late stories, the sense that Henry James had begun to experience wistfulness, even despair, at the narrowing of boundaries and the closing off of options and, perhaps, a concomitant questioning of the validity of his life. If advancing years and poor health did lead to such a preoccupation, its incorporation in his fictions transcends personal indulgence. Nearing the end of his life but still in superb control of his art, his anxieties provide exemplary stories of the eerie and bizarre. No less successful as pure fiction than the stories of his earlier periods, these tales function additionally as speculations on the nature of the unknown, the unlived life, and the might-have-been. One sees in them the gradual movement away from the social realism and irony of his first and middle phases and the emergence of themes increasingly abstract, contemplative, and philosophical.

• • •

It has been the misfortune of Edith Wharton (1862–1937) and Willa Cather (1873–1947) to exist through the decades in the shadow of Henry James: Cather in this or that story is Jamesian or un-Jamesian. Wharton is, variously, a disciple of James, a lesser James, a female James. Indeed, the man who was both friend and mentor to Edith Wharton was to become, finally, her albatross, the titan to whom she was inevitably compared and usually found wanting. The literary characteristics these three share are those that define most traditionalist literature: a deliberate and unhurried narrative; a consecutive chronology; and a solid recognizable social world in which time-honored institutions, the bonds of family and community, the strength and endurance of the human spirit form a moral nexus. And if Wharton and Cather did go to school to Henry James, they took what they could best make use of (clearly, not his far more complex prose style), adding the shape of their own lives and sensibilites: the background of high society New York and frontier Nebraska, and most tellingly, the experience of being a woman. They both worked steadily in the short story form and although, like James, they are better known as novelists, the energy and care they lavished on their shorter fictions make abundantly clear that they regarded the form, not as an exercise, a reprieve from the more taxing demands of novel writing, but rather a vehicle perfectly adapted to the development of specific and highly individual literary ideas.

In the introduction to his two-volume edition of Wharton's stories, R. W. B. Lewis calls attention to the role of the genre in her career: "Edith Wharton began as a writer of short stories, and in a sense, she finished as one." That she had written eighty-six short stories by the end of her life demonstrates the degree to which the form attracted her. She was interested in its methods enough, in fact, to devote a chapter of her book, *The Writing of Fiction,* to an analysis of the short story. In it she distinguishes between novel and story by examining the emphasis in each of character and situation and finding, as others have before and after her, that the test of the novel is that "its people should be alive" and that in the short story, "action is the chief affair." But she evokes the true essence of the form most succinctly, if somewhat impressionistically, in her observation that the successful short story is not a "loose web spread over the surface of life," but rather "a shaft driven straight into the heart of human experience."

Given her interest and, needless to say, that same genius we see at work in her novels, it is not surprising that a number of her stories are fine, many of them unforgettable. (What is surprising is that except for a few, they are rarely reprinted or anthologized.) Her subjects are many: Lewis designates six or seven thematic categories. Among them are tales of the supernatural, and of these, there is at least one that achieves extraordinary effects. Like the best ghost stories, it has the capacity to unnerve, and like the best of any literature, it penetrates beneath the tensions of plot and image to reveal profound psychological and moral truths.

"The Eyes" (1910) begins as so many tales of terror do with a quiet circle of friends in an atmosphere of mystery and gloom (here, further modified by the faint aura of decadence), the suggestion of some terrible evil, the gradual revelation of gruesome or eerie events, and a host who provides the appropriate setting. The host in this instance is Andrew Culwin. Each of his guests has told a tale of a ghostly visitation, and now Culwin, the oldest and most worldly of the group, tells them of his strange experience. That which came to him was not a ghost but only a horrible pair of eyes. They first appeared to him many years ago when, feeling bored, he began a dalliance with a young cousin. She was girl who amused him, not because she was beautiful or intelligent (she was neither of these, he assures his listeners), but because "it interested me to see any woman content to be so uninteresting, and I wanted to find out the secret of her content." The girl falls in love with him, expecting, as a matter of course, marriage. Culwin, feeling trapped, plans to go to Europe. The girl, devastated, collapses, and Culwin, flattered by her devotion, promptly proposes to her. It is on that same night that the eyes first appear to him, staring from out of the blackness, giving off an eerie glow.

They were the very worst eyes I've ever seen: a man's eyes—but what a man! My first thought was that he must be frightfully old. The orbits were sunk, and the thick red-lined lids hung over the eyeballs like blinds of which the cords are broken. One lid drooped a little lower than the other, with the effect of a crooked leer; and between these folds of flesh, with their scant bristle of lashes, the eyes, small glassy disks with an agate-like rim, looked like sea pebbles in the grip of a starfish.

But the age of the eyes was not the most unpleasant thing about them. What turned me sick was their expression of vicious security. I don't know how else to describe the fact that they seemed to belong to a man who had done a lot of harm in his life, but had always kept just inside the danger lines.

The eyes return, night after night, until Culwin, terrified, flees to Europe. Here, he experiences the "bliss of escaping" both the eyes and the embarrassment of an involvement with the young woman.

Some time later, still in Europe, Culwin has taken under his tutelage a young writer, a beautiful young man of no talent but immense charm. Unable to promote his career, but reluctant to give up so amiable, so accommodating, a companion, Culwin leads him on. And now, the eyes appear once more, seeming even more ghastly than the last time.

I saw now what I hadn't seen before: that they were eyes which had grown hideous gradually. . . . There they hung in the darkness, their swollen lids dropped across the little watery bulbs rolling loose in the orbits, and the puff of flesh making a muddy shadow underneath—and as their stare moved with my movements, there came over me a sense of their tacit complicity, of a deep, hidden understanding between us that was worse than the first shock of their strangeness.

At about this time, the young protégé, running out of both hope and funds, decides to leave. When he does, the eyes give up their ghostly vigil.

Culwin pauses in his narrative to glance across at young Phil Frenham, his latest companion and protégé, who had remained unmoving, as though transfixed, all through the tale, his gaze fixed steadily on Culwin's face. Their eyes meet and the young man suddenly flings his arms across a table and drops his face upon them. "Phil," Culwin cries out. "What the deuce? why, have the eyes scared *you*? My dear boy—my dear fellow—I never had such a tribute to my literary ability, never!" Culwin laughs nervously, and moves across the room to Frenham. As he does, he catches the reflection of his face in the mirror behind the young man's head:

He paused, his face level with the mirror, as if scarcely recognizing the countenance on it as his own. But as he looked, his expression gradually changed, and for an appreciable space of time he and the image in the glass confronted each other with a glare of slowly gathering hate.

Much of the story's power can be attributed to a complex play of irony. While Culwin unknowingly reveals the hideousness of his nature, recognizing only at the end that the grotesque eyes are in fact his own, the narrator, just as ingenuously, reveals his own terrible obtuseness, his inability to see and to judge appropriately the evil that confronts him. Throughout, the terms in which he presents Culwin make abundantly clear his host's misanthropy. He was, he tells us, "a spectator, a humorous, detached observer . . . of life." He was a man who "made a study of the human race," and his conclusions were that "all men were superfluous and women necessary only because someone had to do the cooking." As to his young recruits, "he liked 'em juicy," and Frenham, the most recent acquisition, was a "good subject for experimentation." The influence of Hawthorne is plain here: the earlier writer's explorations into the psychology of Faustian egocentricity in, say, "Ethan Brand" or "Rappaccini's Daughter" have the same suggestion of some dark and awful defilement of the human spirit, unspecified, but palpable.

The two unwitting revelations—of Culwin's monstrous ego and the narrator's uncritical acceptance—are twin horrors and in them lie the true subject of the story. In its wonderfully sustained drama and its ironic unfolding of moral degeneration, "The Eyes," is one of Edith Wharton's most perfectly conceived and executed shorter fictions.

Wharton's concern about the nature and function of morality is nowhere more fulsomely addressed than in her stories at whose center is the "marriage question." Although Henry James before her had successfully explored the rituals of courting, marriage, and divorce and those often rigid public attitudes that shape and maintain them, his interest was that of the detached observer. For Wharton, the subject was both more immediate and more vexing because she lived it: although she was independently wealthy and moved with ease among the leisured and cultivated in both America and Europe, she had to do battle with the narrow prejudices of society and was fully aware of the extent to which women, and especially creative and ambitious women, were deprived of opportunity for the development of their true potential, and, as a corollary, were forced to be dependent upon the men in their lives. Further, she had for many years been locked in a marriage devoid of the pleasures of love or companionship, reluctant to divorce her mentally ill husband, Edward, in deference to the traditions of the social class to which she belonged.

In 1899, only a few years after beginning her writing career (a career that began, predictably, with "female" interests: the decoration of houses, landscape design, travel), she published a book of short stories, *The Greater Inclination*. Here, she moved from essays on the decorative and esthetic worlds to fictions on the human one. She had found her métier. Throughout the collection there is evidence of both her ease in adapting to storytelling techniques and her sensitivity to women's issues. One of the finest of the stories is "Souls Belated." It is her earliest and one of her most successful treatments of the conflict between woman's identity and the social world to which that identity must be accommodated.

Lydia and Gannett are two lovers on a train from Paris, having arranged, finally, to be free of those entanglements that had kept them apart. But their hard-won union brings them not joy or contentment but rather self-consciousness, anxiety, silence.

How could it be otherwise, with that thing between them? She glanced up at the rack overhead. The *thing* was there, in her dressing-bag, symbolically suspended over her head and his. He was thinking of it now, just as she was; they had been thinking of it in unison ever since they had entered the train.

The "thing" that lay between them is, ironically, that which unites them— the papers of her divorce. That morning she and lover had been laughing over some foolishness in a local guidebook when the envelope was delivered to her.

Even when she had unfolded the document she took it for some unimportant business paper sent abroad for her signature, and her eye travelled inattentively over the curly *Whereases* of the preamble until a word arrested her: Divorce. There it stood, an impassable barrier, between her husband's name and hers.

The word and the accumulated moral shadings that accrue to it suggest the anomalous position of Lydia Tillotson. As a woman engaged in a long, ardent, and illicit love affair, it is naturally assumed that she will leave one marriage to enter another. She is, then, not the free agent she had hoped to become, but paradoxically even more dependent upon those institutions she is attempting to reject and transcend. She had left a dreary, loveless marriage marked by social obligations and a "sense of proportion" in order to shape her life anew. She loves Gannett but wants desperately to remain separate, autonomous, to be free of those social conventions she had flouted in leaving her husband. But she finds that the coveted freedom is compromised by social pressures that compel her to remarry. She discovers that in divorcing, she has fallen from the publicly decreed state of grace, and it is expected, indeed presumed to be axiomatic, that she will now marry her lover and thus be "rehabilitated." Struggling against this expectation, she tells Gannett that to marry would be fraudulent, a "sneaking back into a position that we've voluntarily forfeited." "It would," she says, "betray the secret longing to be accepted by the very people whose conventional morality we have always ridiculed and hated."

And so they move from place to place, always on the periphery of society, frequently thrown together with its least savory elements. It is this very rootlessness with which Wharton underlines the precariousness of their roles. As the story opens, they are on a train from Paris; the narrative is punctuated by a series of journeys to resorts and hotels across the landscape of Europe; and the concluding scene shows Gannett perusing a timetable of trains. But their wanderings are not those of a romantically united two against the world, but, in Wharton's words, "like the flight of exiles."

The story is extraordinarily modern, indeed prophetic in its creation of a woman whose integrity cries out for a moral code by which she can live but which she finds unacceptable to society; it is wonderfully satiric in its anatomy of the empty pieties and indolence of the well-to-do; and it is sober in its bitter recognition that a woman alone, pitted against the customs and dictates of society, is doomed. Any hope of real and continuing freedom for Lydia Tillotson is subverted by the counterclaims of the "cult of domesticity," the promised nirvana of matrimony and motherhood. The woman who demands more or other is alien, suspect; there is neither place nor identity for her. Gannett, extraordinary in his perceptiveness, states the case admirably:

Where would she go? What would her life be when she left him? She had no near relations and few friends. . . . He thought of her as walking through a stony waste. No one would understand her—no one would pity her.

The story's uniqueness is in its treatment of the complex and shifting attitudes toward divorce and adultery, but its most affecting statement is in its indictment of bourgeois society and its by-product, the miserable, utterly dependent status of women. Wharton renders this most poignantly by way of one image, perfect, irreducible: that of Lydia Tillotson walking away from a boat platform and her dream of independence, and wearily, resignedly, returning to the hotel and Gannett, to marriage, and to that society whose strictures cannot be repudiated. What Lydia Tillotson learns is that life "is made up of compromises." To shun respectability is to be condemned to a fugitive existence, a state that would inevitably destroy the love that holds Lydia and Gannett together. As he tells her: "One may believe in [conventions] or not: but as long as they do rule the world it is only by taking advantage of their protection that one can find a *modus vivendi.*" The words are Gannett's; the concept, clear-eyed and practical if also a conciliation to public notions of morality, is the author's. In it we can see Edith Wharton's longing to be free of externally imposed conventions and proprieties and her recognition that she, like all women of her time, was inextricably bound to them.

Her continuing interest in this subject, in fact her commitment to an analysis of the problems it posed, is demonstrated by the appearance in 1904 of "The Other Two," the most celebrated and anthologized of her shorter fictions and, perhaps, the finest story in English of the plight of the female in a fiercely acquisitive and rigidly patriarchal society.

Alice Waythorn, thrice married, twice divorced, has learned the art of adapting, chameleon-like and with astonishing speed and versatility, to the needs of whatever man she wishes to attract. Her third husband, from whose point of view the story is narrated, slowly comes to realize that the woman he adored for her uniqueness, for the extraordinary originality of her charm, is, in fact, "as easy as an old shoe," taking, as it were, the shape of each successive foot—Alice Haskett, Alice Varick, Alice Waythorn—with a gradual erosion of identity, a leaving behind of a "little of the self where the unknown God abides." Her social progression, through marriage, has been upward—an escalation due entirely to her malleability, to the ease with which she learns what and how to be for the men who provide her with material comfort and social position. But while Waythorn is gradually disillusioned by the blankness he perceives beneath his wife's veneer, he still yields to "the joy of possessorship. They were his, those white hands, with their flitting motions, his the light haze of her hair, the lips and eyes." Finally, seeing her calculated pliancy with Haskett and Varick, "the other two," he recognizes that in his possessing her, he is merely a "member of a syndicate. He held so many shares in his wife's personality and his predecessors were his partners in the business." The story's concluding irony is in Alice Waythorn's inevitable inability to keep her successive roles distinct. Pouring coffee for Waythorn one evening, she is all smiles and grace and flattery, but in a moment of confusion, she pours cognac in his cup—a ritual required not by the tastes and habits of Waythorn, but those of Varick. The obvious moral premise of the piece is that when one partner exists merely to service the needs of the other, both lose equally. If Alice Waythorn has no verifiable character, no true "self," if she is only a series of studied gestures and responses, then Waythorn has not a wife, but rather a custom-tailored and expendable package. But the larger implication of the story is feminist, revealing the utter dehumanization of women in a society in which security and its social manifestation, success, is obtainable only through marriage to the most desirable (which is to say, most economically solvent) man.

In both her novels and her stories, Wharton has traditionally been regarded as an astute observer of New York's high society in its moribund but still glittering years at the close of the nineteenth century. In this sense, her work has the added value and luster of social documentary. Of course, as is customarily the case in fiction of manners and morals, the careful elucidation of setting, costume, and behavior gives us not only the distinctions of class, but the motivations that underlie the characters' being and doing. Thus, Waythorn's observations of his wife's second husband in a restaurant function on one level to reveal the telltale practice of adding cognac to coffee, but additionally, they make wonderfully evident ths scrupulous details of Varick's presumptive and his actual social status.

When Waythorn first saw him he had been helping himself with critical deliberation to a bit of Camembert at the ideal point of liquefaction, and now, the cheese removed, he was just pouring his *café double* from its little two-storied earthen pot. He poured slowly, his ruddy profile bent over the task, and one beringed white hand steadying the lid of the coffeepot; then he stretched his other hand to the decanter of cognac at his elbow, filled a liquor glass, took a tentative sip, and poured the brandy into his cup.

The studied casualness, the beringed fingers, the absorption in effects, the ruddy complexion, are the unmistakable emblems of Varick's "middle-classness," the futility of his attempts to be regarded as aristocratic.

And Haskett's "made-up tie attached with an elastic" is the index to a whole cluster of habits and conventions that define Alice Waythorn's first marriage; it suggests to Waythorn the single overriding purpose of her life—to move, through successive husbands, ever upward on the social ladder:

He could see her, as Mrs. Haskett, sitting in a "front parlor" furnished in plush, with a pianola, and a copy of *Ben Hur* on the center table. He could see her going to theater with Haskett—or perhaps even to a "Church Sociable"—she in a "picture hat" and Haskett in a black frock coat, a little creased, with the made-up tie on an elastic. . . . He could fancy how pretty Alice must have looked . . . and how she must have looked down on the other women, chafing at her life and secretly feeling that she belonged in a bigger place.

Many of Wharton's stories are given shape and direction by this movement up and down the social scale, and they are evidence of the author's own nervousness about the invading "parvenus" who, it seemed to her, threatened much that had been valuable in the elegant world of old money—honor, dignity, culture. But frequently we find as well her concern about the role of woman as commodity. It is precisely this view that is so perfectly adumbrated in "The Other Two," and its importance for the short story is incontestable. Until Wharton's work, we have no record in this form of the haplessness of the female in American culture. Alice Waythorn's sublimation of identity in the service of security, status, and respectability (Wharton calls it the "obliteration of the self") is not idiosyncratic: it is typical, and the author's attitude toward her character is, finally, less scornful than pitying.

In the later "Autre Temps" (1916), the subject of divorce is scrutinized once again, but now in a view both more complex and more bitter. Mrs. Lidcote had scandalized New York twenty years ago by her "rebellion," that is, by her refusal to remain unhappily married. Since that time she has lived in self-imposed exile in Italy, largely to protect her daughter, Leila, from gossip and innuendo. Now she learns that Leila, like her, has divorced and is about to remarry, and she rushes to New York to help her bear up under the strain.

What she finds upon her arrival is that her daughter, far from needing her ministrations, is as respectable and secure as is the impressive "establishment" house that she and her new husband have acquired and that she is eagerly accepted by the smart new social set in whose orbit she unself-consciously moves. But while Leila lives a life unblemished by talk of her divorce and remarriage, Mrs. Lidcote finds, wherever *she* appears, averted eyes, heads drawn together in whispered unison, sudden departures from a room she has entered. Her daughter's divorce seems almost to have been erased, canceled out. But her own follows her about like some noisy and inescapable lapdog. Throughout the years she had grown accustomed to being ostracized, had even come to expect that the divorce "would always be there, huge, obstructing, encumbering, bigger and more dominant than anything the future would ever conjure up." And yet, here *was* the future and it brings, in the benign acceptance of her daughter's divorce, the gratuitous snubbing for her own, a feeling of confusion and humiliation. There is, she says, no sense to it, no sequence. This new world was a "crowded, topsy-turvy world, with its changes and helter-skelter readjustments, its new tolerances and indifferences and accommodations"; it is a world that refuses to extend its generous new attitudes to her. She discovers, too, that the daughter in whom she had invested so much of herself, for whom, in fact, she had exiled herself, is altogether insensitive to her situation; that she finds her mother, cruelly and paradoxically, an embarrassment, an encumbrance. And in perhaps the most disturbing in a relentless series of awful revelations, she watches as Franklin Ide, the one man she has come to trust as being beyond the ugly bigotry of all the others, betrays his own smug and narrow prejudices. Bereft of friends and family, without a framework of social customs and attitudes she can comprehend, there is no alternative for her but to return to Italy.

The thematic richness of the story resides in its dual vision: the past, while shaped by occasional narrowmindedness, is presented as a solidly based structure, as being comprised of a community of values, known and understood, in which the individual can survive and grow. But the present, for all its new (and arbitrarily dispensed) freedoms can be, in Mrs. Lidcote's words, "chaos," a "void." There is, in the peculiar contempt still accorded her, the symbol of a society too hurried, too pleasure-bent to ask the appropriate questions or to formulate adequate responses. It has, quite simply, become the fashion to cut Mrs. Lidcote. Her own assessment of this strangely persistent custom reflects a sad, hard-won wisdom:

It's simply that society is much too busy to revise its own judgments. Probably no one . . . stopped to consider that my case and Leila's were identical. They only remembered that I'd done something, which, at the time that I did it, was condemned by society. My case had been passed on and classified. I'm the woman who had been cut for twenty years. The older people have half forgotten why, and the younger ones have never really known: it's simply become a tradition to cut me. And traditions that have lost their meanings are the hardest of all to destroy.

The passage enunciates the radical disjunction between social attitudes and ethical norms, a rupture symbolic of an all-pervasive moral turpitude. The consequences for the individual of such rapidly fluctuating mores is the inability to understand clearly what is expected of her by the larger world of which she is a part. Unable to decode its shifting, often contradictory messages, she may unwittingly commit public blunders and gaucheries, may even make needless personal sacrifices. This is precisely Mrs. Lidcote's experience. The standards by which she and her daughter are judged for the identical "transgression" are quixotic at best and her bitterness is predictable and just. She is "overwhelmed at the senseless waste of her own adventure, and wrung with the irony of perceiving that the success or failure of the deepest human experiences may hang on a matter of chronology."

If in the character and predicament of Mrs. Lidcote, Wharton shows us once again the price exacted from a woman who defies tradition, she depicts also the collapse of the old order with its reliable—if not always admirable—systems of conduct. In her memoirs, she contemplates the dizzying tempo of the shift in custom: "What had seemed unalterable rules of conduct became of a sudden observances as quaintly arbitrary as the domestic rites of the pharaohs." Edith Wharton recognized the injustice of many of the old orthodoxies, but at the same time, she saw their disintegration as a break in social continuity, which—she maintained steadfastly in nearly all her fiction—ultimately subverts civilized living.

· · ·

Willa Cather is the first writer of the group under consideration to be defined wholly and exclusively as a writer of the American experience. Both James and Wharton chose the Continent as the place most hospitable to their natures and interests and lived most of their lives there. Indeed, their despair at the hordes of "vulgar arrivistes" who increasingly peopled the commercial centers of America was transmuted into thematic material in many of their works. Consequently, one finds in their subjects and settings a degree of sophistication, an ambience of the cosmopolitan and cultivated, a sense of life as it might be lived by the very rich and very poised almost anywhere in Western civilization. But Cather, although well traveled and superbly educated, remained stubbornly rooted in the American scene, and her fictions are given shape and direction by American lives, American struggles, American dreams.

She was brought as a young girl from Virginia to a small desert town in Nebraska, and many of her stories and novels reflect the frontier experience she knew best because she heard its legends, breathed its history. It is for this reason that she has frequently been labeled (and usually in the pejorative sense) a local colorist. But if her subjects are often (and certainly not exclusively) the development of the Midwest and if her theme is often the courage and indomitability of the pioneer spirit, both her intent and the achieved effect are far more vast than the geographic limits would suggest. Her subject is in fact universal: the focus is inevitably upon the special creature engaged in combat with an intractable environment or with obstacles to a passionately declared goal, the conditions of the struggle, and the nature and consequences of the triumph or defeat. It is not surprising, then, that her

other compelling subject is the experience of the artist. Throughout her career, Cather envisioned artists and pioneers alike as those gifted mortals
whose unique vigor, responsiveness, and acuteness of perception—the defining characteristics of the creative spirit—allow them to reshape the raw
material of the world, phenomenal and ontologic, into a place closer to the
human heart's desire, and to bring to those more ordinary souls among
whom they move, a sense of spiritual renewal. She knew, because she lived
this too, the rigorous discipline such dedication requires, not least of which
is the renunciation of ordinary pleasures and frequent isolation from the rest
of the world.

It is this—the special nature of the artistic soul and the loneliness of his
calling—that is Cather's preoccupation in the short stories of 1900–1920. In
1905 a collection of her stories, *The Troll Garden,* was published; it included
four artist stories which were later issued with the addition of three new
works in 1920 as *Youth and the Bright Medusa.* We have in this collection a
convenient grouping of artist tales which additionally reveals a distinct thematic and tonal shift from the early (1900–1905) to the later (1916–1920)
stories.

Cather's world is, in general, one reduced in sound and activity. It is not
nearly so densely populated as Wharton's, in whose fiction one hears the
hum and buzz of witty, animated discourse, the interjection of bright if occasionally shrill laughter, the clatter of china teacups in china saucers, the
strains of violin or harp in a hotel lobby. This is due in part to the subjects
and settings themselves, but it is also in execution of a deliberately conceived
esthetic ideal.

In her essay, "The Novel Demeublé," Cather calls for the "disfurnishing
of the novel," asking that writers "leave the scene bare for the play of emotions, great and little, for . . . to make a drama a man [needs but] one passion
and four walls." It is in this same spirit that she constructed her stories—
many of them are bare indeed—especially and appropriately those at whose
center one finds the solitary, brooding presence of the artist.

"A Death in the Desert" (1903) is an enactment of Cather's proscription
for stripping the fictional world of many of its customary accoutrements.
The plot is nearly nonexistent; the characters are two; the mood, elegiac
as the title predicts it will be, is induced wholly through reverie and
reminiscence.

The pianist, Everet Hilgard, has stopped in Cheyenne, Wyoming, on his
way to the West Coast and discovers that Katherine Gaylord, the great diva
whom he had loved at a distance as a boy, is at her ranch, dying of tubercu-
losis. He goes to see her and remains for several weeks; that which unites

them is Everet's brother, Adriance, who, although never present, emerges through their conversations as the most fully realized character in the story. For Katherine, Adriance has functioned as a source of pain: she has loved him for years, and he, a brilliant and magnetic composer comfortably ensconced in the citadel of art and his own ego, remains blissfully unaware. Everet's relationship to Adriance poses problems of a different kind: the two are so nearly identical that Everet is mistaken for his world-famous brother wherever he goes.

The story is an interweaving of several thematic strands. The least successful of these is the portrayal of Katherine, who in her prolonged and unrequited love and her lingering, feverish, handkerchief-clutching death has too close an affinity to a number of grand opera heroines. But her presence in the story provides another layer of meaning, for in her recollection of one glorious night with Adriance, there are insights into the nature of the creative experience and the uniqueness of the artist's sensibilities:

His first words were not to tell me how ill he had been, but that that morning he had been well enough to put the last strokes to the score of his "Souvenirs d'Automne," and he was as I most like to remember him; calm and happy, and tired with that heavenly tiredness that comes after a good work done at last. Outside, the rain poured down in torrents, and the wind moaned and sobbed in the garden and about the walls of that desolated old palace. How that night comes back to me! . . . Adriance sat staring at the fire with the weariness of all his life in his eyes, and of all the other lives that must aspire and suffer to make up one such life as his. Somehow the wind with all its world-pain had got into the room, and the cold rain was in our eyes, and the wave came up in both of us at once—that awful vague, universal pain, that cold fear of life and death and God and hope—and we were like two clinging together on a spar in mid-ocean after the shipwreck of everything.

The passage is charged with the kind of poetic power that Cather was to become most famous for—a rendering of mood, atmosphere, and emotional state with but a few, carefully selected phrases; it is a clear demonstration of her concept of "disfurnishing," of leaving the scene bare for the play of emotions.

But the most compelling feature of "A Death in the Desert" is the subtle psychological portrait of Everet Hilgard, the less gifted, less charismatic brother, who is everywhere reminded of that genius in whose shadow he walks: his brother is "the only subject people ever seemed to talk to him about." He tells Katherine of his suffering as a child, his likeness to his brother acting as a constant reminder to his mother of the preferred Adriance. "She'd have made burnt-offerings of us all for him any day. . . . She used sometimes to call me to her . . . and kiss me and then I always knew she was thinking of Adriance." For Everet, this reunion with the dying Katherine is bitterly ironic, for his ability to ease her pain, to meet her emotional needs, "lay solely in his link with his brother's life." In her last words to him, the identification has become complete: "'Ah, dear Adriance, dear, dear,' she whispered."

Left once again to minister to "one of the broken things his brother had abandoned," Everet Hilgard emerges as the true center of decency and compassion in the story. In Everet there is an insistence on the eternal verities: concepts, for example, of loyalty and selflessness; and while these are revealed as the cornerstone of human relations in Cather's fictional universe, they are frequently ceded, as in the relationship of the two brothers, to the higher demands of art. "How many souls," the author once asked, "must be sacrificed to make up the life of one gifted artist?"

"The Sculptor's Funeral" puts the question another way: for what kind of people is the true artist sacrificed? The answer comes from Sand City, Kansas, where Harvey Merrick's body has been brought for burial. As his kinsmen and neighbors gather in the Merrick home to pay their last respects to the famous sculptor, their mean-spirited smugness and resentment of his success is revealed: "Too bad the old man's sons didn't turn out better"; "He hadn't it in him to be sharp"; "he shore was never fond of work." The general consensus is that what Harvey Merrick needed was "a course in some first class business college."

Witness to the desecration of Harvey Merrick's creative spirit is Henry Steavens, the young student who has brought the body home. Much of the story is presented from his point of view, a device that enables the reader to apprehend with him the rottenness that had, miraculously, spawned Harvey Merrick. Steavens and Jim Laird, the town lawyer, are the lone voices of integrity in the story; their observations are set in deliberate and essential counterpoise to the self-serving commentary of the townspeople. It is in their vision of him that the real meaning of the sculptor's life resides.

As Steavens sits in the Merrick parlor, a room whose gaudy pretentiousness is wholly out of character with the simplicity and naturalness of the sculptor, he begins to understand the mystery of Harvey Merricks's life.

Steavens went on and on, reconstructing that whole miserable boyhood. All this raw, biting ugliness had been the portion of the man whose mind was to become an exhaustless gallery of beautiful impressions. . . . Steavens understood now the real tragedy, . . . the yearning of a boy, cast ashore upon a desert of newness and ugliness and sordidness, for all that is chastened and old, and noble with tradition.

His reflections are interrupted by the words of Jim Laird whose own capitulation to the code of Sand City has led to a life of drunkenness and despair. He reminds his listeners that all the young men of Sand City have been tragic failures—suicides, gamblers, alcoholics, convicts, degenerates of every description, because their elders had "drummed nothing but money and knavery into their ears" from the time they were born. "There was only one boy raised in this borderland between ruffianism and civilization who didn't come to grief, and you hated him more for winning out than you hated all the other boys who got under the wheels. Lord, Lord, how you did hate him!"

These words are more than bitter pronouncements on the true meaning of Merrick's success for the people of Sand City; they express Cather's personal views on the narrow limits of small-town life and her growing pessimism about the possibility of redemptive relationships. Here, as elsewhere in her work, communication is shown to fail; the special individual is not esteemed but ridiculed and, in order to survive, must move on to an environment more conducive to his uniqueness. In much of Cather's fiction, the oppressive and constricting features of small-town life (commentators have termed it her "revolt from the village") reflect her own early disenchantment with the provincial character of Red Cloud, Nebraska. And her story, "Paul's Case" (1905), doubtless springs from the same cluster of longings and resentments, but here transposed to Pittsburgh, that city in western Pennsylvania where she lived and worked early in her career.

Although Paul is not, strictly speaking, an artist, Cather's inclusion of the story in *Youth and the Bright Medusa* makes clear her own view of the protagonist and of those aspects of the creative life that continued to both fascinate and trouble her. For while Paul has no visible talent and directs his energy to no esthetically attributable ends, he shares with the true artist several critical characteristics. He has a rich imaginative life; he finds it difficult, if not impossible, to conform; he regards himself as singularly important; and he is, without question, an outsider. It is, then, clearly, the differentness of the artist, or in this case, the artist manqué, that Cather continues to pursue as material for her fiction.

The characterization of Paul is complex. Neither admirable (he embezzles funds from his employer) nor even particularly likable (he is by turns flippant and morose), he yet embodies a number of universal human impulses: he feels a deep sense of frustration at a world he can neither adapt to nor manipulate with success; he is contemptuous of surroundings that yield only the mediocre; estranged from all ordinary sources of psychic nurturing, he yearns for a world of beauty and glamor with which to transform his grim reality. Cather's attitude toward him is an admixture of pity and irony, with enough of the former to engage our interest and sympathy and enough of the latter to avoid the bathetic.

This carefully controlled dual vision is in evidence from the first. Called into the faculty room to face accusations of laziness, rudeness, and arrogance, he is suave and smiling but also frayed and worn, hysterically defiant, but also polite; he shrugs deferentially, but his fingers tremble and his mouth twitches. The counterpointing of intrepidity and fear, of charm and awkwardness, form a continuing pattern in the story so that at times we are drawn to this strange, unhappy boy and at others, repelled by him. It is clear, however, that the work's great success (it seems to be everybody's favorite Cather story) is finally determined by the degree of reader identification it achieves. There are several means by which this is established.

There is, of course, Paul's unremitting aloneness: he is in every sense an isolato, and if this state is elicited by his impertinence and his refusal to conform, it is brought about as well by the inability of all those around him to perceive either his uniqueness or his pain. Added to this is the sordidness of the boy's surroundings placed repeatedly in contrast to his sensitivity to the beauty of the natural world. The drabness of mediocrity is increasingly Cather's subject, and in none of her fiction is there a more compelling indictment of it than in the description of Paul's home, his neighborhood, and his father.

[He] never went up Cordelia Street without a shudder of loathing. His home was next to the house of the Cumberland minister. He approached it tonight with the nerveless sense of defeat, the hopeless feeling of sinking back forever into ugliness and commonness that he had always had when he came home. The moment he turned into Cordelia Street he felt the waters close above his head. . . . [He felt] the loathing of respectable beds, of common food, of a house permeated by kitchen odors; a shuddering repulsion for the flavourless, colourless mass of everyday existence; a morbid desire for cool things and soft lights and fresh flowers. The nearer he approached the house, the more absolutely unequal Paul felt to the sight of it all; his ugly sleeping-chamber; the cold bathroom with the grimy zinc tub, the cracked mirror, the dripping spiggots; his father, at the top of the stairs, his hairy legs sticking out from his nightshirt, his feet thrust into carpet slippers.

Perhaps one is especially drawn to this odd young man because so much of the perplexity and desperation of youth is embodied in his character. Eudora Welty, commenting on Cather's enormous responsiveness to young people, has said that "the burning drive of the young, the desire to live, to do, to make, to achieve, no matter what the sacrifice, is the feeling most surprisingly alive to the author, most moving to us. Life had made her terribly certain that being young in the world is not easy." Welty finds in Cather's fiction "a world with the power to crush and suffocate . . . a world to promise everything, and to deny everything; a world to open a way for living, or to close in life's face." This is agonizingly true for Paul: "It was at the theater and at Carnegie Hall that he really lived; the rest was but a sleep and a forgetting. This was Paul's fairy-tale, and it had for him all the allurement of a secret love." It was during these moments that "he felt within him the possibility of doing or saying splendid, brilliant things."

When these avenues of escape are removed from him in the attempt to force him to conform, he is, indeed, crushed and suffocated, denied everything. Deadened by Sunday school pieties, front-stoop economics, and the stench of his crowded neighborhood, he steals money from his employer, runs away to New York, and there lives out the most extravagant fantasy for one week: a suite at the Waldorf, fashionable clothes, champagne dinners, a box at the opera, and always and everywhere, flowers. When he is discovered (the news makes headlines in the Pittsburgh papers with assurances by employer, minister, and teachers that they will reclaim the soul of the "motherless lad"), Paul knows that now and forever all the world would be Cordelia Street. Unable to face that death-in-life, he pins a red carnation in his lapel, rides to the outskirts of town, and throws himself beneath the wheels of a train.

Commentators are agreed that Paul is marked for catastrophe from the start; but to see him, as some do, as "clearly deranged," or as a "homosexual touched by madness" is surely a reductive reading, one in which the narrative is essentially a clinical investigation and Paul a character in search of a psychoanalyst. While he is unquestionably "different," he engages interest by that very fact; that is, he suggests the sense in which each of us is somehow "alien to" or "other than," and suggests as well the necessity of being sustained by a dream, even when that dream has been shaped in the mind of an inexperienced boy by the illusory gleam of superficial opulence. It is the struggle itself that is of interest to Cather; it is at the core of all her best work, and when that subject disappears from her stories, they tend to become flat and lifeless.

Such is the case in her late artist stories, those from *Youth and the Bright Medusa* written between 1916–20. Cather had by this time befriended the great Wagnerian soprano Olive Fremstad and other notables from the worlds of theater and opera in New York. It seems likely that her close proximity to the lives of these celebrities gave her a "warts and all" view, one that led to a much more cynical treatment of the artist subject. The focus of "The Diamond Mine," "A Gold Slipper," and "Scandal" is on the exploitation of the artist by those merely ordinary human beings—the entrepreneurs, the money managers, the sycophants, the bored—who surround him. "Coming, Aphrodite!" is a strange intertwining of two stories, one the journey to a hard-won, unheralded, but genuine success of a young painter bent on following his own creative impulse rather than the fashionable trends of the New York art establishment; the other, the portrait of a woman he had once loved, a physically beautiful but spiritually flawed singer for whom success is measured not in terms of creative growth but only by the increasing accumulation of money and fame. The effort expended in maintaining these ephemeral rewards has left her hard and sullen and ugly.

It is precisely this characterization of the artist figures and their satellites in the late stories, which is to say, the portrayal of human beings as crass, acquisitive, exploitive, that defines and thus weakens the fictions. There are few psychologically convincing characters; indeed, most are more nearly stereotypes: the melancholy violinist, the materialistic, vacuous beauty, the avaricious Jew. One misses the poignancy of the early stories, a quality derived, no doubt, from their origins in Cather's own lived experience. In each, the sensitive soul is contrasted to the narrow smugness of provincial types whose combined meanness and power lead inevitably to the suffering or death of the artist. In each, the extraordinary use of imagery—the sobbing and moaning of the wind during Katherine Gaylord's one night with Adriance Hilgard; the gaudy, pretentious sitting room where Harvey Merrick's body rests; the bright red carnation in Paul's lapel—heightens the sense of pathos and tragedy. In each, technique is deployed in such a way that the achieved effect is elegiac, perhaps occasionally rhapsodic, but never mawkish. In each the emphasis is clearly on the struggle of the gifted soul, the value of the prize, and the philosophical considerations such subjects yield.

Perhaps the success of the early stories is attributable to Cather's distance from her subject. Although the struggle of the creative being was one she knew all too well, character and plot were, in the main, imaginative projections. The result is a clear demonstration of her mastery of the short story form: a compression of events, an amalgam of sympathy and observation, and a brief revelation of the mystery of things. The proximity to her subject in the late artist stories yields not poetry, but reportage, a journalism too singularly bent on exposing the petty concerns of mean-spirited people, too little defined by those larger questions about art and life whose answers, however tentative and groping, evoke in us an awareness of the authentic and profound. Still, the late stories do function as an interesting bridge from the nineteenth-century idealism and optimism at the core of even the darkest works of James, Wharton, and early Cather to the anxiety and skepticism expressed in her famous words: "The world broke in two in 1922 or thereabouts."

• • •

Whereas James, Wharton, and Cather wrote at some remove from the sordidness of experience (their financial independence providing a kind of insulation), other writers were emerging whose early careers plunged them hip-deep into it. These were the young journalists, Dreiser, Crane, and Hemingway among them, whose reporting of desperate human events were to shape their attitudes toward life and their ideas about fiction writing. Of these, Theodore Dreiser (1871–1945) is the most paradoxical: known (and often criticized by his detractors) as a writer of sprawling, expansive, loosely constructed novels, he was able to turn to the shorter form and achieve, at least occasionally, extraordinary effects. Two of his short stories are especially worthy of study, not only because they are fine examples of the genre, but because they lay to rest the view that Dreiser was unable to control, by compressing, his material.

"The Lost Phoebe" published in *Free and Other Stories* (1918) gives us Dreiser's natural affinity for storytelling, his rootedness in the oral tradition of the folktale: a conversational idiom, an implied listener, and the subtle use of suspense. These strategies are in evidence from the first paragraph:

They lived together in a part of the country which was not so prosperous as it had once been, about three miles from one of those small towns that, instead of increasing in population, is steadily decreasing. . . . Their particular house was part log and part frame, the log portion being the old original home of Henry's grandfather. The new portion, of now rain-beaten, time-worn slabs, through which the wind squeaked in the chinks at times, and which several overshadowing elms and a butternut tree made picturesque and reminiscently pathetic, but a little damp, was erected by Henry when he was twenty-one and just married. That was forty-eight years before.

What follows is a strange and brooding tale of an old farming couple who have lived alone for years in an isolated part of the country. So defined is each by the other that when his Phoebe dies, old Henry cannot abide the loss, and so he conjures her up again. Now, convinced that her absence is a kind of mean and willful prank, he plays (with the nonexistent Phoebe) a continuing game of hide-and-seek around the property and then in the countryside beyond. Each night he awaits her return; each morning he goes out again looking for her, calling to her. Finally, after seven years of this strange, unwavering pattern, the aged and feeble Henry finds his lost Phoebe. She has, in his weary and deluded vision, been transfigured into the lovely young girl she once had been and beckons to him now from the edge of a cliff: "Oh, Phoebe!" the old man calls. "Oh, Phoebe! Oh, no, don't leave me!" He feels the "lure of a world where love was young and Phoebe, as this vision presented her, a delightful epitome of their quondam youth." Enraptured, he calls out gaily, "Oh, wait, Phoebe!" and leaps.

A bare plot outline cannot suggest the power of this story: it is a great deal more than the record of an old man's bizarre hallucinations. It depicts with the unerring simplicity of a folktale not only Henry's mystical and futile search but the dreary routine, the petty quarrels, and the peevish silences of the old couple as they lived together through the years. It juxtaposes in so skillful a way the lyrical and the prosaic, the eerie and the mundane, that it conveys a haunting, poignant vision of aging, loneliness, and loss.

"Nigger Jeff" (its unfortunate title dates the story) appeared in the same 1918 collection of Dreiser's short works. It is much closer to the lived event, precisely because it grew out of Dreiser's own experience as a cub reporter in St. Louis. In it, Elmer Davies, confronted for the first time with mob violence during the lynching of a black man, is led to discover new truths about his own life, about the larger culture of which he is a part, and about the complex issues of morality and justice. In its dramatizing of the horrific and in revealing the gradual change in young Davies as he is exposed to it, the story is in the traditional pattern of initiation-ritual fiction.

At first, Davies appears as a "vain and rather self-sufficient youth, who was inclined to be of that turn of mind which sees in life only a fixed and ordered process of rewards and punishments. If one did not do exactly right, one did not get along well. On the contrary, if one did, one did. Only the so-called evil were really punished, only the good truly rewarded—or Mr. Davies had heard this so long in his youth that he had come nearly to believe it." Assigned to cover the story of the rape of a white woman by a black man, he is swept along and defined by the brutal impulses of the mob. As the story unfolds, he discovers—and we with him—that the black man, while not blameless, is both responsible and loving. He had raped the woman in a state of stupefied drunkenness and was caught because he had come home to see his mother once again before fleeing.

The narrative is composed of two elements in careful and pervasive counterpoise: the stark horror of the lynching and the extraordinary beauty of the natural world, beyond and utterly indifferent to the agonizing moment of the human event. Here is the description of the hanging:

Then came the concerted action of a dozen men, the lifting of the black mass into the air, and then Davies saw the limp form plunge down and pull up with a creaking sound of rope. In the weak moonlight it seemed as if the body were struggling, but he could not tell. He watched, wide-mouthed and silent, and then the body ceased moving. . . . As he still sat there the light of morning broke, a tender lavender and grey in the east. Then came the roseate hue of dawn, all the wondrous coloring of celestial halls, to which the waters of the stream responded. The white pebbles shone pinkily at the bottom, the grass and sedges first black, now gleamed a translucent green. Still the body hung there, black and limp against the sky, and now a light breeze sprang up and stirred it visibly.

The body moves soundlessly in the soft wind and, inanimate now, is rendered as just one more element in the cosmic design.

In thematic terms, the story could easily have been a miniaturization of Dreiser's naturalistic novels in which the individual is seen as a helpless victim of society or circumstance, engaged in a struggle he can neither win nor even understand. Hurstwood's exhausted question at the moment of his suicide in *Sister Carrie* is the consummate expression of this deterministic view: "What's the use?" But in "Nigger Jeff," the hanged man is treated less as suffering victim (to the author's everlasting credit this is more than a tale of social protest) than as the means by which the young reporter begins to accept his responsibilities as journalist and as human witness. Having come to the dead man's cabin, and hearing the sobs of his mother as she sits in the dark by her son's body, Elmer Davies recognizes that it was not always exact justice that was meted out to all and that it was not so much the business of the writer to indict as to interpret. The last words in the text are those that Davies cries out as much to himself as to the mourning woman: "I'll get it all in! I'll get it all in!"

In an early edition of *Free and Other Stories,* James Farrell's introduction hails Dreiser as one of the best short story writers in America. The praise is, unquestionably, excessive. Too often, the author's bitterness at the inequities of the social system give us stories energized by a zeal for reform rather than an impulse of creativity. And yet, the power of these two stories—the spare, mythic quality of "The Lost Phoebe," the stark human drama of "Nigger Jeff"—does substantiate Sherwood Anderson's more generalized and more accurate assessment of Dreiser's skill: "If there is a modern movement in American prose writing, a movement toward greater courage and fidelity in writing, then Theodore Dreiser is the pioneer and the hero of the movement."

• • •

That Sherwood Anderson (1876–1941) recognized and responded to the "modern" in Dreiser is not surprising. So altogether different in method, configuration, and effect from traditional modes are his own *Winesburg, Ohio* stories (1919) that it is as though a new genre had been born. The influence of the work cannot be overstated: as a consequence of its publication, the American short story was never to look the same again.

Anderson's distinctiveness becomes most obvious when his techniques are contrasted to those of the writers discussed earlier in this essay, who, although nearly contemporaneous with him, were rooted in and shaped by literary modes and strategies very different from his own. The imaginative impulse of their stories is nearly always the same as that of their novels. It is abbreviated, of course, and modulated or intensified by the requirements of the shorter form, but it is essentially an outgrowth of related thematic ideas and is organized around conventional notions of fictional form: a verisimilitude of character and place; a fundamentally Aristotelian plot structure in which a situation is introduced, and conflicts emerge and are enlarged upon and, in one way or another, are resolved; and an orderly, which is to say linear, chronology. The narrative is shaped as a logical progression of events that inevitably leads either to a dramatic alteration of external circumstances or to a new condition of being for one or more characters (e.g., John Marcher's devastation, Mrs. Lidcote's sad recognition, Paul's suicide, Elmer Davies's maturity), and this, seen in the light of all that has gone before, reveals an identifiable moral nexus; that is, an implicit value judgment is made upon the character, the world with which he is in conflict, or both. Equally important is the degree to which all these authors assume, even as they despair its passing, an available code of conduct.

In Anderson, the representational mode, the tripartite structure, the assumption of verifiable patterns of behavior and the moral concomitant disappear. In their place is a form at once more allusive and epigrammatic, more mystical and poetic, and more psychologically suggestive than anything that had gone before it in American fiction. The effect is that of the Joycean epiphany in which a single gesture, a perception, or a bit of dialogue is caught, rendered permanent, and although never interpreted, dissolves into a myriad of implications for the reader. Fundamental to this form is that it shows a life, not in process, but revealed by a moment's flickering light in its quintessential meaning.

"I have come to think," Anderson was later to write, "that the true history of life is but a history of moments. It is only at rare moments that we live." The theory is not original. Walter Pater in the nineteenth century and Virginia Woolf early in the twentieth had both embraced this view, and

Woolf's novels are the consummate expression in British fiction of the way in which life is composed of a series of "moments." But Anderson is the first writer to articulate this vision in the American short story, allowing the "moment" to reveal a hidden and not altogether flattering element in American experience.

This was a new kind of truth, one that gave the lie to the comfortable and cherished view of the health of the state. Anderson was peculiarly qualified as spokesman for this darker perception. In a sense he had seen it all: as a laborer, soldier, and business executive; as a boy in a quiet, tradition-bound Ohio town; and as a man in the huge, complex metropolis of Chicago. Born and reaching adulthood in the nineteenth century, he lived for nearly half of the twentieth. Clearly, then, he was witness to the rapid and extraordinary shift in the American ethos and to the sudden displacement in sensibility it created. That which he saw was the deadening effect of urbanization and technocracy, the erosion of religious faith and its usurpation by the money-god, the separation of men and women from work that provided a sense of purpose, and a consequent drift toward bewilderment, malaise, and despair. To illuminate this other reality—the one beneath the smiling benignity of American progress—Anderson dramatized a single, often bizarre moment in the lives of his characters.

His perception of an all-pervasive cultural hypocrisy led to his candid treatment of sexual longing, a treatment that by today's standards is timid stuff, but in 1919 was, doubtless, regarded as shocking. His focus on sexuality ("the terrible importance of the flesh in human relations") is not sensationalist, but is part of a larger, clearly authentic, interest: the mysterious psychic history of modern men and women, who, thwarted by the increasing impersonality of the new age, became isolated, silent, and withdrawn, and thus could be rendered knowable only by way of a frozen moment in time that reveals the private, often sexually repressed self.

Through the decades, Anderson has frequently been disparaged as a writer of intuition but no ideas. As is so often the case with sweeping generalizations, the crucial terms of the statement—intuition, ideas—remain undefined so that the concept is more a convenient tag for dealing with a new and unusual form than it is a valid assessment. It would be more accurate simply to acknowledge that in the introductory chapter to *Winesburg*, the author claims more philosophical content for his stories and characters than they demonstrate. He says that the people in Winesburg ("grotesques," he calls them) embody different kinds of truths, and in the moment that "one of the people took one of the truths to himself, called it his truth, and tried to live his life by it, he became a grotesque and the truth he embraced became a falsehood." His statement implies that, first, his characters define "truth"; then, that having established these truths as moral principles, they live by them; and last, that having done so, they find that they have been deluded. The theory does nothing to clarify the stories whose "truths" emerge without the aid of embellishment and whose characters are energized and defined not by their intellects but by their behavior.

There is, too, the matter of Anderson's style. None of the pellucid prose of Willa Cather appears here, nor the brilliant irony of Edith Wharton, and most assuredly, none of the modulations and refinements of language of Henry James. Instead, the narrative is composed of two seemingly irreconcilable, but as interwoven here, enormously effective patterns: the cadences of natural speech, approximating the beat and sense of immediacy of the oral tradition; and the highly stylized rhetoric of biblical prose—syntactical inversions, formal diction, controlled rhythms. There is a consequent tension in the prose, a quality at once native and oracular, recalling the character of Walt Whitman's poetry.

Anderson is said to have seen *Winesburg* as a novel, and, to be sure, there is a sense in which the Winesburg setting, the presence of the young newspaper reporter, George Willard, in many of the stories, the consistency of mood, and the cumulative power of the pieces give the work that continuity associated with the longer form. But the best of the stories are enormously effective as they stand alone; the least of them are not missed when they are omitted; and Anderson's method, as true of his novels as of the *Winesburg* stories, is by nature anecdotal and episodic, lacking that sustained momentum and integration of material essential to novelistic structure. Further, the focus on individual lives at a given moment in time—the very substance of these stories—is inappropriate to the longer narrative form with its requisite sequentiality and connectedness. The book is, in fact, a story cycle, the first of many in American fiction and the progenitor of the Nick Adams stories of Ernest Hemingway (a debt Hemingway later grudgingly conceded) and the Miranda stories of Katherine Anne Porter. But in Anderson, the emphasis is not on the growth to maturity and wisdom of the unifying character as in Hemingway and Porter, but rather on a succession of separate, isolated lives. Thus, while some of the stories can be seen as rites of passage for the young George Willard, their impact derives mainly from the odd creatures who shuffle awkwardly through the streets of Winesburg, Ohio, and whom George observes with sympathy and often with confusion. All are marginal types, those strange, unhappy beings who are increasingly to inhabit the American short story: men and women withering in the face of perplexing circumstances, unfulfilled capacities, atrophied emotions, and terrible loneliness. The unrelieved isolation and repressed longings of the characters are expressed by way of an obsession, a physical defect, or a sudden, quirky act so that they become, in an almost Dickensian way, identifiable by their peculiar traits or tics. But Anderson's interest is in penetrating beneath the visually discernible to a buried world that clarifies the surface one; and what he finds and illuminates there is an admixture of innocence, bewilderment, yearning, and pain. In "Paper Pills," the second story in the collection, the author describes the apples of the Winesburg orchards, those left after the pickers have removed the more perfect fruits: "On the trees [each fall] are only a few gnarled apples that the pickers have rejected. . . . One nibbles at them and they are delicious. Into a little round place at the side of each apple has been gathered all of its sweetness. One runs from tree to tree over the frosted ground picking the gnarled, twisted apples and filling his pockets with them. Only the few know the sweetness of the twisted apples." The image of the twisted apple with its spot of sweetness resonates throughout the stories, acting as a metaphor for all the lives within.

Epitomizing the pattern is Wing Biddlebaum, the central character of "Hands." A man old and wizened far beyond his years, he had arrived in Winesburg twenty years earlier under circumstances never revealed to the townspeople and accessible to the reader only through the words of a narrator who reconstructs the events. Biddlebaum had lived in a town in Pennsylvania where he had been a gifted, indeed inspiring, schoolteacher. His extraordinary ability with the young boys who were his pupils was reinforced by the expressiveness of his hands: "Here and there went his hands, caressing the shoulders of the boys, playing about the tousled heads." As the teacher spoke, his voice became soft and musical. It was as though through his tender touch and voice the schoolmaster tried to "carry a dream into the young minds." A half-witted boy misunderstands the schoolteacher's gestures, has erotic visions of him in his dreams, and reports them to his elders as lived events. The townspeople, resenting the teacher's awakening the imaginative and poetic in their sons, now find the opportunity to be rid of him; they brutalize him publicly and hound him out of town. Biddlebaum spends the rest of his years in Winesburg as a laborer, remaining wholly confused about what had happened to him. He only knows in some half-realized way that his hands must be to blame.

A moment of transfiguration ends the story. As Wing Biddlebaum prepares himself for bed, he sees some bread crumbs from his evening meal still on the table: "Putting the lamp upon a low stool he began to pick up the crumbs, carrying them to his mouth one by one with unbelievable rapidity." In the dim light of the single lamp, "the kneeling figure looked like a priest engaged in some service of his church. The nervous expressive fingers, flashing in and out of the light, might well have been mistaken for the fingers of the devotee going swiftly through decade after decade of his rosary."

In *The Lonely Voice: A Study of the Short Story*, Frank O'Connor, writing of Gogol's "The Overcoat," says: "What Gogol has done so boldly and brilliantly is to take the mock-heroic character, the absurd little copying-clerk, and impose his image over that of the crucified Jesus, so that even while we laugh, we are filled with horror at the resemblance." It is precisely this amalgam of eccentricity and tenderness that characterizes Wing Biddlebaum. By way of the strange, ritualized hand motions, Anderson creates a being whose very awkwardness ennobles him. Like Gogol's clerk or the biblical Jesus, he is a man whose differentness makes him peculiar and alien, while at the same time it suggests the quiet suffering, strength, and innocence of martyrdom.

The midwestern rural setting of *Winesburg, Ohio* has led some commentators to read the work as Anderson's "revolt from the village," that too facile rubric attached to numberless fictions in the early decades of the century. But, taken together, the stories are clearly a great deal more than a statement of disillusionment at country freshness gone stale or pastoral innocence tattered and vulgarized. The frightened and lonely lives exposed by Anderson's method transcend time and place, expressing less a cynical than a tragic view, less a local or even national condition than a universal one. Settings and atmosphere work against the sense of a fallen agrarian world; indeed, it is most often in silent streets that characters are seen in their fugitive and puzzling encounters. The rare glimpses of a green world are on the outskirts of town in an open field or wooded area, settings not of pastoral serenity but of violent acts and terrible misunderstandings. Whatever the time of day, one has the sense of failing light, of the obscurely visualized, of a nighttime world whose gloom is wholly consistent with the mood of melancholy, inward-turning experience.

Nor are the creatures of Winesburg rustics. Rather, they form a procession of single souls, estranged from their environment and from one another, displaying a suspicious unease which at times erupts into lunacy. They do not live so much as they merely endure a joyless existence—joyless because devoid of love, companionship, sexuality, art, and faith, those timeless, unalterable, and absolutely essential sources of spiritual nourishment. And so they sit alone in the drab rooms of boardinghouses endlessly waiting; or they move woodenly through the nearly empty streets unremarkable but for the one convulsive moment in which Anderson catches and reveals them.

There are a number of characters whose frustration is of a specifically sexual nature. Such a character is Alice Hindman in "Adventure." She has waited years for the return of her one young lover, rejecting other suitors in her steadfast and, as it turns out, fruitless loyalty. She becomes increasingly withdrawn and peculiar as the silence and loneliness of the years accumulate. Increasingly, she becomes attached to inanimate objects, creating fantasy lovers in her bedroom, arranging blankets so that they resemble human forms lying between her sheets. Caressing these mute and passive surrogates, she whispers over and over, "Why doesn't something happen? Why am I left here alone?" Finally, one cold and rainy night, half-mad with the desire to "find some other lonely human and embrace him," she rushes naked into the streets.

Others in the town are thwarted by the absence of love, by the unfulfilled yearning for sexual experience. Kate Swift ("The Teacher") is regarded by her students as cold, forbidding, unapproachable. The townspeople view her as a confirmed old maid who speaks sharply and lacks all human feeling. But "in reality, she was the most eagerly passionate among them," who often walks the streets of Winesburg at night, tormented by memory and desire. On one such night, she goes to see young George Willard at the office of the *Winesburg Eagle*. She has been drawn to the boy, recognizing in him the seeds of something fine and sensitive. She has told him in the past that he must try to experience all he can so that he won't become a "mere peddlar of words." Now, in the newspaper office, they sit by the stove, he watching and listening, she speaking, passionate, inspired. Her eagerness to reach the boy and the appeal of his quiet charm combine to arouse her sexually: "As she looked at George Willard, the passionate desire to be loved by a man, that had a thousand times before swept like a storm over her body, took possession of her. In the lamplight George Willard looked no longer a boy, but a man ready to play the part of a man." For a moment she yields, the strength goes out of her body, and she falls against him. Then, just as quickly, she repels him, beating him on the face with her fists. Kate Swift runs out of the office, and the baffled George Willard is left to pace up and down, "swearing furiously."

As George functions to illuminate the complex nature of Kate Swift, so she serves in "The Strength of God" to reveal that of the Reverend Curtis Hartman. He is much admired in Winesburg because he is quiet, unpretentious, and refined. But Curtis Hartman is haunted by twin specters: he feels the absence of God's spirit within him; and he is obsessed by the physical loveliness of Kate Swift whose bedroom is opposite the bell tower of his church. Finally, the longing for spiritual faith is superseded by the longing for the teacher, and he makes an opening in the leaded window that allows him to see her lying on her bed: "I will beseige the school teacher. I will fly in the face of all men and if I am a creature of carnal lust, I will live then for my lusts." For a time, the distracted man trembles from head to foot and "came near dying from the effects of waiting" and watching. But as he gazes at the naked woman, she begins to weep, to beat upon her pillow, and then, to pray. In the softly lit room, her body suggests to him not that of a sexually desirable woman, but that of a young boy attendant upon Christ. Astounded, the Reverend Curtis Hartman cries aloud and runs out of the church and down to the newspaper office where he announces to the startled George Willard: "The ways of God are beyond human understanding. I have found the light. After ten years in this town God has manifested himself to me in the body of a woman. . . . God has appeared to me in the person of Kate Swift, the school teacher, kneeling naked on a bed."

The desperate need to make human contact, to move beyond the narrow limits of self, precipitate the abrupt, peculiar actions of each of the men and women in the *Winesburg* stories. In "Godliness," Anderson states the case for all of them: "It seemed . . . that between [each of them] and all the other people in the world, a wall had been built up and that [each remained forever outside] the warm, inner circle of life." What Anderson catches and dramatizes with stunning economy in the stories is the profound paradox of human existence: while we live in a world crowded with others, we are, in fact, each of us, quite alone.

In his treatment of isolation as the defining characteristic of experience and in his recognition of the sexual impulse as an attempt to assuage it, Anderson is extraordinarily innovative and influential. No serious writer of the short story who followed him could fail to treat the twin issues of loneliness and sexuality. The writers before him had either avoided these subjects altogether, disguised them tactfully, or used them artfully in the service of some larger concern.

Of course, earlier writers had assumed a world, if not always moral, at least knowable, manageable, all of a piece. *Winesburg, Ohio* was published just at the ending of World War I. The agrarian dream had long since died; the humanist one was dying. Industrialism—the new reality—gave experience an odd shape: fragmentary, anonymous, nervous, unpredictable. It is just this quality that Anderson epitomizes in both vision and method in the *Winesburg* stories. In the best of them, he achieves nothing less than the literary metaphor by which the citizens of a radically changing culture could know themselves; in *Winesburg, Ohio,* the American short story was suddenly and resoundingly thrust into the twentieth century.

Ellen Kimbel

Pennsylvania State University

THE "LESSER" RENAISSANCE:
THE AMERICAN SHORT STORY
IN THE 1920s[1]

The 1920s are still as controversial and as exciting as ever. In *The Familiar Faces* (1962), David Garnett remembered that there were those who looked upon the decade as the "dirty twenties." To him, however, they were "years of joy, of freedom and of enlightenment." To others, it was the Age of Flaming Youth, the Jazz Age, the Turbulent 1920s, the Terrific Twenties, the Roaring Twenties, the Era of Wonderful Nonsense.

It was also the Literary Decade. World War I had catapulted a provincial-minded America onto the international scene. Following the war, the country redirected its newfound stature and energies not only to areas like politics and economics, but to cultural affairs. Some of its soldiers-turned civilians remained in Europe or returned there as expatriates. They used Paris as their foreign capital, involving themselves in new philosophical theories and newer literary techniques, writing in a variety of forms and styles, and even establishing publishing enterprises. By their actions, these expatriates were contributing to America's impulse toward modernism and cosmopolitanism.

All the arts boomed until the stock market crash of October 1929. Surprisingly, the stronghold of provincialism—the Midwest—dominated in fiction, especially in the short story. It was as if W. J. Cash's well-known remark in *The Mind of the South* ("Anybody who fired off a gun in the region was practically certain to kill an author") could have been used to characterize the rich creative outburst by the midwestern writers of the 1920s. Looking back from F. Scott Fitzgerald's "Babylon Revisited" (1931), however, the decade changed; it seemed like a time of dissipation that had turned into a nightmare, into spiritual as well as material bankruptcy, where young writers suddenly felt old and tired, and attempted to recoup something by seeking rehabilitation or another rebirth.

71

In the 1920s, the cultural boom occurred in many fields: in painting, music, sculpture, and architecture. The strides made in literature were extraordinary. The novel was experiencing a robust renaissance, as seen in the published works of Fitzgerald, Sinclair Lewis, Ernest Hemingway, Edith Wharton, Ellen Glasgow, Sherwood Anderson, John Dos Passos, Thomas Wolfe, and many others. Poetry was experiencing a similar renaissance, with such diverse talents as T. S. Eliot, Robert Frost, Ezra Pound, e.e. cummings, Wallace Stevens, William Carlos Williams, Robinson Jeffers, Hart Crane, Carl Sandburg, John Crowe Ransom, and Marianne Moore. The drama was coming out of the dark ages, led by that somber giant Eugene O'Neill and more modest playwrights, Elmer Rice and Maxwell Anderson. An impressive renaissance was also clearly taking place in the short story; it seemed hardly noticeable because of the attention being given to the novelists, poets, and playwrights. Short story writers were considered a lesser breed.

Publishers and editors, critics and readers, even the writers themselves, were to blame for the lesser status accorded to the short story in the 1920s. True, short stories were in great demand in the commercial, mass audience magazines, and even in the avant-garde little magazines. In the commercial magazines, they were useful as attractive fillers for the growing number of advertisers and their advertisements.[2] In this medium, moreover, they were handled very much like the news in the daily newspapers; they were of transitory value. If short stories were collected in volume form and assumed the size of a novel, they were still not much read nor taken seriously by critics, publishers, and readers (just as in times past). In the 1920s especially, short story collections were often used to keep a novelist like Fitzgerald before the general public until he produced his next bona fide novel.

Maxwell Perkins, the premier editor of the decade, treated short story collections in very practical terms. More than once, he tried to get Ring Lardner to write "that 40,000 word story, or novel, or whatever it ought to be called." When he failed, he packaged collections with care. He began Lardner's How to Write Short Stories with a piece ("The Facts") that would appeal to both sexes. He placed the satiric comedy "Some Like Them Cold" next, followed by the baseball story "Alibi Ike," making certain another kind of story intervened before the boxing story, "Champion."[3] Perkins did not stop here. He had Lardner write a brief preface, along with commentaries for each story. In putting together another short story collection in 1925, Perkins was worried about size; he felt that the volume needed to have at least 60,000 words to approximate the length of a novel.

Many good short stories were published in the 1920s by young and older writers, some of whom were primarily known or anxious to be known as novelists. The new and distinct talents included Sherwood Anderson, Wilbur Daniel Steele, Fitzgerald, Lardner, and Hemingway. Of these, Steele seemed destined to become the outstanding short story writer of the decade because he collected awards almost on a yearly basis from the two annuals, *The Best Short Stories* (edited by Edward J. O'Brien) and *O. Henry Memorial Award: Prize Stories* (introductions by Blanche Colton Williams). Others tried their hand at random stories, hoping to embark on careers in fiction or keep established careers alive. They included Ruth Suckow, Conrad Aiken, Ben Hecht, Edith Wharton, Joseph Hergesheimer, James Branch Cabell, Floyd Dell, Jean Toomer, Ellen Glasgow, Thomas Boyd, Zona Gale, Willa Cather, William Carlos Williams, Dorothy Parker, Theodore Dreiser, Thomas Wolfe, Kay Boyle, Djuana Barnes, Stephen Vincent Benét, William Faulkner, Glenway Wescott, and Katherine Anne Porter. Many other short story writers of the decade, now almost completely forgotten (e.g., Konrad Bercovici, Rupert Hughes, Elinor Wylie, Morley Callaghan, Irvin S. Cobb, Richard Connell), can be found in the O'Brien and Williams annuals.

There were outstanding short story collections too, although some received belated or little recognition: Cather's *Youth and the Bright Medusa* (1920), Anderson's *The Triumph of the Egg* (1921), Cabell's *The Line of Love* (revised edition, 1921), Fitzgerald's *Tales of the Jazz Age* (1922), Anderson's *Horses and Men* (1923), Toomer's *Cane* (1923), Lardner's *How to Write Short Stories* (1924), Hemingway's *In Our Time* (1924; revised editions, 1925, 1930), Aiken's *Bring! Bring!* (1925), Boyd's *Points of Honor* (1925), Fitzgerald's *All the Sad Young Men* (1926), Lardner's *The Love Nest* (1926), Suckow's *Iowa Interiors* (1926), Hemingway's *Men without Women* (1927), Wescott's *Good-Bye Wisconsin* (1928), Boyle's *Short Stories* (1929), and Lardner's *Round Up* (1929). Various other kinds of collections were published during the decade—*The World's Best Short Stories, The Best Love Stories,* and *Stories from Vanity Fair*—suggesting a potentially larger market and interest in the lesser genre.

With their literary beginnings in the Midwest, the pivotal short story writers (Anderson, Fitzgerald, Lardner, Hemingway, and others like Suckow, Boyd, and Wescott) conjure up all kinds of associations. For example, there is D. H. Lawrence's phrase "spirit of place," or "regionalism" as defined in those provocative essays by members of the southern literary renaissance, Allen Tate, Eudora Welty, and Flannery O'Connor. The spirit or the sense of place—Ohio, Michigan, Illinois, Iowa, Minnesota, Wisconsin—meant the world of small towns, rural farm areas, the frontier, the good earth, along with the simple life and simple virtues of ordinary people trying to hold at bay the machine and factory, attempting at the same time to protect and sustain their individual character and their traditional values.

The new writers of the Midwest were a paradoxical blend of humanists, traditionalists, provincials, and rebels. A case in point was Edgar Lee Masters, who almost single handedly put the Midwest on the literary map with his unorthodox *Spoon River Anthology* (1915), and who recognized the inevitable incompatibility of country and city: "The city is facts, is hard reality, is lifeless stone. The country is the haunt of something universal and deathless and infinite which broods upon the earth and reflects itself in it. In communion with nature we can wrest from the gods ideas identifying life with eternity."[4]

Unfortunately, writers like Masters were labeled regionalists and provincials in the narrowest sense; this meant that they were crude local colorists, according to sophisticated eastern and European-oriented standards. Yet the emerging writers of the Midwest were a godsend. Generally, they were self-reliant and tough-minded, removed from the standardized and conforming patterns of the East, and closer to the pulse and beat of past traditions, the heritage of America. They recorded with remarkable fidelity the native American values and colloquial speech patterns. In the woods of northern Michigan, Hemingway would come face to face with the frontier, with nature in the raw, with the elemental forces of life, which gave him the ability to see and feel into things freshly and closely, in both specific and universal terms. The midwestern writer also had a closer identification with the romance of sports—baseball, football, fishing, hunting, horse racing—making him more conscious of violence and order and things masculine. In his stories, the midwestern writer would be more sensitive to the myth of the hero as well as to the day-to-day struggles of the common man, recording his responses to fear, pride, honor, and courage. The Midwest itself was the new battleground between preservation of the land and humanism on the one hand and the steady encroachments of industrialism and mechanization on the other. These and other factors gave the midwestern writer special advantages that led to a revitalized short story in the 1920s.

Meanwhile, the publishing world clamored for short stories that satisfied the palates of middlebrow readers and advertisers. This meant the tried-and-true formula stories, and well-plotted and innocuously light stories. Fitzgerald knew exactly what publishers and audiences wanted, and he gave it to them. He once confessed to Hemingway that "he wrote what he thought were good stories and then changed them for submission, knowing exactly how he must make the twists that rendered them salable to the magazines." (Hemingway thought his friend was "whoring.")

Despite this, commercial magazines still sought fresh voices and fresh stories; they made concessions. A powerful editor like George Horace Lorimer of the *Saturday Evening Post* was not rigidly conservative in his literary tastes;

in some ways he was adventurous. Beginning in 1914, he published Ring Lardner's crude and ungrammatical baseball stories in the *Post* with great success; these stories were later collected as *You Know Me Al*. Lorimer also published the young and effervescent talent, Fitzgerald, who became the *Post*'s most popular writer of the 1920s. There was a growing and keen competition for short stories among the many other magazines of the day: *Cosmopolitan, Collier's, Metropolitan, Century, Bookman, Liberty, McCall's, Scribner's Monthly, Smart Set, Red Book, Woman's Home Companion*, and *American Mercury*. For those writers unwilling to make concessions—that is, to craft formula stories—there were the little magazines (e.g., *Dial, Double Dealer, transition, Little Review, Contact*, and *This Quarter*), doing direct battle with the commercial magazines and the formula stories.

Short story writers of the 1920s had a special bonus available to them. Once their stories appeared in magazines they could reappear in the two popular annuals, *The Best Short Stories* and *O. Henry Memorial Award: Prize Stores*. These annuals brought into sharper focus problems that were already subtly suggested by the kinds of stories the *Post* usually accepted and the kinds accepted by *transition* and the *Dial*. In his review of the *O. Henry* annual for 1924, Edward J. O'Brien made several observations, only one of which was complimentary. He approved of the attention being lavished on Steele (although he should have been critical of the author, who was an exemplar of the well-plotted story). But he complained that his rival annual gave no place to deserving new talents, to Anderson, Cabell, Hemingway, Westcott, Suckow, Cather, Lardner and Waldo Frank. O'Brien complained further: "And from year to year it [the *O. Henry* annual] has thus consistently put itself on record as provincial in its judgment and unimaginative in its contact with reality." He warned of the "machine-made commercial product" reflected in its pages; it was "impressed by the artificial mechanics of plot rather than by the fresh living presentation of life."[5]

One of the judges of the *O. Henry* annual, R. L. Ramsay, in his response to O'Brien's charges, exposed deeper divisions over the short story in the 1920s. Ramsay thought that O'Brien was eccentric, narrow, and dogmatic, and was drawn to his own special kind of formula—"sophisticated irony, mingled with psychoanalysis." Ramsay prided himself and the *O. Henry* annual for remaining provincial and therefore American. As he saw it, O'Brien was overly concerned with satisfying the foreign audiences of the American short story. To Ramsay, the *O. Henry* annual remained faithful not only to things American, but to the many types and moods of stories that O'Brien excluded from his own annual.[6]

•   •   •

In his critical studies—*The Advance of the American Short Story* (1923) and *The Dance of the Machines* (1929)—O'Brien continued his battles against formula or standardized stories. To him, the great enemy was the "machine," the industrial and technological progress taking place in America, which made it almost certain that standardization and conformity would rule in all phases of life and the arts. Continually, O'Brien looked to one American writer to champion his cause, and this writer happened to be as concerned, probably more so, with the harmful effects of the "machine" on American life. If O'Brien was trying to dismantle the formula short story through his editorial policies and his critical pleadings, Sherwood Anderson was challenging it with his own kind of formless short story in *Winesburg, Ohio* (1919), which became a model and inspiration for many of the younger talents of the 1920s, especially Hemingway and Faulkner.

In *Winesburg*, Anderson brought the short story down to earth, back to human nature as well as to the humdrum day-to-day lives of ordinary people confronting their "ordinary" problems. By doing this, Anderson was proving how machined the short story had already become under the influence of Edgar Allan Poe, Bret Harte, and O. Henry. The chief villain was plot, for it usually led to smartness and trickery, to something slick, artificial, and formulaic. It also led to the coldly impersonal story and to the overly intellectualized one (e.g., the stories of Henry James). In place of plot, Anderson brought back the tradition of the storyteller, that is, the spoken word (colloquial speech) and a loose, rambling narrative, which meant more intimate and seemingly casual relationships among characters and between the writer and the reader.

It was indeed significant that in the subtitles to his first three short story collections—*Winesburg, Ohio, The Triumph of the Egg,* and *Horses and Men*— Anderson employed the word *tales.* As he seemed to regress in terms of the form of the short story, he went forward in subject matter, widening the areas for presentation in fiction, thereby helping to break the shackles of Victorianism and Puritanism that had limited the scope and depth of the short story. In his stories, Anderson demythologized the idyllic image of town and rural life. At the same time, he explored taboo areas of human relationships and human problems, making the short story a greater instrument for serious moral and psychological scrutiny rather than merely light escapist entertainment.

As the "throwback modern," Anderson softened and humanized the short story without necessarily sentimentalizing it. Yet his disarmingly honest and shapeless narratives (they were really carefully crafted) were to be transformed by the end of the decade, because of the magazines and their policies, the times, and the talents, like Dorothy Parker, who reintroduced sophistication and smartness, along with a brittle irony and a cynical satire. The short story was to be hardened all over again, with another kind of formula story.

In his collections of the 1920s—*The Triumph of the Egg* and *Horses and Men*—Anderson continued the characteristic themes and techniques so central to the earlier *Winesburg*. These stories are richer and denser than the *Winesburg* stories; that is, they are filled with the details associated with naturalism. They are also more literal and more sophisticated, thus losing some of the haunting quality of *Winesburg*, with its mystical, mysterious, and primitive strains. Anderson may well have been heeding the advice of some of his critics and the policies of the commercial magazines. He acted as if he were trying to reach a larger audience and to satisfy those who looked with disfavor on his "fuzzy mysticism" by communicating his materials more directly. His short stories became more artful, less artless.

In "The Egg," the prose is formal and literate; the colloquial materials are less in evidence. The clumsy and honest artlessness found in "Hands" is now tightly controlled to better achieve the effects of irony and symbolism so important to "The Egg." As in *Winesburg*, Anderson delves beneath the surface of lives. Here he shows a father, instilled with the American passion for getting ahead, trying to fulfill himself. But the father is locked into a "dreadful cycle" of nature, like the hens laying eggs; he moves from one failure to another, from chicken farmer to restauranteur. The prophetic line—"Grotesques are born out of eggs as out of people"—echoes throughout the story; it endows the father's vision (as well as the son's) with sterility and inevitable doom, as he is conquered by the egg. It is a grim story, far grimmer than anything in *Winesburg*, even though there are clear overtones of humor. Anderson starkly reveals man's entrapment, along with the perplexing and painful riddle of life itself.

In another well-known story, "I Want to Know Why," Anderson may have made no concessions to his audience, but interestingly it first appeared in the *Smart Set*, which prided itself on being the magazine of cleverness. Irony and paradox do stand out in "I Want to Know Why." On one level, it is naturalistic, in that it is full of the precise details of the horse-racing world. It focuses on an adolescent, on his loss of innocence and the accompanying painful crisis of maturation. He tries to straighten out things that cannot be straightened out, partly because he now has a glimpse of the more complex adult world. By the end of the story, the boy is overwhelmed by confusion, pain, and anger. He is unable to understand the adult world and the way it is attracted to beauty and to ugliness, as if they were one and the same thing.

The trainer Jerry Tillford loves the horse Sunstreak the same way he can love an ugly prostitute. To the boy, good and evil, purity and impurity, are separate entities. His adjustment to adult life will not be easy. With great skill, Anderson employs a dramatic monologue and a rambling style to create another one of his circular and unresolved stories. He effectively captures the mixed feelings and inner turmoil of his adolescent hero. Nonetheless, "I Want to Know Why" reads like an orthodox story when compared to the unorthodox and "bitter pills" of *Winesburg*.

From the collection *Horses and Men*, "I'm a Fool" serves as a companion piece to "I Want to Know Why." Again, it focuses on the world of horses in order to understand the world of men. The more the adolescent hero of the story talks about getting "everything straight," the more he is like the captive hero of "I Want to Know Why." His ego overtakes him; his pride clouds his reason; he traps himself by telling a lie in order to impress the girl of his dreams. By the end of the story, the boy is bewildered, hurt, angered, and isolated by a dilemma of his own making. There is no resolution in sight. In this and other stories, Anderson remains close to the world of nature, the pagan world, as he enters into private lives. He dramatically highlights the natural world and the "unnatural" behavior of people, especially the purity of youth and its anxiety and frustration over love, over conventions and traditions.

• • •

Although admired by a small circle of writers and critics, Anderson's "formless" stories were too private, too depressing, too removed from the mainstream of American life for him to have any kind of popular and mass acceptance. But another and younger writer emerging in the same Midwest— F. Scott Fitzgerald—received almost instant recognition because he supplied just what the major commercial magazines were looking for: mainstream stories. They could be light, silly, frivolous, cute, even slick and sophisticated, so long as they were well-plotted and entertaining. In contrast to Anderson's private stories, Fitzgerald's were public, mirroring the life of the city, families, friends, and crowds, a world of vitality, excitement, whirlwind romances, and brisk adventures, with an overlay of optimism and hope—all far removed from the brooding melancholy, the terrible desolation and emptiness of Anderson's rural country.

Unlike Anderson, Fitzgerald did not believe in the "tragedy in the American countryside because all the people capable of it move to the big towns at twenty." Although he was from the Midwest (Minnesota), Fitzgerald was by nature an Easterner and cosmopolite. In his stories, he suggests his weariness with the West by continually talking about the East—about New York City, the Yale Club, and the Ritz. In his subject matter, Fitzgerald focuses on the world of adolescents, on prep school and college students from well-adjusted middle-class families. Their major concerns are with status symbols and love entanglements; their tragedies are often trivial and temporary. The plot lines of the stories seem far more important to Fitzgerald than the characters and their development; they are full of clever twists and turns, and abrupt climaxes and surprise endings. They echo the plots and ingredients found in the Roman comedy of Plautus and Terence: mistaken identity, deception, trickery, suspense, farce, buffoonery, and satire. The actions are sprinkled with frivolous, sometimes witty, dialogue. Periodically Fitzgerald even introduces racy materials. In various ways, then, he was contributing to the stereotyped popular story, the *Saturday Evening Post* story, where many of his writings first appeared. Besides these breezy, mischievous, and irrelevant popular stories, however, Fitzgerald was to produce some serious, relevant, and mature stories, especially in the mid-1920s. More than once, though, he confessed that he wrote short stories rapidly, for quick money, in order to finance his major interest, writing novels.

Although the *Post* preferred light entertainment, the happy story with the happy ending, escapist romances and detective stories, it was not hopelessly narrow and conservative in its tastes. Its editor, George Horace Lorimer, was fond of "style" and even intrigued by "radicalism," as Fitzgerald himself once noted. Yet there were certain guidelines imposed by the nature of the magazine. Not only the editor and publisher but the advertisers were very sensitive to taboo subjects; the *Post* audience was never to be offended. Also, because of the many advertisements, much more space was available for fiction, so that *Post* stories frequently approached the novelette in length, as did stories in the *Smart Set*. This situation aggravated Fitzgerald's writing problems; many of his *Post* stories are full of excessive details, padding, redundancies, and outsized plots.

Widely admired in its day, "Bernice Bobs Her Hair" is a good popular story of its kind; everything is on the surface, the only subtleties being the twists and turns of the plot. For its time, "Bernice" was considered racy—with mention of "kissable mouths," bobbed hair, and the fast woman, the vamp. What stand out are the concerns of middle-class youths: manners, poses, fads, and the social passions (golfing, dancing, parties, kisses). Fitzgerald creates a modern version of the ugly duckling theme; the wallflower, Bernice, gets her revenge on Marjorie, the girl who has everything. Behind the story's superficial action, Fitzgerald reveals his shrewd insight into the feminine sensibility, into the prosaic talk of youth (interlaced with the sophisticated wit and banter of the decadent Oscar Wilde), and into the rebellious stance of the young generation, as it discards the traditional views of womanhood, modeled after Louisa May Alcott's *Little Women*.

In other early *Post* stories, Fitzgerald demonstrates his serious side. A story like "The Ice Palace" was controversial; the *Post* received letters of protest and had to pacify readers from both the North and the South. In the story, Fitzgerald contrasts the two cultures. The softness and romanticism of the South, where girls are brought up on memories, not money, with a respect for the past and a sense of family, is counterposed to the bigness, coldness, and masculinity of the North and its gloomy Ibsenesque moods. In other stories of the period—"The Diamond as Big as the Ritz," "The Jelly-Bean," "The Dance," "Family in the Wind," "The Last of the Belles"—Fitzgerald further tapped the southern theme. With Sherwood Anderson, he was helping to pave the way for the southern literary renaissance and its impressive array of young talents (e.g., William Faulkner, Katherine Anne Porter), who were to draw on their own region in their stories of the 1920s.

It was fortunate that the *Post* was not Fitzgerald's sole market for short stories. On occasion, the *Post* rejected his work; two of his better efforts, "May Day" and "The Rich Boy," were turned down because they were "too realistic." Both probed deeper, more controversial moral and political issues than any of his popular stories. "May Day," for example, draws on the political tensions of the times; they serve as a backdrop to an intricate and ambitious plot, which links an individual's tragedy (Gordon Sterrett) to the age. Luckily, other markets like the *Smart Set* were available to Fitzgerald. As early as 1919 he had published "Babes in the Woods" in the magazine. "May Day" and "The Diamond as Big as the Ritz" were just right for the *Smart Set,* edited by iconoclasts H. L. Mencken and George Jean Nathan, both of whom relished controversial subjects and satirical exposés of middle-class· values and prejudices.

If markets like the *Smart Set* had not been available and his shrewd editor, Maxwell Perkins, had not encouraged him to turn away from the flapper stories, Fitzgerald might well have remained a topical, superficial, and popular short story writer. For he was an effective reporter of the contemporary scene. He accurately observed the changing tastes and interests of the youths of his day. It is easy to see why he was looked upon as the oracle of the Jazz Age and why he relished his role as social historian.

Another kind of early story, "The Diamond as Big as the Ritz," stands out as an example of the richer, more varied nature of Fitzgerald's talent; it

makes use of parody, social satire, romance, fantasy, classical myth, and tragedy. Fitzgerald said that the story was written for his own amusement, that
he was "in that familiar mood characterized by a perfect craving for luxury
and the story began as an attempt to feed that craving on imaginary foods."
Using imagery that echoed Keats and made the story more like a lyric poem
than a short story, Fitzgerald found the opportunity to present some naughty
and bold ideas: "I've always heard that a girl can have more fun with a man
whom she knows she can never marry"; "God had His price, of course." He
did not forget to make a wise comment about youth: "Everybody's youth is
a dream, a form of chemical madness." Nor did he forget that exotic dreams
inevitably lead to disillusionment. Most important, he attacked the false luster of wealth that was corrupting and dehumanizing the American character.

Some of Fitzgerald's stories of the mid-1920s, like "Absolution" and "The
Rich Boy," are even more probing, more mature, and more subtly ironic.
Once meant to serve as a prologue to The Great Gatsby, "Absolution" is a
dense psychological tale, exploring the world of Catholicism, of sin, guilt,
and redemption, the attraction to both sensuality and religion. Uncharacter-
istic of Fitzgerald's earlier short stories, it anticipates the moral ambiguities
and dilemmas he explored in his novels. In "The Rich Boy," his irony is much
more subtle than it was in "The Diamond as Big as the Ritz," as he dramatizes the sensibility, superiority, and psychology of the rich. The narrator
announces his subject at once: "Let me tell you about the very rich. They
are different from you and me. They possess and enjoy early, and it does
something to them, makes them soft where we are hard, and cynical where
we are trustful, in a way that, unless you were born rich, it is very difficult
to understand." The reader follows the career of Anson Hunter, who demonstrates the paradox of wealth. He is rich only in the material sense; he has
little or no redeeming spiritual values, no real moral backbone. Although he
seems to be moving in three worlds at once, he is going nowhere. His life is
sterile; he cannot cope with responsibility and maturity. The older he gets,
the fatter he gets; he ends up alone and a very "poor" boy.

· · ·

Even with his reliance on plot and entertainment values in his popular stories, Fitzgerald nowhere achieved the artifice, the rush of rhetoric, the intricacies of plot, coincidence, surprise, intrigue (some of which echoed the
style and manner of melodramatic theater) that Wilbur Daniel Steele refined
into his popular short stories of the twenties. In a letter of March 1938,
Fitzgerald himself complained: "Why Wilbur Daniel Steele, who left no
mark whatsoever, invented nothing, created nothing except a habit of being

an innocuous part of the [Edward J.] O'Brien anthology?" Steele was a prolific writer, publishing several short story collections during the 1920s: *The Shame Dance and Other Stories* (1923), *Urkey Island* (1926), *The Man Who Saw through Heaven and Other Stories* (1927), and *Tower of Sand and Other Stories* (1929). He also appeared in the O'Brien and Williams annuals in the years 1915–22, 1924–26, 1928–31; sometimes he appeared in both annuals the same year.

In his work, Steele demonstrated that the traditions of Edgar Allan Poe and O. Henry, along with that of the well-made story, were durable and very much alive. Steele had the master's touch, with all the plot formulas at his command; the subtleties and intricacies of plotting were far more important to him than any moral theme or serious issue he may have wished to explore. As a "romantic realist," he was often attracted to the primitive, the exotic, and the remote; it would not be long before he satisfied the escapist hunger of the audiences of the day. A student of impressionistic painting, he could create atmosphere as arrestingly as Poe; and his lifelong interest in the theater as a practicing playwright reinforced his devotion to the mechanics of plot.

A popular anthology piece even today, "Footfalls" is a good illustration of the typical Steele short story. Minus Poe's fantastic and nightmare imagery, it has the Poesque ingredients of coincidence, surprise, suspense, mystery, terror, inevitability, and death. "Footfalls," however, remains a drawn out and implausible story; it is forced and redundant, reading like shrill melodrama. A blind cobbler, Boaz Negro, waits patiently for nine years to vindicate himself and his son and to punish a villain, former lodger Campbell Wood. Having taken the law into his own hands to recoup his honor, Boaz experiences self-doubts, worrying that he has murdered an innocent man. The story reads like a detective mystery, with clever delays, turns, and surprises.

Many of Steele's other stories, like "Bubbles" and "When Hell Froze," have the same kind of formula. They are well-made, full of rhetorical flourishes, mystery, and intrigue. At times, Steele could turn his popular liabilities into strengths; he fused romance and reality to create his best story, published in the 1930s, "How Beautiful with Shoes."

One of Steele's stories of the twenties was a "sleeper"—"The Man Who Saw Through Heaven"—a striking and innovative effort, in which he combines romance, the exotic, and the strange with creative insight and power. He makes an imaginative excursion not only into history and science but also into the realm of the supernatural and God to trace the haunted life of a missionary in search of his universe. Reverend Hubert Diana, the hero in "cosmic flight," journeys back to man's beginnings, to the world of idolatry and elemental life. He attempts to understand the history of civilization and "all space and all time" in order to achieve his "cosmic reckoning."

While there were subtle and unsubtle reactions to Steele's kind of short story—at least by his fellow writers—he proved how difficult it was to replace the standards of the short story set by Edgar Allan Poe and maintained by magazine and book publishers and editors of the 1920s. Years later, in 1950, Steele confessed that his kind of story "had gone radically out of style." He knew he was being replaced by the "rough boys," by Ernest Hemingway and the new breed of writers who received their literary training in advertising agencies or newspaper offices. In covering police and fire beats, the courts, and sports events, newspaper writers developed a sharp eye for irony and a tough realism that was inevitably and unfairly labeled as cheap cynicism. When they wrote short stories, they framed them in simple declarative sentences; they had little use for the "romance of words" and for exotic settings and light entertainments.

• • •

Steele's reputation, then, was short-lived. His kind of writing, generally somber and humorless, reflects one side of the writing of the decade. It took a writer with Ring Lardner's sensibility to right the balance, to bring back the American tradition of humor, along with its accessories, irony and satire. Lardner also brought a special creativity developed from his famous baseball column "In the Wake of the News." His years as a newspaperman had taught him how to hold the reader's interest. He understood the importance of a tight narrative, of pace, tone, and voice; and of appeal to eye and ear. Humor and satire were central to his vision; partly he was inspired by his own innate abilities, partly by the examples of his fellow midwestern humorists, George Ade and Finley Peter Dunne.

To the 1920s, Lardner brought not only a new lightness and tightness, but a new kind of short story. He emphasized the masculine personality, the world of sports, the wise boob as hero. It did not matter that Alibi Ike, one of Lardner's inimitable creations, was semiliterate. The fact that he was a baseball player was enough to cover him with glory. He was a reincarnation of the frontiersman, carrying a bat and a glove instead of a musket and powder. He displayed the all-American virtues of speed, agility, strength, endurance, along with the ethics of fair play and team play. While he was crude and naive, with an excuse-a-minute, a character like Alibi Ike (and Jack Keefe) passed into American folklore.

More important, Lardner brought to the American short story a renewed and deeper interest in the colloquial tradition, the vernacular speech patterns and rhythms that were typically full of redundancies, awkward phrasings, grammatical lapses, and malapropisms. With his phenomenal ear for everyday speech, Lardner forced the reader to translate his fractured monologues and dialogues into literate terms. In this way, the reader became more active, doing more than simply extracting a story from its plot. Lardner's characters were more significant than the plot; how they talked and what they talked about illuminated their values and their states of mind. Lardner also brought pointed irony to his stories, which, although humane and compassionate, unfortunately were too often seen as misanthropic.

Despite this, Lardner never completely rid himself of the haste and attention to facts associated with newspaper writing. He did not always develop his stories; sometimes they were anecdotal or cartoonlike; they remained topical, and topical stories, like the day's news, are stale by tomorrow. His humor and satire could be self-serving, showing off his cleverness.

Although in the literary histories, Lardner is classified as narrow in range, he did write some serious and substantial stories about the human comedy. His chief subject was the average person and his average mind. In "The Golden Honeymoon," the husband confesses, "Do you expect everything I say will be something you ain't heard me say before?" Lardner developed his instruments—the monologue and the letter—into a fine art.

Dealing with average sensibilities in everyday situations, he created characters, not caricatures. They may be well-meaning, but they are also foolish, stupid, selfish, hypocritical, or vulgar. One of his best stories displays his uncanny ear for speech and the habits of the average individual—"Some Like Them Cold." Following a chance meeting at a Chicago train station, a young couple, Charles Lewis and Mabelle Gillespie, carry on a correspondence. Lardner studies this trite situation with imagination and captures the psychology of the male and female minds. At first they are coy; gradually they become familiar with each other; finally they try to solidify their relationship. At one point, Mabelle pathetically tries to lure Charles into a marriage proposal. When Charles announces that he is marrying someone in New York, they continue their correspondence, although the tone of their letters changes. The ever-present ironies are softened by the comic situation and the use of language that reflects the personalities of the couple. The ironic close to the story is not simply a variation of the O. Henry snapper; irony permeates the entire story. The characters are both individualized and made into types. Charles is more critically portrayed, with his egotism, vulgarity, and insensitivity. Mabelle, by contrast, is trying to be sincere, in making herself available to a prospective mate. "Some Like Them Cold" may not be a deep story; it was not meant to be. What Lardner has effectively done is to dramatize a train station romance and its outcome.

In his justifiably famous story, "The Golden Honeymoon," Lardner again handles monologue and dialogue with great skill. He captures the "hardening" effects of a fifty-year marriage, as he follows a couple on a golden anniversary trip. They are tedious, quarrelsome, short-tempered, childish, and silly, especially the husband, who shows his jealousy in front of his wife's old beau. Lardner does not miss other problems of old age: the growing smallness of their world (the husband finds comfort and meaning in reporting the minor details of the railroad timetable) and their pathetic attempt to hold onto their lives and their love as time is running out. The close of the story may seem slick: "Here comes Mother, so I guess I better shut up." But all along Lardner has shown the irony and pathos of old age. He convinces us that people, although they are often caricatures of themselves, do not really lose their basic humanity.

Although Lardner works within the narrow compass of the monologue once more in "Haircut," he also demonstrates his range, for in mood and tone this story is quite different from "Some Like Them Cold" and "The Golden Honeymoon." Clearly, "Haircut" has a sharp cutting edge. The grotesque pranks of Jim Kendall are treated as comic relief in this grim story. It is the barber who exposes the mentality of the small town as well as of himself. What he talks about and how reveal his limited reasoning abilities, his insensitivity, and his primitive humanity. The end of the story is not simply a clever one-liner: "Comb it wet or dry?" All along, the barber has assumed he is an objective reporter; in reality, he is a biased and shallow person with warped values.

Despite stories that are flippant and predictable with shrill and obvious ironies, miniature pictures of the social history of the 1920s, Ring Lardner proved that he could rise above the rules imposed by the style books and formulas of the magazine and newspaper world, for he wrote some first-rate short fiction. He never took himself seriously enough, however; he wanted to be a successful musical comedy writer. Fitzgerald assessed the tragedy of his friend: "Ring got less percentage of himself on paper than any other American author of the first flight." In part, this was also true of Fitzgerald's own experience as a short story writer.

• • •

One of Ring Lardner's admirers was Ernest Hemingway, who drew much from others, too, during the early phase of his writing career: Sherwood

Anderson, James Joyce, Gertrude Stein, Ezra Pound, and T. S. Eliot. Hemingway was a remarkably quick learner. In a short time, he proved himself to be equal or superior to his mentors. He declared his independence in some of the great short stories of the decade: "Big Two-Hearted River," "Soldier's Home," "The Battler," "The Killers," "In Another Country," and "Hills Like White Elephants." When these stories and the collections *In Our Time* (1925) and *Men without Women* (1927) are placed alongside the efforts of his contemporaries, one recognizes, especially from the hindsight of the 1980s, that Hemingway was a leading contributor to the art and themes of the twentieth-century short story. Unfortunately, critics and students, almost from the first, battled over the idiosyncrasies of his personality, so that they never really knew what he accomplished in the 1920s.

The other arts had a pronounced effect on Hemingway's short stories. Earlier, Anderson had drawn on Whitman's poetry as well as on the colors and moods of impressionistic painting. Fitzgerald's dramatic and lyric gifts were helped along by his love of the theater and poetry. Both Lardner and Steele learned a good deal from the theater in composing their stories. But no one was able to absorb so well and so deeply the worlds of music, painting, architecture, drama, and poetry as did Hemingway. His recently published letters contain countless proofs of the influence of the other arts on his work. He mentions how he carried over painterly qualities in a story like "Big Two-Hearted River," where he was "trying to do the country like Cezanne." In another letter about the story, he adds: "What I've been doing is trying to do country so you don't remember the words after you read it but actually have the Country. It is hard because to do it you have to see the country all complete all the time you write and not just have a romantic feeling about it."[7] He pays homage to music, to Bach, to harmony and counterpoint, things he learned as a youthful cello player.

Over the years, Hemingway also reflected on his major goals in fiction. For one, he wanted to explore the many levels of reality, even striving for the fifth dimension. In *Green Hills of Africa,* he said, "There is a fourth and fifth dimension that can be gotten." There is still no consensus on how far Hemingway traveled in his short stories, but he traveled farther and deeper than any other American writer of his day. Some of his theories he acquired from his newspaper experience; others he developed as an expatriate student, absorbing the wisdoms of Stein, Joyce, and Pound. He aimed for careful selection, condensation, and an austere prose, where nothing would be lost, and in fact, much would be gained: "I always try to write on the principle of the iceberg. There is seven-eighths of it underwater for every part that shows. Anything you know you can eliminate and it only strengthens your iceberg. It is the part that doesn't show." His goal was the "absolutely true," far beyond the literal accuracy and the factual details he was trained to report in his newspaper copy: "A writer's job is to tell the truth. His standard of fidelity to the truth should be so high that his invention, out of his experience, should produce a truer account than anything factual can be. For facts can be observed badly; but when a good writer is creating something, he has time and scope to make it of an absolute truth."

By thinking about and testing various arts and theories, Hemingway added new perspectives and dimensions to the short story. If Anderson's stories unearthed the contemporary themes of violence, terror, and aloneness, Hemingway dealt with all these themes more acutely and more disturbingly; his stoic and understated manner created profounder aftereffects. If Anderson's stories were masculine, they seemed feminine along side those of Hemingway. If the colloquial tradition was realistically presented in Lardner's stories, then Hemingway captured the subtler world of speech, not only what characters said and how they said it, but what they did not say, their voices of silence. By this, Hemingway achieved a heightened realism in his sparse stories.

In the beginning, however, he was content to follow the traditional path to success, hoping to publish in the *Saturday Evening Post,* as if he would be satisfied to become just another popular short story writer. Luckily, he was rejected by the mainstream commercial magazines, and he had the patience to wait for acceptance in the avant-garde magazines, like *Transatlantic Review* and *This Quarter.* No one else seemed interested in his stories, which editors "would never call . . . stories, but always anecdotes, sketches, contes, etc." He learned that there was a great disparity between what he wanted to do and what publishers wanted to present to their audiences.

In 1923, Hemingway described one of his trials to Edward J. O'Brien: "I remember sending a story about an Italian gun man to the Red Book, Karl Harriman editor, back four or five years ago and getting a long letter from them written by Kennicott or someone like that name saying that the story lacked heart interest. That if I would make the gun man the sole support of an aged mother and have him reform in the end it would be a corking yarn."[8] In 1925, he tried and failed to induce George Horace Lorimer to consider a "real bull fight story" ("The Undefeated") for the *Post.* Nor could he find an outlet for the boxing story, "Fifty Grand" (in places like *Collier's,* the *Post,* and *Liberty*), because it was "quite hard in texture." These doubts and rejections on the part of the mass circulation magazines toughened Hemingway. He kept faith in his craft and vision, eventually winning an audience for his kind of story.

Hemingway's short stories derived from his midwestern heritage, his experiences in World War I, and his expatriate life in Paris. In his early work, he echoed his mentors, especially the atmosphere and themes of Anderson's *Winesburg, Ohio*. At the same time, he was exploring and discovering his own personal themes of illusion and reality, loneliness and alienation, violence and death. These and other themes found expression through one character, Nick Adams, who appears in many of his stories. Nick tries to confront reality, or he is witness to conflicts in nature or human nature. In his adventures, Nick desperately searches for a separate peace and meaning within himself; he finds only chaos and disorder in the world at large.

In some of his first stories, Hemingway focuses on the concrete and fuller details of the literary naturalist, making himself appear to be a physical writer of action stories. In reality, he was attempting to reach the deeper world hidden behind facts—the emotional life of the individual, his state of mind, and his crises. Thus, Hemingway was essentially a spiritual writer.

"Up in Michigan" displays his tough and naturalistic manner. It is a masculine story, hard and brittle. It is full of facts; almost everything remains on a one-dimensional plane. The only time Hemingway gets beyond the naturalistic surface is when he repeats the word *like*, hoping to open up the subjective layers of his story of sex and love. In this, he is imitating Gertrude Stein's "art of words." "Up in Michigan" ends as a "pointed" story, closer to a sketch or an anecdote.

In "My Old Man," an early imitation of Sherwood Anderson, Hemingway explores the world of European racetracks and the fate of an American father and his son. While Hemingway's ear for colloquial speech develops, the story is overwritten; at the same time, it treats too cryptically several things—the relationship between father and son, the effect of people and events on the boy's sensibility, and his initiation into violence and corruption. The reader does not really empathize with the boy's bewilderment and pain following his father's death. George Gardner does his best to console the boy: "Don't you listen to what those bums said, Joe. Your old man was one swell guy." Hemingway is here too close to his models—"I Want to Know Why" and "I'm a Fool."

Flatness, dullness, literalness, and reportorial and naturalistic details are tediously repeated in another early story, "Big Two-Hearted River," suggesting that while Hemingway was not developing as an artist he was at least developing a manner. It took more than a decade for critics and readers to discover the meaning and value of this "underground story," a classic example of his style and vision. "Big Two-Hearted River" gets far beyond its closely packed details. It is a dark journey into a man's private world, a study

in exorcism; the hero, Nick Adams, struggles to move toward light and harmony, toward meaning and order in his personal life, despite the meaning-
lessness of the larger world. A remarkable psychological study, "Big Two-
Hearted River" captures the lingering effects of the war experience on a
returning veteran. (In a letter, Hemingway pridefully, and rightly, stated that
he never once mentioned the word *war* in the story.) The narrative concerns
Nick's fishing expedition, which becomes an expedition into the psychic
wound he is trying to nurse. The several rituals in the story—fishing itself,
camping, and eating—obliquely reflect the hidden traumas in Nick, who acts
like a Dostoevskyan double, both escaping from and trying to confront himself and his crisis. On the one hand, Nick relishes elemental acts, like eating,
in order to recover his basic sensations and to fight off any drift toward his
"mind working." The positive poetic refrains (used incrementally)—"They
were satisfactory," "happy," "glad"—are ways in which Nick tries to cope
with the destructive effects of the war and to overcome the dark and omni-
present forces—symbolized by the swamp—still awaiting him in the future.

> Nick did not want to go in there now. He felt a reaction against deep wading
> with the water deepening up under his armpits, to hook big trout in places impos-
> sible to land them. In the swamp the banks were bare, the big cedars came together
> overhead, the sun did not come through, except in patches; in the fast deep water,
> in the half light, the fishing would be tragic. In the swamp fishing was a tragic
> adventure. Nick did not want it. He did not want to go down the stream any further
> today.

With great sensitivity, Hemingway reveals how long and slow is the process
of rehabilitation and recovery. He suggests this by the subdued and tor-
tuously painful movement of his prose.

It took more than a decade for critics and readers to appreciate the acuteness and subtlety of Hemingway's "baby talk," which is still being criticized.
Here is a sample:

> Inside the tent the light came through the brown canvas. Already there was some-
> thing mysterious and homelike. Nick was happy as he crawled inside the tent. He
> had not been unhappy all day. This was different though. Now things were done.
> There had been this to do. Now it was done. It had been a hard trip. He was very
> tired. That was done. He had made his camp. He was settled. Nothing could touch
> him. It was good place to camp. He was there, in the good place. He was in his
> home where he had made it. Now he was hungry.

In this and other scenes like it, Hemingway approximates the workings of
Nick's mind. In a sense, Nick is learning to write prose all over again. He is
trying to rehabilitate himself by reducing things to simple, controllable units

and to bring order and harmony to his world within the peace and stability of a pastoral environment—"home."

This kind of writing (and thinking) is repeated, underscoring Nick's tensions and fears. Mainly, his story is told by means of the rhythm and cadence of the riveting sentences, which both lock and unlock the depths of his wound. Once critics and readers became aware of Hemingway's technique and style, "Big Two-Hearted River" was transformed from "a nice dull fishing story" into one of the major short stories of the century. Very early, with this story, Hemingway achieved the "real thing," the "sequence of motion and fact which made the emotion and which would be as valid in a year or in ten years or, with luck and if you stated it purely enough, always."

If Anderson's stories could be called formless, then Hemingway's major stories are "pointless."[9] Many stories by other writers of the 1920s were of course "pointed," in that they were well-made and well-plotted, with actions direct and on the surface so that they could not be missed by the average reader. Hemingway's stories, by contrast, are oblique; they reverberate, in the Chekhovian manner, with aftereffects. The reader of the 1920s was basically a passive reader. To him, there was no story in "Big Two-Hearted River" because nothing happened, nothing moved; there was no beginning, middle, and end. Hemingway's story needed, even demanded an active and imaginative reader. To understand and appreciate other dimensions and perspectives of this story, one needs to go to "Soldier's Home" in order to get another glimpse of Nick's problems in "Big Two-Hearted River." One also needs to go to the collection *In Our Time* and locate the story within the context of a cycle of stories and vignettes. In the end, "Big Two-Hearted River" encompasses the personal, the contemporary, and the universal at one and the same time.

To get a fuller sense of Hemingway's evolving craft as a short story writer, one should study the three published versions of *In Our Time*. The 1924 version is made up of vignettes. In 1925, these vignettes serve as interchapters to a group of short stories: "Indian Camp," "The Doctor and the Doctor's Wife," "The End of Something" "The Three-Day Blow," "The Battler," "A Very Short Story," "Soldier's Home," "The Revolutionist," "Mr. and Mrs. Elliot," "Cat in the Rain," "Out of Season," "Cross-Country Snow," "My Old Man," and "Big Two-Hearted River." In 1930, Hemingway added an introduction. All these versions show that he was trying to extend the possibilities of the short story cycle, which Anderson had experimented with earlier in *Winesburg, Ohio*.

The experimental *In Our Time* helped Hemingway to achieve larger and deeper effects in his later short stories. The lack of transitions between vignettes and stories; the incongruous juxtaposition of scenes and moods; the contrasts of order, harmony, and rationality with disorder, disharmony, and irrationality; closeups and long shots; the convergence and separation of people and events; things in and out of focus; panoramic views; the hardness and sterility of the prose—all gave Hemingway valuable lessons relating to the ever-shifting nature of reality and the complexity of truth.

In his other important stories of the 1920s, Hemingway journeyed farther and deeper than his readers realized. "The Killers," for example, was looked upon as a "pointed" story, involving gangsters. Hemingway's larger purpose was missed. The blunt and sinister style of the story and the stance of the two gangsters, Al and Max, demonstrate how the raw power and faceless force of violence and death can intrude upon the orderly routine of everyday life. The sardonic playfulness of the two gangsters—they look like comics, "a vaudeville team"—reflects the real grimness of the story and the helplessness of those, like Nick, who are witnesses to a present and future action. Ole Andreson refuses to leave his room and passively awaits his execution; Nick cannot understand Ole Andreson's position, and the helplessness of people generally to fight off violence and evil; George remains philosophical. In "The Killers," Hemingway has created a modern Greek drama of inevitability and the fates.

Although both "In Another Country" and "Hills Like White Elephants" were viewed as anecdotes or sketches in their day, they are highly complex. The Italian major attempts in the story, "In Another Country," to rehabilitate himself from a war wound and face up to the loss of his bride; the story expands into a deeper realm, for it is a paean to man's grace under pressure. "Hills Like White Elephants" deals with far more than abortion. Hemingway captures the terror and pain of impending separation and loss for the young girl, Jig. In this barren story of the end of an affair, the tragedy is the girl's. This story explodes a long-held myth, that the "male chauvinist" Hemingway created only stereotyped women, either bitches or goddesses. Jig is a real girl; Hemingway displays her genuineness, unselfishness, and courage. Her lover is arrogant, egotistical, dishonest, and "reasonable." Their story transforms into a drama with large overtones: the sterility of rationalism and the beauty of irrationalism, the impotence of selfish love and the power of selfless love.

In his "pointless" stories, Hemingway expanded the horizons of the short story, adding a series of "layerings" (as Vladimir Nabokov would put it) to get far beyond what Poe and his followers thought was the genre's main purpose—to aim for and achieve one single effect. Hemingway's important contributions have been underrated. Leon Edel insists that he is really an artist of "evasion," who resorts to tricks, cleverness, and superficial action to "suggest" much when he presents very little. Frank O'Connor also questions Hemingway's value as a short story writer: "The rest of the time I merely ask myself if this wonderful technique of Hemingway's is really a technique in search of a subject or a technique that is carefully avoiding a subject, and searching anxiously all the time for a clean well-lighted place where all the difficulties of human life can be comfortably ignored." The "evasions" and the "technique" found in Hemingway's major stories of the 1920s were central to the reality and truths he was exploring and defining.

Before long, there was a whole school of writers imitating Hemingway's "style," trying to carry his technique to perfection. He was very difficult to imitate, however, because he was more than just a stylist. His disciples were clumsy and shallow; some of them became unintentional parodists.

• • •

It was one thing for Dorothy Parker to review Hemingway's *Men without Women* (1927) in glowing terms in the *New Yorker;* she claimed that he was "the greatest living writer of short stories." It was another thing for her to be influenced by him in her own stories. Moreover, her embittered life, her literary training with the sophisticated magazines *(Vanity Fair, Vogue, New Yorker),* and the lessons she learned from Lardner and Fitzgerald—all helped Parker to "harden" the short story in the late twenties, even though she never forgot one of the ideals of Hemingway's craft, his iceberg theory.

The slick professionalism and smoothness of her ironical stories gave Dorothy Parker a certain fame for a time, but her reputation was to rest on her clever poetry and her legendary wit. Many of her stories remain superficial exercises in pain and depression; they lack the full range of emotions found in human beings and in life. As they rehearse her cynical view of the stupidity and meanness of the nature of things, they yield to formula, to what became popularly known as the Dorothy Parker story.

Parker's limited success with the short story could be blamed partly on the literary environment of the decade. She once admitted: "Silly of me to blame it on dates, but so it happened to be. Dammit, it *was* the twenties and we had to be smarty. I *wanted* to be cute. That's the terrible thing. I should have had more sense." Dorothy Parker became a "smart cracker." Her main weapon was satire, and she recognized the problem with it: "Successful satire has got to be pretty good the day after tomorrow." Her satire was often so pointed and sharp it blunted the possibilities for larger nuances and meanings. Nonetheless, she pleased the editors of the day (like Mencken and Nathan) as she contributed stories like "Too Bad" and "Mr. Durant" to the *Smart Set* and the *American Mercury,* doing her utmost to "aerate Puritanic tradition," to debunk the myths associated with marriage, romance, love, family life, and worldly success. She used the short story to advance her modern ideas concerning the plight of oppressed people, especially women, struggling for their rights and their independence.

On the surface, Parker's work was experimental in style and progressive in ideas; in a short time, much of it became "terribly dated." Her heavy reliance on slick plots, her corrosive irony, and her cynical outlook—all inevitably led to one-dimensional themes and characters who dwindled into caricatures.

"Too Bad" reviews the banal style and pace of a supposedly happily married middle-class couple. However, Grace Weldon is really full of despair: she rearranges the furniture in her apartment; she attempts to find some value in material objects while her husband is away at work; she suffers through an evening of empty talk with him. An imprisoned housewife, Grace hungers for creative outlets. Meanwhile, her husband Ernest spends his free time reading the newspaper. Grace uses various ploys, like "fresh" language ("daffy-down-dillies" for daffodils), to get his attention. When they do converse, the talk is of tomato soup and pie. Grace tries to remember what they talked about before their marriage; but then she had heard that "true love was inarticulate." Now almost inarticulate, they can still find flaws in each other: she has long fingernails; his hair is falling out. Their friends, who appear in the foreword and the afterword to the story, underscore further the smallness of lives and the emptiness of friendships. Mrs. Marshall and Mrs. Ames gossip about the separation of the "ideal" couple; they wonder if Grace and Ernest have had illicit affairs.

"Mr. Durant" recounts the infidelity of a happily married man of forty-nine, who assumes he is cultured because he reads books. He idolizes youth, so he gets involved with a girl of twenty named Rose. As her suitor, he is gentlemanly, but when Rose becomes pregnant, he turns into a self-centered and irresponsible monster. He thinks he is being gallant when he helps the girl get an abortion, although this disturbs his orderly daily routine and makes him unhappy. Meanwhile, his devoted wife wonders if he is not well when he refuses a second helping at dinner. Mr. Durant has no appetite because he cannot find a simple solution to a problem of his own making. In a contrived and ironic ending, he insists that his children get rid of a stray dog they have picked up, especially since it is a female, a reminder of Mr. Durant's predicament with Rose.

Similar stories by Parker, when closely analyzed, have superficial themes and plots, ironies, and formulas. In "Wonderful Old Gentleman," she debunks (again) the notion of the happy family. A brother, his sisters, and their father are lacking in virtue; they are stupid, cruel, hypocritical, or snobbish.

There may be echoes of Shakespeare (references are made to King Lear and Cordelia), but this middle-class family is devoid of tragedy. All the characters move about like automatons; they belong in a soap opera.

A long-admired short story, "Big Blonde," breaks through the formulas, the shallowness, and the unrelieved cynicism of Parker's other work. "Big Blonde" remains harsh and ironic, yet its heroine, Hazel Morse, rises above caricature and melodrama. In fact, she comes to symbolize the broken and futile life, the physical and psychological deterioration taking place at the end of the twenties. Hazel epitomizes the popular girl, the good sport who attends an endless round of parties. Then she nears thirty and marries. Her partying degenerates into a dull and dreary domesticity. When her husband leaves her, she is taken up by other men (Ed, Charley, and Sydney); her life becomes a "haze." She loses her sense of time, even her own identity. She attempts suicide and fails. Although the life has gone out of her, she is kept alive. "Big Blonde" is a danse macabre, a potent and effective study of a woman and an entire generation moving from fun-filled youth to bankrupt age, finding little solace in alcohol, and longing for death.

• • •

With writers like Dorothy Parker relying heavily on irony, plot, and formula and on the standards set by the commercial magazines, the short story of the twenties found itself in a predictable location: a dead end. City life was a factor too; after all, it was the spawning ground for the literary naturalists who concluded that an advanced civilization meant determinism, fatalism, and materialism and the loss of one's individuality and spiritual identity. As a city writer, Parker viewed contemporary life as "closed."

This was a sharp contrast to the beginning of the decade where, in the environment of the Midwest and an agrarian society, the short story was "open"; it had liberated itself from the restrictions and conventions of Poe's theories. Nonetheless, whether the writer was identified with the country or with the city, the short story—thematically speaking—did not radically change. The themes of false illusion, loneliness, alienation, and depression were analyzed and reanalyzed. For beneath its sentimentalism, romanticism, glitter, and gaiety, the twenties was a tragic age. Fitzgerald, Parker, and others came to the same conclusion: the tragedy of youth—the 1920s—was age—the 1930s.

There were subtle new stirrings, however, in the short story of the twenties. Minor voices that would become major voices were being heard in the country again, anticipating another renaissance—not a "lesser" one but one that would remain virtually "hidden" until the 1940s, the southern literary renaissance. In his essay of 1920, "The Sahara of the Bozart," H. L. Mencken dealt what he presumed was a lethal blow to any possible literary aspirations in the New South; the only southern writer he took seriously was James Branch Cabell. Mencken's scathing attack on the barrenness and backwardness of southern culture was to have a reverse effect; it inspired young talents like William Faulkner, Katherine Anne Porter, and Jean Toomer to tap the resources of the region. Their efforts helped to activate not only the southern renaissance but the Negro or Harlem renaissance as well.

Like the Midwest, the South of the 1920s was involved in its own war with the machine and the city. A group of Southern artists, philosophers, economists, and historians defended the agrarian life against the new wave of science and industry; this culminated in a manifesto, *I'll Take My Stand* (1930). Moreover, the Civil War had made the South more southern. It wanted to preserve its moral and spiritual integrity, its bond with the land, its reverence for nature. It wanted to defend its humanism (with its roots in the classical tradition) against the artificial and anonymous urban environment. It wanted to maintain a sense of the past and a sense of family.

As to the preservation of the arts, Donald Davidson was convinced that they flourished best in a "stable, religious, and agrarian" society. This meant the ideals of the pastoral heritage—innocence, simplicity, beauty, individuality, and community. This would be an effective way to ward off the corruption of city life and technological progress, which inevitably led to materialism and a shallow culture.

The new short story writers of the South found themselves at the crossroads: between pastoralism and civilization, between the machine and the garden. They respected the legend and memory of the Old South as they confronted the New South. They never forgot the Civil War and their Fall. As Flannery O'Connor put it: "We have gone into the modern world with an inburnt knowledge of human limitations and with a sense of mystery which could not have developed in our first state of innocence—as it has not sufficiently developed in the rest of our country." Nor could the new writers forget the heritage of the Bible and their earlier oral literature (folk tales, legends, songs, and stories).

•   •   •

When Katherine Anne Porter drew upon the South and Mexico in her first short stories, she was not retreating to the nineteenth century, to the local-color tradition, and to an almost literal transcription of the manners, dress, and customs of her region; she was, rather, the experimental writer, focusing on primitive civilization better to understand modern civilization and life in general terms. Her experimentalism was different from that of the Parisian expatriates. Years later, she was to weigh the achievements of the decade with great skepticism: "Even now when I think of the twenties and the legend that has grown up about them, I think it was a horrible time: shallow and trivial and silly. The remarkable thing is that anybody survived in such an atmosphere—in a place where they could call F. Scott Fitzgerald a great writer!"

At first, Porter praised the experimentalism of Gertrude Stein; later, however, she was critical of Stein and the "modern school" of writing, for "poverty of feeling and ideas were disguised, but not well enough, in tricky techniques and disordered syntax." She even turned against the experimental magazines. Her "Magic" and "The Jilting of Granny Weatherall" appeared in *transition,* which she was to call a "sinister" magazine because "its real voice was hoarse, anxious, corrupted mysticism speaking in a thick German accent"; it was hostile to "reason" and defended "the voice of the blood"; it advocated "the disintegration of syntax."[10]

In going to Mexico and writing about it in her first short story, "María Concepción," Porter was an expatriate writer with a difference. She reacted against the advanced civilizations of Europe and America, and their hollow sophistication. She sought deeper, more universal values in a primitive culture like Mexico, studying the natives and their "complication of simplicities," their "passion for individual expression without hypocrisy." Porter's fiery independence and her humanistic impulse also reinforced her hostility toward the mechanics of the plotted short story and formulas. As a student of Henry James, she respected "form" and "discipline"; however, they were to be in the service of art, a kind of religion to Porter. As she saw it, the short story allowed one to cope with the violence and disorder in the world; she aspired to the Greek ideals of moderation and order.

Porter's characteristic themes were universal ones: good, evil, betrayal, treachery, self-deception, justice, and order. She treated these themes without sentiment or romance. A no-nonsense clinical realist, ironist, and satirist, she had a male's "toughness" and admired the "just cruelty" she was to find in other southern writers who came after her, like Eudora Welty and Flannery O'Connor. As she probed legend and memory, the psychology of character, she lifted her stories to lyric and symbolic levels.

Porter's inimitable treatment of a primitive culture and primitive emotions is forcefully and effectively presented in a story like "María Concepción." In some ways, the proud heroine reminds one of the imposing gallery of Greek heroines, those with a male's strength, like Clytemnestra, Medea, and Antigone. María endures her trials with patience and in silence. Her husband Juan has run off with a fifteen-year-old, María Rosa, who later bears him a child. María Concepción takes justice into her own hands and kills the girl with a butcher knife, the same knife she uses to kill chickens for the marketplace. She takes María Rosa's infant as her own, thus replacing the child she herself has lost. In her simplistic way, María Concepción moves from death to resurrection. Meanwhile, the community accepts her action, and even defends her against the authorities of law and order. While Juan is punished for his sin, by having to return to labor for an archeologist in a "buried city," María finds happiness with her new child.

Into the foreground and the background to this simple plot, Porter has woven a complexity of issues and emotions. There are the elemental and ancient themes of the curse, evil spirits, revenge, sin, mystery, violence, personal justice, fate, and religious belief. As Porter translates these themes into contemporary terms, she highlights a paradox: good can come out of an "evil" action.

Almost from the beginning, Porter demonstrates her versatility and maturity as a short story writer. She takes the basic themes of "María Concepción—betrayal and justice—and reintroduces them into an advanced culture, the middle-class world of the American South, headed by a matriarch. The brooding and primitive violence and disorder of "María Concepción" are replaced by a sophisticated comic satire on pride and vanity, fidelity and infidelity, in "The Jilting of Granny Weatherall." Porter probes with deft psychological insight an old matriarch's nagging complaint that has hounded her for her entire life (she is nearly eighty as she expires): she was once jilted by her bridegroom. Porter's subtle use of the dimensions of time (past, present, and future), her representation of inner and outer reality, and the constant drift between dream and waking—all reveal that beneath this domestic story and the old woman's frustrations are universal concerns: the need for a strong will and a sense of family to survive and endure misfortune.

None of Porter's other stories of the twenties—"Magic," "Rope," "He," "Theft," "Virgin Violeta," "The Martyr"—has the freshness, originality, and keenness of the art and vision found in "María Concepción" and "The Jilting of Granny Weatherall." True, Porter does prove her gift for irony, satire, and caricature in these stories, but they are "pointed" and lacking in range, depth, and power.

• • •

At the time that William Faulkner met Sherwood Anderson, he was an unknown quantity compared to Katherine Anne Porter. But their meeting in New Orleans in 1924 was a symbolic moment; the mantle of the short story was to pass from the Midwest to the South. Anderson and Faulkner became friends; they collaborated on writing tall tales; they compared notes about the characters they created. Because of the bardic and epical nature of his craft and vision, however, Faulkner once stated flatly, "I am quite sure that I have no feeling for short stories; that I shall never be able to write them."

Sometime before 1925, William Faulkner did write short stories and fictional sketches. They reveal that like other short story writers of the twenties he was also a student of the arts of poetry, drawing, and painting. In addition to his sketches, which appeared in the *Double Dealer* and the New Orleans *Times-Picayune* (one of them, "The Liar," was a forecast of Yoknapatawpha County), he wrote numerous stories that remained virtually unknown for years until they appeared in *Uncollected Stories* (1979). These included "Nympholepsy," "Adolescence," "Al Jackson," "Don Giovanni," "Peter," "Moonlight," and "The Big Shot."

Like his later famous stories, these early pieces by Faulkner never had a direct influence on the American short story, as did the work of Anderson and Hemingway. They had, however, a more subtle and roundabout impact through his novels and "communal" stories. While Faulkner's early work clearly lacked the ambiguity, implications, and perceptions of his later stories, they suggested the larger designs of his major fiction. Faulkner's stories, to begin with, were not meant to be self-contained units, as were the typical stories of the day. They were parts of a cycle, gradually filling in and developing his mythical country of Yoknapatawpha. By continually returning to and reusing stories, legends, myths, themes, characters, and situations, Faulkner was experimenting with and extending the world of the short story. His "communal" stories were always in the process of being transformed and redefined.

These qualities were hinted at in Faulkner's stories of the twenties. "Nympholepsy" reveals his descriptive powers, his striking use of poetic images, and his attempt to link man and nature, myth and symbol. Although "Nympholepsy" has no real story line, it echoes the future Yoknapatawpha County. "Adolescence" does have a story line; it is a study of the backwoods South, a beginning portrait of the Bundren family of *As I Lay Dying*. Here Faulkner creates a pastoral idyl; Juliet and Lee are like "two animals in an eternal summer." The threads of later themes are here too: sex and adulthood, transience, violence, and death. Faulkner also shows his early skill with the local dialect of his people. Another story, "The Big Shot," is of interest mainly because its first portraits of Popeye, Thomas Sutpen, Wash Jones, and Flem Snopes. "The Big Shot" demonstrates that Faulkner is equally at home in the city environment; the tough and literal naturalistic style of the story serves as a foundation for the lyric, symbolic, and mythic levels of his later and more famous work.

• • •

The Negro characters found in the work of Faulkner, and earlier in the stories by Anderson and Hemingway, helped to create a greater respect for the Harlem renaissance, which received modest recognition by March 1924. The year before, in *Cane* (1923), Jean Toomer gave the Harlem renaissance added impetus in the direction of modernism and experimentalism, and away from the long-lived "plantation-school" image. In the past, Negro stories had generally reflected a placid life, romance, and sentiment, with Negroes devoted to the status quo and stereotyped roles.

On the surface, Jean Toomer appears to be a plantation-school writer. The settings in *Cane* are often the cane fields of the South; they recall the literature of the soil, primitivism and pastoralism, the preservation of traditional codes, and biblical and spiritual themes. But here the connection ends. For like other writers of the emerging southern renaissance, Toomer was sensitive to the debilitating effects of modern industrial society, which meant the supremacy of rationalism and materialism. Like D. H. Lawrence, Toomer warred against science and the intellect. He was vitally concerned with protecting and exalting the individual's inner freedom and his sexuality, especially in women, who were subjugated and oppressed by men and society.

In his work, Toomer drew upon and extended the style and technique of Sherwood Anderson's *Winesburg, Ohio.* He reintroduced the lyricism and symbolism of Walt Whitman; the colors and moods of impressionistic painting; the freshness and sharpness of imagist poetry; the philosophy of Eastern mysticism; and the folk songs, jazz, and spirituals native to southern blacks.

All these qualities can be found in *Cane,* a volume that is hard to categorize even today. Some insist it is a novel, but it represents a variety of other genres: sketches, vignettes, poems, plays, and short stories. It is hard to assess the full impact of *Cane* on the Harlem renaissance, which by the thirties was deeply committed to social questions. However, *Cane's* critical acceptance was important; it gave confidence to the black short story writers who came after Toomer.

The daily lives and actions of the Negro characters in *Cane* are not treated in the peripheral way they were represented by white writers. Toomer sees his Negro characters from the inside out and independent of white culture. The most widely discussed story in *Cane* is "Fern." While it has a more literal plot line than "Karintha," it radiates with imagery and symbol, with exotic and erotic overtones. "Fern" is another study in possession. Early, Fern is sexually possessed by men. But men can only bring their bodies; therefore she is left with a sense of the joylessness of life. "Fern" also foreshadows life in the urban North (portrayed in later sections of *Cane*), where the Negro heroine sits at a tenement window "looking down on the indifferent throngs of Harlem," when she belongs amidst the "folk-songs at dusk in Georgia." Like others of the southern renaissance, Toomer understood the inevitability of things: the pastoral and the primitive would be overtaken by "industry and commerce and the machines. The folk-spirit was walking in to die on the modern desert."[12] In *Cane*, Toomer was singing a swan song, the end of an era; blacks were leaving one kind of bondage for another.

• • •

From the beginning to the end of the twenties, from Sherwood Anderson's Ohio to Jean Toomer's rural Georgia, the short story was extraordinarily productive. Although the popular story, slick entertainments, and formula plots still flourished, the new short story—in the hands of Ernest Hemingway it resembled an antistory—was coming to the forefront. Experimental magazines in Europe and America, with their modern views of art and reality, helped to create the climate for highly individual "formless," "pointless," and "communal" stories. As the writers themselves drew upon the other arts, they were making the short story genre into an art form. Although the short story was beginning to be taken seriously in the twenties, there was an inevitable lag, with critics and readers, editors and publishers, not fully aware of what was happening. As writers became more adept in style and technique, they reflected life more realistically; they became bolder in their themes, with controversial subjects and moral and ethical issues usually reserved for the novel. They wedded pleasure and purpose, entertainment and moral values, things that seemed contradictory to the popular short story writers and the middlebrow readers.

The writers of the twenties found their richest resource in the provincial, the regional. Katherine Anne Porter claimed that "all true art is provincial in the most realistic sense." Flannery O'Connor stated flatly, "The best American fiction has always been regional." Another important resource was the city. The new writers of the decade, in viewing both worlds, were better able to study closely the local and the private and from it draw larger meanings. Already the short story writers were finding the universal in the personal, the absolute in the relative. Collectively, they mirrored the tragic conflict of the age—the rise of material progress and the spiritual wants and needs of democratic man. The short story in the 1920s may have been looked upon as a lesser renaissance in its own time, but it left an impressive legacy of experimentation, diversity, and density to future generations of readers and writers.

Thomas A. Gullason

University of Rhode Island

THE AMERICAN
SHORT STORY:
1930–1945

Contours

The years 1930–45, from the start of the Great Depression through the end of World War II, mark the most prolific outpouring of American short fiction in the history of our national literature. It is a climactic period, representing the high point of an era that H. E. Bates, in his 1941 book *The Modern Short Story,* described as a modern American renaissance begun by Sherwood Anderson, taken up by Ernest Hemingway, and carried into the 1930s by William Faulkner, Erskine Caldwell, Katherine Anne Porter, and William Saroyan. Anderson had uncovered the true American subject matter in *Winesburg, Ohio* (1919), Bates said, turning from unwieldy national perspectives to stories based in regional realities. Hemingway had crafted it— "sheared away the literary woolliness of English,"—in the stories of *In Our Time* (1925) and *Men without Women* (1927). And following their examples, "a whole generation of American short-story writers turned round to American earth, American cities, small American towns, American homes, American politics, and American hopes and troubles, to find waiting for it the limitless untouched raw materials of a new American tradition."

Today only two of the then still emerging generation of short story writers Bates identified are recognized as masters of the form: William Faulkner's reputation rests on his more than one hundred short stories published between 1930 and 1950, Katherine Anne Porter's on her twenty-six stories. Overshadowed by Faulkner and Porter and their successors in the South, Caldwell mastered the subject matter of the new movement but not the technique. Saroyan really never mastered either one. Nonetheless, Caldwell published fifteen volumes of short fiction beginning with *American Earth* (1931), and Saroyan claimed to have written nearly five hundred stories, sketches, and self-portraits during the 1930s alone. Theirs, along with a score of other names, swell a rich undercurrent in American writing of the 1930s and 1940s that includes the short fiction of Conrad Aiken, Kay Boyle, James T. Farrell, Langston Hughes, Mary McCarthy, John O'Hara, Dorothy Parker, James Thurber, John Steinbeck, William Carlos Williams, and Richard Wright. At the top of the list, ranked with the work of Faulkner and Porter and the late Hemingway, are some late stories of Scott Fitzgerald, Thomas Wolfe's collection *From Death to Morning* (1935), and the first two of Eudora Welty's collections, *A Curtain of Green* (1941) and *The Wide Net* (1944). This, briefly, is the core of the generation of the "new American tradition."

Literary America has a long-standing fascination with traditions, hardly less with those manufactured out of whole cloth than ones honestly inherited. In his preface to *The Marble Faun* in 1860, Nathaniel Hawthorne lamented the lack of an American literary tradition rooted in a dark American past like that which had captured his imagination in England and Italy in 1853–59. In 1919, in "Tradition and the Individual Talent," T. S. Eliot insisted that such a tradition not only was available to the modern writer but was the one essential context in which his individual achievement could be defined. Eliot argued, however, that "if the only form of tradition, of handing down, consisted in following the ways of the immediate generation before us in a blind or timid adherence to its successes, 'tradition' should positively be discouraged. We have seen many such simple currents soon lost in the sand; and novelty is better than repetition. Tradition is a matter of much wider significance. It cannot be inherited, and if you want it you must obtain it by great labour." As we shall see, there are good reasons for discussing the American short story writers of the 1930s and early 1940s in the context of an evolving modern tradition—somewhat better ones, in fact, than H. E. Bates could have seen from his standpoint in the midst of that tradition in 1941.

These have to do, as so much of American literature has to do, with the opposition of contrary elements: with, on the one hand, the unique social realities of the Depression that demanded literary expression and, on the other, the emergent American sense of literary modernism as an alternative mode to social realism. These powerful forces generated productive tensions that mark the short fiction of the period as not only "new" but wholly American. In the best such work, there is a complex fusion of the two amounting to the double awareness Eliot described as making a poet traditional—"a sense of the timeless and of the temporal together," the consciousness, as he concluded, "not of what is dead, but of what is already living." That there were European models for that awareness there is plentiful evidence in Eliot's own poetry and the writing of numerous Americans educated by him, including Hemingway, Faulkner, Porter, and Wolfe. But in the "new American tradition" of the short story as they represent it, there is the strongly felt presence of an older tradition as well, rooted not in Europe but in the America of Hawthorne and Melville and Twain and Henry James. In their own short fiction, the writers of the modern renaissance of the 1930s powerfully recreate the subjects, the themes, and in the case of the short story itself, the modes of expression of the American renaissance of the nineteenth century.

Unlike the Great War, the Great Depression pointed the need for no radically new modes of expression. Rather, it nurtured intensities and uncovered materials already existing in American writing of the previous decade and the previous century. Paul Fussell has said in *The Great War and Modern Memory* that, for the English imagination, the Great War is where the modern irony and absurdity began; that "relying on inherited myth [as a mode of expression], it was generating new myth, and that myth is part of the fiber of our own lives." In America in the early twentieth century, the two "myths" were more nearly complementary than antithetical: irony and nightmare and irresolvable contraries were already firmly imbedded American literary realities, and American writers had long struggled with their expression. The Manichaean paradoxes inherited from American Calvinism produced a literature in the nineteenth century that challenged transcendental oversimplifications, said no thunderously, and investigated the ambiguities inherent in both the whiteness of the whale and the blackness of darkness. Broken from the preceding decade by no event so cataclysmic as world war, the writers of the 1930s drew on the experiments of the 1920s in the contexts of broader national subjects—young Americans, initiations, death and dying, fantasies. They worked, too, with broader national themes that evoked the psychological and emotional undercurrents of American life, even when the subject matter was most topical—what Hawthorne identified as "the truth of the human heart" and Faulkner was to call "the old universal truths lacking which any story is ephemeral and doomed—love and honor and pity and pride and compassion and sacrifice." And they turned again—turned naturally, one is tempted to say—to the short story. Whatever the directions that American modernism takes, and there are several; whatever the forms it assumes, and they are various; by 1930 it had rooted itself deep in the tradition of American romanticism.

• • •

In the 1930s a significant portion of the American reading public found itself unable to afford the luxury of buying books. In *The Popular Book. A History of*

America's Literary Taste, James D. Hart points out that from 1929 to 1933 publication figures for new books fell from 214,334,000 to 110,790,00; many of those that were published in 1933 were never bound or presented for sale. The exigencies of personal finances, together with the limits on library budgets and reading room space, brought about the rise of rental libraries. The twenty-five-cent Pocket Book series initiated publication with James Hilton's *Lost Horizons,* and there was a vast increase in magazines of all kinds and persuasions, from *The Anvil: Stories for Workers* (1933) to *Esquire.* Americans, weary of the daily realities of the Depression and burdened with more unpaid free time than ever before, turned naturally to the multivarious entertainments of literature, and if books were in limited supply, magazine fiction might fill the void. This created a vast market for short fiction to which writers began immediately to respond. The commercial magazines, of course, had thrived for years, and many serious writers were drawn to them by the large fees they paid. F. Scott Fitzgerald was accustomed to receiving $3,600 per story from the *Saturday Evening Post,* which paid a total of $22,050 for his stories in 1928 and $27,000 in 1929. Even in 1930–31 at the start of the Depression, his five *Post* stories about the adventures of the adolescent Josephine Perry brought him $18,000. His royalties and other writings that year earned only $439.07. Other magazines that paid well for slick short fiction were *Redbook, McCall's, Cosmopolitan, Collier's,* and *Woman's Home Companion.*

There were two literary reactions to the demand for short stories and the popularity of this sort of story in particular. One was aesthetically derived, the other founded primarily in social ideologies and outraged indignation. Both were revolutionary.

By the time *Winesburg, Ohio* was published in 1919, Sherwood Anderson and others were vocally protesting the formula fictions published by commercial magazines which, in their view, expressed nothing so much as the dangerous standardization of life in America. In an essay titled "New Orleans, *The Double Dealer* and the Modern Movement in America" (*Double Dealer* 3 [March 1922]), Anderson complained of the "strange exterior semblance of life" that magazines presented as images of America. The modern movement, as he called it, was an effort to reopen channels of individual expression closed by the failure of public taste and the self-serving editorial policies of the *Saturday Evening Post.*

A magazine having a circulation of a million is in a rather ticklish position when it comes to handling any such matters as honest reactions to life. There are so many things the editors of all such magazines have to be careful about. All such basic human attributes as sex hungers, greed and the sometimes twisted and strangely perverted desires for beauty in human beings have to be let alone. The basic stuff of human life that all real artists, working in the medium of prose, have handled all through the history of writing has to be thrown aside. The writer is perpetually called upon to seem to be doing something while doing nothing at all. There is the perpetual tragedy of unfulfilment.

Serious short story writers, taking their cue from Anderson, from Chekhov, Maupassant, and Joyce before him, and from his immediate disciples such as Hemingway, reshaped the forms and formal strategies of the short story as the Depression went on. They published their work in magazines like *American Mercury*, edited by H. L. Mencken, *Atlantic Monthly*, and *Scribner's Magazine*, where the discerning editor Alfred Dashiell held sway. Some found a publisher in the *New Yorker* and founded what they did not even know was a school based on the tastes of Harold W. Ross. There is a lively and powerful modernist strain in the work of all of these, and the major short story writers in America between 1930 and 1945 can be defined by their relation to this aesthetic and its broad-ranging manifestations.

The second social response was supplied by the little magazines, many of which provided a much needed outlet for protest against those repressive elements in American society that Hart Crane laid at the door of "the czars of golf in plaid plus-fours." The greatly increased numbers of little magazines in the 1930s made up for their relatively limited readership: according to Frederick Hoffman, Charles Allen, and Carolyn Ulrich, in *The Little Magazines*, the number of new little magazines published, primarily in the United States, rose from eighteen in 1931 and fifteen in 1932 to forty-three in 1933 and a remarkable forty-nine in 1934. The titles suggest a common revolutionary bias: the *Anvil*, the *Left*, *Masses*, and *Blast* are typical. All published more than one issue; some were fairly long-running. Nearly all of them published short stories. Founded in the spirit of conscientious revolt against received standards and public taste, and given to experimentation and novelty, they formed an advance guard to the commercial magazines.

They published the work of nonpolitical writers, of course, as well as that of inspired fellow travelers, but their emphasis was on stories depicting actual social injustices. Some, like *Story*, were exclusively dedicated to sponsoring genuine talent and encouraging the highest development of the short story form regardless of ideology. Founded in 1931 by Whit Burnett and Martha Foley, *Story* published the work of Conrad Aiken, Kay Boyle, and William Faulkner among many others. Other magazines were openly political. In his essay *A Note on Literary Criticism* (1936), James T. Farrell tried to distinguish between Marxist art and Marxist propaganda by calling for a literature in the tradition of Anderson's stories, stripped of preachiness of whatever persuasion and simplified "to the point of obviousness and even downright banality." Farrell envisioned a literature shaped by "social structures" rather than social function, and his stories and novels of life in the Irish immigrant communities of Chicago exemplify his conception. The literature of social function was championed by figures such as Jack Conroy: an accomplished writer of short stories himself and editor of the *Anvil*, subtitled "Stories for Workers," he viewed art as a weapon against the bourgeoisie. He once editorialized, "We prefer crude vigor to polished banality." Whatever the editorial outlook of such magazines—they ranged from "A Review of Ideas and Personality" *(Contempo)* to "A Magazine of Proletarian Short Stories" *(Blast)*—and whatever the length of their careers—*Story* published regularly from 1931 to 1948 and intermittently thereafter into the 1960s, *Kosmos* ran only from November–December 1933 to July–August 1935—together they were responsible for a steady stream of short fiction in the decade of the Depression.

There is no more thorough perspective on the history of the little magazines than Hoffman, Allen, and Ulrich's book. One telling comment on the contribution of the little magazine to the rise of the short story is their contention that "in the thirties the short story came into its own, to meet a literary need. Writers experimented in a variety of ways with the form, favored by an editorial generosity which is characteristic of the little magazine in general." But editorial generosity, while it fostered experimentation, ironically permitted some of the same standardization in avant-garde magazines that they were supposedly rebelling against in commercial ones. It constituted a risk as well as a resource. The risks lay in oversimplifications and formula stories, and the aesthetic outcome was the same whether the magazine was *Esquire* or *Leftward*. Fitzgerald's Josephine stories, for example, are sentimental, melodramatic, and romantic in the pejorative sense of that word. But they were popular. Like the companion pieces about Basil Duke Lee that Fitzgerald sold to the *Post* in 1928–29, they are imitations of fully imagined story masterpieces such as "Mayday," "Winter Dreams," and "Absolution." Fitzgerald aimed at diverting his readers from the realities of the Depression, the proletarians at arousing their outraged indignation. But too often the results in the proletarian stories were as predictable as the names on Josephine's dance card. Hoffman, Allen, and Ulrich say this of social realism, the form in which leftist literature was frequently written:

Selecting a scene, an event, or a person, the author relied upon the facts themselves to tell the story and announce his attitude toward it. The subjects were starvation, strikes, poverty, proletarian heroism. The formula for melodrama, which assumes clear-cut personal representatives of villainy and virtue, was often employed to give reportage an editorial slant, so that the moral might be made more explicit. The writing is marked by self-confidence: the hero, though imprisoned actually or spiritually, is consoled by the thought that his imprisonment is a temporary thing; it will be relieved by death or by some other form of deliverance. This current of comment runs through many of the tales: prejudice, injustice, or oppression are absurd; men act this way only when they are victims of an intolerable economic system; once the system has been smashed, men will be good and above all sensible.

To this formula the short story was particularly well suited; its shortness was suited to the portrayal of emblematic lives, and it was versatile enough to accommodate authorial moralizing. Examples of social realism may be found in sometimes quite good stories about urban horrors by Farrell, Benjamin Appel, Paul Corey, and Langston Hughes, and in stories about regional rural hardship, published in little magazines like the *Midland* and the *New Mexico Quarterly*, by Loren Eiseley, Meridel Lesueur, William March, and Ruth Suckow.

According to Hoffman, Allen, and Ulrich, the little magazines since 1912 have sponsored fully 80 percent of the most important American writers and every noteworthy literary movement in America. Today few stories by any but the best social realists have even the appeal of Fitzgerald's slick fiction; few, even of the best of those writers, achieved his sometimes stunning power. But like him and his imitators, the social realists and their imitators made notable contributions to the short story. The frequent failings no less than the considerable achievements indicate how delicate the form is, and how demanding and unforgiving.

• • •

Thinking of those stories now, with the purpose of describing the literary contours of the period, their diverse and open forms are more striking than any narrow formulas they may have popularized. The good stories published in magazines and gathered in anthologies seem as different, as individual in conception and achievement, as the men and women who wrote them. And so they should. There is after all no exclusively American subject matter or ideology nor, though the short story has been called American, an exclusive genre. But there are recurrent subjects and themes and ways of expressing them in every literature that together do define its national identity and suggest the outlines of a tradition. One such compound, that R. W. B. Lewis calls the central figure in "an emergent American myth," is the American Adam. In his book of that title, Lewis traces the Adamic image in American thought and expression from its emergence in the second quarter of the nineteenth century as far as selected avatars in the twentieth. By its recurrence in American short stories, it provides a point of common reference for a discussion of several writers of short fiction in the second quarter of the twentieth century who appropriated Adamic materials into their work as the naturally available, traditional matter of American literary expression.

This is to say what is perhaps obvious: the sons and daughters of Young Goodman Brown, Ishmael, Huckleberry Finn, and Christopher Newman were born into the twentieth century with the names George Willard and Nick Adams, Miranda Rhea and Isaac McCaslin; and their reappearance in such numbers is one clear indicator of the relatively seamless tradition available to American writers from Anderson and Hemingway, in the years after the war, to Porter and Faulkner and their contemporaries who made literary reputations in the following decade. Lewis described the American Adam as "a figure of heroic innocence and vast potentialities, poised at the start of a new history." Modern versions are perhaps less sanguine. In the short fiction of the 1930s, Adamic protagonists are portrayed typically in imagery taken from Genesis by way of the Puritan concept of America as a New Jerusalem. They are loners, outcasts, and principled nay-sayers, and they are wanderers in wildernesses that stretch from the streets of Los Angeles to the Mississippi River Delta. They are tormented by sexuality, social difference, innocence— any one of which may prove mortally dangerous. Their world is one forever ambiguous and forever young, where family and societal restrictions heighten the impulse toward individual freedom and temptations are sharpened by personal inhibitions. Like the protagonist of William Saroyan's story "Snake," they are likely to undertake their rites of passage "in the garden with the snake, unnaked, in the beginning, in the year 1931."

But this resource, too, embodies risks. The range of uses to which such materials were put, and the delicacy required to keep them from their own sort of formulary, can be shown in the early autobiographical stories of three men who, by some definitions, were themselves outcast sons of America in the 1930s: William Saroyan, James T. Farrell, and Richard Wright.

Like many of his young heroes, Saroyan was an Armenian-American, born in northern California, and acutely sensitive to his immigrant antecedents. His first collection of stories, *The Daring Young Man on the Flying Trapeze,* was published in 1934. As the title of the book suggests, he conceived of growing up in America as a public performance that uncovered, tested, and more often than not confirmed the veracity of personal principles already latent in the individual. When the performance is sexually motivated, as it is in the story "And Man," the agonies and the rewards increase proportionately. The narrator of "And Man" is a fifteen-year-old boy who says of himself:

I was as large physically as a man, larger, for that matter, than most men. It was as if I had leaped suddenly from the form of myself as a boy to the vaster form of myself as a man, and to the vaster meaning of myself as something specific and alive. Look at him, my relatives were saying, every part of his body is growing, especially his nose. And they made sly jokes about my private organs, driving me out of my head with shame. How about it? they asked, even the ladies. Is it growing? Do you dream of big women, hundreds of them?

Of course he does dream of women, of one in particular, a schoolmate. Daringly one morning he plays truant to walk in the country pondering these changes and compulsions. At school the next day, his grown-up airs earn him a public spanking from the principal and the mocking laughter of the girl he loves. Denied the Adamic garden of innocence symbolized in the country retreat and unfit now for the social refuge of childhood represented by the school, the hero asserts his self-reliance in a secular platitude: "the truth was myself and I was man." Here and throughout the collection, Saroyan insists on himself as a writer, embodiment of the Word as he says in one story, but too often in these autobiographical sketches and self-portraits the only "Word" he can summon is a self-conscious cliché of his own or a fragment from another writer. T. S. Eliot, Ezra Pound, and Ernest Hemingway are favorite sources. His formula responses to his American material suggest that, however sensitive he was to uncovering it, he never achieved the objective control to put the rites-of-passage plot to expressive individual use. The material is not distanced, the characters are not individuated, and the stories are not self-contained.

James T. Farrell's early stories of fallen innocence are equally personal and frequently more successful. In "Studs," from which the Lonigan trilogy evolved, he tells the story of the boyhood, dissipation, and untimely death of the proto-typical urban American hero, Studs Lonigan. But the story is not a sentimental eulogy for a heroic have-not nor paean to an immigrant athlete dying young. The autobiographical narrator is both part of and apart from the life he describes: his empathy with Studs is distanced by his recognition that long before Studs's death the adventurous boy who once inspired "the pride and the glory" in him had disappeared in "slobbish dissipation." Studs's story is "the usual commonplace story," the narrator says: commonplace, we understand him to mean, not only in the closed world of Chicago's South Side he so realistically describes, but in America itself where the rites of passage from boyhood are too often destructive of the man. In his moral and physical decline, Studs represents the failure of the American dream of possibility, and only by escaping Studs's influence has the narrator escaped Studs's fate. By contrast, Studs's respectable boyhood cronies turn endlessly to the romanticized past, mythologizing their reckless days of urban innocence and longing a little wistfully for the drunken pranks and poker games, prostitutes and petty thievery of their late adolescence. In Farrell's lost Eden of America, the American Adam is a boy named Tommy Doyle or Paulie Haggerty or Red O'Connell, a would-be sexual "stud" unwittingly come to mourn his own manhood at Studs Lonigan's funeral.

Like Saroyan's protagonists, Farrell's narrator is a writer; like them, often, he is the familiar stranger, the man between cultures. But the achievement of Farrell's narrator, and of Farrell himself, is to undercut cultural platitudes with irony. He knows that Studs will be miserable in the Heaven the priests and Old World custom have sent him to, that "he will find the land of perpetual happiness and goodness dull and boresome, and he'll be resentful." His condemnation of that heavenly paradise condemns America as well, a "dull and boresome" land where the death of the individuated character signifies the meaningless lives of the generation of his survivors.

If there is little hope of redemption for the Studs Lonigans of twentieth-century America, there is less still for Richard Wright's young black protagonists growing toward manhood in Mississippi and Chicago in the 1930s. Wright's Adamic man stands in the same ironic relation to the American mythos as Farrell's, but his pariah-hood is more severe and the fault more clearly America's. In Wright's most autobiographical heroes, as in Saroyan's, there is even a tendency toward public performance, as if the lives he depicts in his fictions are moved by the same impulses that moved Wright to assert his own identity in written performances. In this, whatever his considerable individual achievement, Wright represents more clearly, and more agonizingly than either Saroyan or Farrell, the need of the minority writer in America to define his situation by describing it and by describing, protest it. As Wright demonstrates in the 1938 collection *Uncle Tom's Children,* the initiation plot and its associated themes and imagery served these ends with special force. Two stories that illustrate the range of the dilemma as Wright conceived it are "Big Boy Leaves Home" and "Down by the Riverside," the opening two stories of that collection.

There are two epigraphs to the book. The first announces a new day: "Uncle Tom is dead!" The second, drawn from the lyrics of a popular song, indicates that there still is no place in America for the children of Uncle Tom:

Is it true what they say about Dixie?
Does the sun really shine all the time?
Do sweet magnolias blossom at everybody's door,
Do folks keep eating 'possum, till they can't eat no more?
Is it true what they say about Swanee?
Is a dream by that stream so sublime?
Do they laugh, do they love, like they say in ev'ry song? . . .
If it's true that's where I belong.

Here is a myth to be spiked. Wright's stories demonstrate too clearly and all too violently that the America of Dixie is not "true" and is not the place where his black characters "belong." His long expatriation in Europe is evidence that the same was true for Wright himself. In Dixie and in America, Wright is saying, the children of Uncle Tom are doomed to be just that— children—and never more than children. "Big Boy Leaves Home" deals literally with boys, "Down by the Riverside" with a man named Mann killed for asserting his manhood. In both, the male protagonists are treated as "big boys," denied access to either childhood innocence or redemptive maturity. This double-edged syllogism Wright phrased from the Book of Genesis: the fall of the Adamic man, in "Big Boy Leaves Home," and the purgation by Flood, in "Down by the Riverside."

"Big Boy Leaves Home" is the story of four black friends who swim naked in a forbidden swimming hole one hot Mississippi afternoon, encounter a frightened white woman, and are shot at by her husband. Two boys are killed before Big Boy seizes the gun and shoots the white man. He and Bobo flee for their lives, Big Boy arranging to be smuggled by truck to Chicago the following day. He spends the night in a wet hole in the ground beside the highway, first killing a snake there. During the night Bobo is murdered on the hill above him: tarred and feathered, castrated, and burned by a white mob chanting "we'll hang ever nigger to a sour apple tree." Sour indeed. The snake and the apple tree are not accidental, and the Edenic parallels they suggest are pointed and bitter. Bobo and Big Boy are punished not by a vengeful God but by an avenging mob, not for eating of the Tree of Knowledge but for being black boys naked in a demoniac garden. Like Adam, Big Boy crushes the serpent beneath his heel, but the garden from which he is driven is a place of burning and mutilation.

Similar inversions haunt the world of "Down by the Riverside," where a black farmer tries to save his family in a small white boat from a flood. Again the racial symbolism is overt and ironic: the white boat that sustains him on the flood is his undoing. Like a lonely Noah struggling toward Mt. Ararat, Mann is beset on the water by frightening "dim figures in a sick dream." The green hills, when he reaches them alone, relieve some of the terrors of the flood but not of the nightmare, and he prays there, "Lawd, save me now. Save me now." As in the Negro spiritual that gives the story its title, he does lay down his sword and shield "down by the riverside," but only to be slaughtered by white National Guardsmen:

> One of the soldiers stooped and pushed the butt of his rifle under the body and lifted it over. It rolled heavily down the wet slope and stopped about a foot from the water's edge; one black palm sprawled limply outward and upward, trailing in the brown current.

Stylistically, these stories are in the naturalistic tradition revived by the social realists, where moments in impossibly barren lives are presented to speak for themselves of the inequities and iniquities they depict. The heavily dialectic speech of Wright's characters, the detailed horrors of Bobo's lynching, and the overt naturalistic symbolism of Big Boy's fight with the snake and Mann's bare-handed struggle against the current of the flooded river are examples. But if strategies of style insist on the differences between black boys and white men, the strategies of form insist upon their inescapable similarities.

The Adamic forms Wright adopted in the 1930s were not clichés then any more than they are in the 1980s or will be in 2001. New voices in American writing shape traditional materials to their individual needs in every generation, and Wright's is no exception. In her biography, *Richard Wright,* Constance Webb quotes an unpublished preface to *Uncle Tom's Children* in which Wright says that he discovered as he wrote the stories that "the images, symbols, and attitudes of Christianity were the highest crystallizations of the Negro's will to live he had made in this country . . . embodied in a complete system of images, symbols, attitudes." But these are American as well as Negro-American modes of expression, as common to Hawthorne's paradoxical allegories of the Fall as to Richard Wright's. What distinguishes Wright and the black writers of the 1930s is that their voices were literally new—the voices of heretofore "invisible" men and women that had been all but inaudible in previous American generations. In an essay titled "Voices from the Veil: Black American Autobiography,"[1] Gordon Taylor proposes that that invisibility and long silence account in part for the autobiographical tendency in black American writing, including the act of self-narration in works of fiction. Such modes of expression, he says, are responses to a problem of identity simultaneously literary and literal. For Wright, as for W. E. B. DuBois, James Weldon Johnson, James Baldwin, and Malcolm X—to name only those writers Taylor names—the problem is as American in its curious doubleness as it is black.

It is an effort to establish a voice in which to speak oneself into being, to enter through words the world from which one feels oneself an exile since long before one's personal birth. The sense of urgency about most such efforts suggests the close proximity between the issues of literal and literary survival. Questing for human individuality, identifying the personal with the race's general condition, believing that while this condition persists it will be America's national condition as well, claiming a representative role not only in relation to American blacks but also in relation to the idea of America—on each level, for these self-narrators, the human predicament and the compositional problem are essentially one.

Writing inescapably from his own experience as a black man in America, Wright turned American materials back upon themselves in stories that are as intensely assertive of American ideals as they are grimly naturalistic denunciations. Held in a tension between the individual and the traditional, the Adamic forms by which he portrays his characters' rejection by America are the vehicles of his insistence that they are in fact America's native sons.

• • •

Other native sons and daughters whose work significantly contributed to the contours of the short story between the wars include two at apparently opposite ends of the spectrum: the American expatriate writer, Kay Boyle, and the doctor-poet of Rutherford, New Jersey, William Carlos Williams. Expatriate and poet are delimiting labels for these two, but they help to account for divergences in the pattern I have been tracing. In her stories, many of them in the 1930s and 1940s written in England and Austria and France, Kay Boyle appeals obliquely to the rich resources of the Adamic myth. Her sophisticated short fiction draws on the American Adam as a frame or context for plots and values in the way that the poetry of T. S. Eliot and Ezra Pound draws on myth and literary precedent as artificial ordering devices. It is a sign of her modernity and her Americanness.

William Carlos Williams commonly abjures such literariness. He relies instead on acute attention to the telling concrete details of American life to give his stories their shape and significance. His long battle against Eliot's classroom classicism carried naturally from his poetry into his fiction, where likewise the ideas in things have metaphysical value. What Boyle works for through tradition, Williams tries to do with bare perception. Yet they are not so different as this makes them appear, and given another axis of comparison they might occupy some of the same space. In an essay titled "Style and Sacrament in Modernist Writing,"[2] Herbert Schneidau says of twentieth-century prose generally that it "seems to welcome more poetic effects and structures than does that of the preceding century. . . . This poetic quality is not a matter of atmospherics, nor even of reliance on images; at bottom we may see that it is the metaphoric pattern of language that is being used to cross-fertilize prose." Boyle's and Williams's stories mark an advance over those of Farrell and Wright and others of the second level of American short story writers in this regard. With some reservations for individual writers and individual works, the very best American short fiction is characterized by its range and intensity of poetic effect.

Kay Boyle published three books of short stories in the 1930s: *Wedding Day and Other Stories* (1930), *First Lover and Other Stories* (1933), and *The White Horses of Vienna and Other Stories* (1936). She won the O. Henry Prize for short fiction in 1936 for "The White Horses of Vienna," a story that forecasts the human failings toward which Europe was then driving, and in 1941 for "Defeat," where those forecasts are confirmed in the fall of France. A regular contributor to the *New Yorker,* she was a member of the *New Yorker* school of sophisticated short story writers that included, at various times and in their various ways, men and women such as John O'Hara, Irwin Shaw, Dorothy Parker, E. B. White, and James Thurber. Thurber and White shaped the *New Yorker* school as editors of the magazine as well as by the example of their own work, and in the early years there appeared Shaw's famous story "The Girls in Their Summer Dresses," Thurber's "The Secret Life of Walter Mitty," and the first of a host of stories by the preeminent practitioner of *New Yorker* fiction, John Cheever. Boyle's 1931 story "Kroy Wen" is an example of the form. An American moviemaker, voyaging to Europe to recuperate from an emotional breakdown, is drawn back to his cinematic art by a striking Italian couple aboard the same cruise ship. They are circus acrobats, returning to Italy so their child will be born at home, and Mr. Wurthenburger arranges to film them. When a storm at sea brings on the woman's early labor, both plans are upset. The ending of the story, typically, resolves nothing: the frustrated Wurthenburger is trying to direct an artistic childbirth, the woman can respond only to obstetrical imperatives, and the acrobat husband is caught between the two. "'Maybe it hurts her,' said the Italian. He didn't know what to do." The unstated theme of this concluding tableau—that art and life, acting and living, have been reversed—is suggested in the title of the story: "Kroy Wen" is *New York* spelled backward.

But Boyle's story reverses more than art and life. Her extended metaphor also inverts American myth. In "Kroy Wen" it is the American Mr. Wurthenburger who represents Old World weariness and contempt for life, and the Italians aboard the ship *New York* are emigrants, bound away from New York's Ellis Island. Yet Boyle describes them as Adam and Eve, at ease in their self-defined garden of innocence: "They had sought out the gentlest corner, the farthest on the lower deck of the ship, and there they had turned about upon imaginary grasses and sat down close to one another in the sun." There Mr. Wurthenburger finds them with his camera, and there he threatens their fall. "'Listen,' he said with a cold terrible patience. 'Just let your jaw fall open and scream. . . . Won't you open your mouth and scream?' he was whispering to her persuasively."

In Boyle's fictional world, no less than in Richard Wright's, the generative American myths of innocence and opportunity are dispelled by inversions that assert, by mocking, the national identity. In the postlapsarian darkness of the 1930s, her stories of idealism wasted and abused take place always in broken gardens, lonely corners, and isolated lives. Her 1932 *New Yorker* story "Black Boy," for example, makes the beach where the child narrator and her black friend meet into childhood's last refuge: she calls it "the forsaken part, . . . the other end of the city," where waves "as indolent as ladies gathered up their skirts in their hands and, with a murmur, came tiptoeing in across the velvet sand." All too predictably, American racism intrudes on the metaphoric garden, in the person of the girl's grandfather, to drive the children into the world. "Keep Your Pity" (1936) tells the opposite story, of sheltered love impoverished by selfishness and hardened by pride, and of the unredeeming idealism of a well-meaning American innocent abroad named Mr. Jefferson. Like some underdeveloped Jamesian hero, Jefferson's innocence remains undisturbed and ironically unbetrayed by the equally symbolic Benedict Wycherley and his witchy wife.

The title story from the same collection puts such overtly American materials at a still further remove from America proper. "The White Horses of Vienna" also is set in a place apart, this one a white house high on a mountain above an Austrian village. The time is the mid-1930s. Austria is politically in disarray. Boyle's protagonist is a doctor, a former prisoner of war in Siberia, who intends his house on the mountain as a refuge from the world. In this reconstituted Eden, however, white is not only the color of the doctor's idealism but also of his blonde Nordic wife's belief in racial supremacy. The doctor injures a leg at a secret political rally, and the replacement called from Vienna turns out to be a Jew, Dr. Heine. Heine's story of a crippled Lippizaner stallion at the Spanish Riding School in Vienna symbolizes lost Austrian ideals and forecasts the doctor's destruction. And his own. The anti-Semitic wife accuses him of money grubbing, serves him pig for dinner, and in one terribly prophetic scene actually sets him afire. The situation of

European Jews as Kay Boyle envisions it in this fine story is as severe and as frightening as that of American blacks in the stories of Richard Wright. And it is cast in the same metaphoric form as Wright's. Boyle uses the fall of the doctor's family as an allegory of the coming fall of Europe, but the Adamic substructure, like the allegory itself, makes it a particularly American expression. If the values and the dreams at issue here are not specifically American, the method and materials of the story are. In the words of a more famous American expatriate, in his memoir *A Moveable Feast,* "all generations were lost by something and always had been and always would be." Hemingway was speaking of Paris in the 1920s and of mental carelessness, but whether the something was carelessness or racism or fascism, destructive pride or simple American cupidity, the common sense of loss and the common forms of its expression underlie the short fiction of this as well as his own American generation.

William Carlos Williams came to these themes differently, as he came by different ways to the short story form. For two decades a poet, though not yet the poet of *Paterson,* he published two volumes of short fiction in the 1930s, *The Knife of the Times* (1932) and *Life Along the Passaic River* (1938). In his 1949 retrospective essay, "A Beginning on the Short Story (Notes)," he said that the heterogeneous character of the people was centrally responsible for his coming to the short story in the early years of the Depression. "I lived among these people," he said. "I know them and saw the essential qualities (not stereotyped), the courage, the humor (an accident), the deformity, the basic tragedy of their lives—and the *importance* of it. You can't write about something unimportant to yourself. I was involved." Williams was involved aesthetically as well as personally, as a poet as well as a doctor, and in both cases he was ideologically involved. He despised the institutions of the church and state that falsified by stereotyping such lives, and he found in the short story the artistic means to raise people from "that Gehenna, the newspapers, where at last all men are equal, to the distinction of being an individual." "The pure products of America / go crazy," he had written in 1923 in the poem "To Elsie," and it is significant of his social idealism that he chose to publish five stories in the little magazine *Blast: Proletarian Short Stories.* Yet Williams was no Marxist. His objections to social formulas made him impatient, too, of formulas of objection, and the best of his stories are no more typical of proletarian realism than of any other convention of expression, including conventionally American ones.

He could not, in any case did not, name a character of his Adams, as Hemingway so pointedly did. Nor does he appeal to mythic models to portray Passaic River lives in the way that Farrell does to express immigrant hopes, or Wright the hopelessness of black Americans. Williams's America of the 1920s and 1930s is less bound by traditions; it is more fragmentary and, in that, more modern. "How shall we write today?" he asks in "A Beginning on the Short Story." "The hero? Who is a hero? The peasantry? There is none. Men and women faithful to a belief? What belief?" Whatever the quality of their disaffection, Farrell and Wright (not to mention Saroyan) *want* to believe in the American Adam, and the myth informs their fictions. Because of the allegorical implications of that myth, their stories have a finished quality and a sense of closure that Williams's often do not. Kay Boyle's carefully made stories are still more finished: she is less concerned with the substance of the Adamic story than with its outlines, less inclined to it as a system of values than as a pattern of human behavior.

Williams claimed membership in no school of storywriters, subscribed to no modernist or even national creed. His characters seem often to enter and leave his stories as his patients entered and left his office. They come briefly under his eye and hand and are gone, fragments themselves of a hardly definable whole. Yet the stories are carefully, often poetically crafted. Whatever Williams might have seen that was Adamic in the people of Rutherford, to portray them in terms of a national literary convention would have been to sentimentalize their lives and condition. He was interested in overcoming traditions, not copying them. He tried, as he said, to impose form on material in such a way as "to wed the subject to its own time," and of that conjunction the result is "life, not morals. It is THE LIFE which comes alive in the telling. It is the life under specified conditions—so that it is relived in the reading—as it strikes off flashes from the material. The material is the metal against which a flint makes sparks."

In the best of Williams's short fiction, both the subject matter and the form are revolutionary in this way. Each of the first four stories in *The Knife of the Times,* for example, deals with a sexual relationship that violates social norms: lesbianism in the title story, adultery in "A Visit to the Fair" and "Hands across the Sea," and bisexuality in "The Sailor's Son." Each subject is figuratively a *knife* of the times, a painful fact of the heterogeneous life in Depression-era America that challenges social definitions of love and family and upsets preconceptions of normalcy. In "The Knife of the Times," a middle-aged married woman is courted in letters and then in person by a childhood friend, herself a married woman and a mother. At first Maura shares Ethel's newsy letters with her husband, but the personal note becomes more confidential, then passionate, until the letters are "full love missives . . . without the least restraint." Maura is simultaneously frightened and attracted by them: now she hides them from her husband with Ethel's gifts, indulges Ethel's franker and franker fantasies, and finally agrees to meet her friend in New York. There Maura's last reservations about the relationship are overcome. Ethel draws her into a pay toilet where she kisses and caresses her, and though Maura tries to appease the passion she cannot modify it. At a public luncheon, she frankly responds to Ethel's under-the-table pressures. All these elements—the letters, the fetishism, the pay toilet, and the excitement of forbidden caresses—might be no more than symbolic elements in a loveless woman's fantasy life were they not first so frankly granted as realities. Maura is not a frustrated wife in a loveless home, and however abnormal her attraction to Ethel's advances, Williams is at pains to show that it is not entirely unnatural. The opening sentence establishes that "the girls who had been such intimates as children remained true to one another," and the intimacy of shared secrets gives way naturally to that of shared love, first in Ethel's letters and then in their lives. At the conclusion of the story, Ethel begs her lover "to visit her, to go to her, to spend a week at least with her, to sleep with her," and Maura's answer is, "Why not?" Knifelike itself, the story cuts away the easy affirmations and surface assumptions of the times to pose the same question that Maura asks herself. Given the importance of life in its essential qualities—not stereotypes—*why not* be true to the imperatives of intimacy, in life and in art?

Speaking of such stories in 1949, Williams acknowledged with a wry sexual twist and a jab at the *Post* that he had remained true to this principle. He said, "This wasn't the 'acceptable,' the unshocking stuff, the slippery, in the sense that it can be slipped into them while they are semiconscious of a Saturday evening." What writers for the *Saturday Evening Post* accomplished by innuendo or altogether ignored, Williams tried to portray frankly in individualized characters. Unsparing of his patients in his "doctor" stories, he was as unsparing of himself. The life that interested and involved him in the stories of *Life along the Passaic River* was "THE LIFE which comes alive in the telling," his own included, and he resisted the slippery standards of *Post* fiction with the same fervor he reserved for the Gehenna of the newspapers. The knife-cuts that reveal the deformities, the tragedies, and the courage of his patients in "A Face of Stone" and "Jean Beicke" and "The Use of Force" also uncover the buried life of the doctor-narrator. In these opening sentences, for example, the doctor's stony reserve is no less a mask than the expressive face of the patient as he describes it: "He was one of these fresh Jewish types you want to kill at sight, the presuming poor whose looks change the minute cash is mentioned. But they're insistent, trying to force attention, taking advantage of good nature at the first crack. You come when I call you, that type." A "type" at the outset, the patient emerges as a father and husband, and the doctor's stone face cracks to reveal his compassionate nature. They are softened into individuality by their shared concern for a third masked character, the patient's deformed but stoic wife, whose sudden smile concludes the story.

In "Jean Beicke" the doctor's compassion slips past the mask of cynicism he constructs to hide it; his otherwise inexpressible feeling finds expression in its opposite. "Give it an enema," he says of a starving child, "maybe it will get well and grow up into a cheap prostitute or something. The country needs you, brat." Too many of his "brats" will grow up to be cheap prostitutes, he knows, but when they fail to get well the failing is his, not society's. "We did everything we knew how to do except the right thing," he says of Jean Beicke's death. But in "The Use of Force" the right thing is drastically wrong and another kind of failure. Mathilda Olson has diphtheria, which she hides by clamping her jaws shut and refusing to be examined. The doctor describes her initially as "one of those picture children often reproduced in advertising leaflets and photogravure sections of the Sunday papers." But Mathilda's violent resistance to the "nice man" who wants to look at her throat belies the newspaper stereotype: she rises above it to "magnificent heights of insane fury of effort bred of her terror." Simultaneously, the doctor's professional zeal becomes "a pleasure to attack her," and he forces her mouth open with a cooking spoon. The scene is elemental, savage, sexually charged, and he knows it:

> The damned little brat must be protected against her own idiocy, one says to one's self at such times. Others must be protected against her. It is social necessity. And all these things are true. But a blind fury, a feeling of adult shame, bred of longing for muscular release are the operatives. One goes on to the end.

At the end, the doctor and Mathilda have used force against each other: he to confirm his diagnosis, she to express her fear of him. Typing each other, each fails to communicate with the other, and their mute frustrations erupt into violence that reveals while it demeans their individual dignity.

Like this one, many of Williams's stories are concerned with obstacles to communication, in life and in art. Mathilda Olso refuses to speak; the wife in "A Face of Stone" speaks English haltingly; Jean Beicke cannot speak at all and so she screams. The problem for the doctor-narrator of the stories is to understand, so that he can treat, people who cannot or will not express themselves—the physically ill and the deformed, the children, and all the impoverished of language who come to him in need or hide in fear. The problem for the storyteller, of course, is to express them himself: to assert his authority as author over their limitations and his own in order to make stories. In this large sense, Williams's work in the short story is one attempt of many significant attempts to make the fragmented modern world possible for art. Some American writers found a solution in the Adamic forms of Hawthorne and Melville and Twain, others, like Kay Boyle, in the mythical method of Joyce and Eliot. Declining the formulas of tradition and the acceptable contemporary conventions, Williams chose to state frankly the intimate passions and passionate brutalities that he said were flashes struck from the materials of life. His stories fall into that space between revolutionary fictions and the fiction of revolution, and if he is less sure of his form than the great innovators, his stories are more powerfully expressive than those of the committed ideologues. The short story, he said, "must be written so well that that in itself becomes the truth while the deformity informs it."

Some of William's stories meet that high standard, and some do not. As a poet writing short stories, he was not always at home with his own form as he was not always at ease in his time. But the best of his work weds the materials to the form the times dictated, as he said, and marks a significant contour of the genre. Such contours are shaped by no single writer, of course, but by the collective stories of them all—stories written by fictionists and poets, here and abroad; delicate stories and brutal ones, that range from moral allegories to slices of life; and stories of celebration and condemnation, portraying a broad spectrum of social consciousness and psychological insight. The careers of some few of the best practitioners of these in America in the 1930s and 1940s are examined in the pages that follow.

Careers

On 14 October 1938, Charles Scribner's Sons published *The Fifth Column and the First Forty-Nine Stories* and brought to an end one of the great careers in American short fiction. *The Fifth Column* represents an experiment with drama that was not repeated. The stories, however, are essential Hemingway, and the title of the collection alone suggests that neither the author nor his publisher imagined then that he would write no more of them. Increasingly busy with other books in the 1930s, he had worked less steadily but with great care on his short fiction since the publication of *In Our Time* (1925) and *Men without Women* (1927). *In Our Time* was reissued by Scribner's in 1930 with a critical introduction by Edmund Wilson, and a third collection called *Winner Take Nothing* appeared in 1933. In the summer and fall of 1936, three masterpieces were published based on Hemingway's visits to Africa and Spain early in the decade: "The Short Happy Life of Francis Macomber,"

"The Horns of the Bull" (retitled "The Capital of the World" in 1938), and "The Snows of Kilimanjaro." These stories and the 1938 news dispatch "Old Man at the Bridge" were gathered with the three collections to make *The First Forty-Nine Stories.* In his preface Hemingway wrote, "I would like to live long enough to write three more novels and twenty-five more stories. I know some pretty good ones." But barring the inclusion of *The Old Man and the Sea* (1952), there would be no more short stories. Nor by 1938 would there be more stories from Hemingway's earliest mentor, Sherwood Anderson, whose last collection, *Death in the Woods and Other Stories,* was published in 1933. Nor, in a sense, from his most famous American contemporary then, F. Scott Fitzgerald. Although Fitzgerald continued to the end of his life to send hackwork to *Esquire,* the last book of stories published in his lifetime was the 1935 collection, *Taps at Reveille.* The title suggests the end of a beginning—appropriately so, as it turned out.

The careers of Anderson, Fitzgerald, and Hemingway were and continue to be immensely influential in shaping the American short story. Entangled together, personally and professionally, in the end they were almost totally independent of one another. Their achievements are unique and demonstrably their own. Yet each published his last book of stories in the two-year period 1933–35. What these last books have in common is their retrospective character, found sometimes in a single fine story such as Fitzgerald's "Babylon Revisited" and sometimes in several late stories together. Looking back on earlier materials, on ways of telling, even on themselves, each writer brought his short story career to closure in self-assessment. Implicitly reflexive, their last stories demonstrate the excellence and the failings of the careers they reflect upon.

• • •

The title story from Anderson's collection is something of a capstone of the canon, an excellent story in itself that contains the elements of fine earlier stories. "Death in the Woods" is about a "bound girl" who is seduced by a farmhand and becomes the figurative bound girl of her husband and sons. All her life is spent serving "horses, cows, pigs, dogs, men." Lonely, inarticulate, ignored, she nonetheless possesses a buried life magically revealed when she dies. With her dogs leaping about her body in the winter woods, Mrs. Grimes is transformed for the narrator into a snow maiden, her figure "girlish," her frozen flesh as white and lovely for a time as marble. The narrator recalls, "She did not look old, lying there in that light, frozen and still. One of the men turned her over in the snow and I saw everything. My body trembled with some strange mystical feeling and so did my brother's." The scene is reminiscent of sexual revelations in many early stories and reminds one of Anderson's objections to the surface life of popular magazine stories and newspaper pieces.

Recast from the narrator's memories and from his brother's first unsuccessful telling of it, the story of Mrs. Grimes's death in the woods is also very much about the Teller and his Telling. Like the old writer in "The Book of the Grotesque," the narrator has stories "stuck in my mind from small-town tales when I was a boy." Like Anderson, who revised "Death in the Woods" through one unpublished and three published versions, the narrator says that the reality of the scene in the woods lies in his telling of it. Looking back, he understands that the mystical experience was "the foundation for the real story I am now trying to tell. The fragments, you see, had to be picked up slowly, long afterwards." These fragments include bits of his own experience, grafted to the story of Mrs. Grimes to complete the telling. As her story is in part his in its substance, so the narrator's method of telling is Anderson's, and his judgement of it is an approving authorial self-criticism.

If the focus of Anderson's story is himself as Teller, Fitzgerald's in "Babylon Revisited" is himself as himself or rather, himself as he wished to be. Charlie Wales's attempt to reclaim his daughter, Honoria, from the wreckage of his alcoholic past is a romanticized version of Fitzgerald's attempt to rescue his own daughter, his honor, and himself from the same past and present dissipation. When Charlie's memory is sparked by a voice from his past, Fitzgerald writes, "His first feeling was one of awe that he had actually, in his mature years, stolen a tricycle and pedalled Lorraine all over the Étoile between the small hours and dawn. In retrospect it was a nightmare." Fitzgerald made fictions of his dreams very often in his prime and made his reputation by them. Living well, he lived heroically through his heroes— Dexter Green of "Winter Dreams," Rudolph Miller of "Absolution," and the sad young men of his tales of the Jazz Age. But "Babylon Revisited" is a story without such rewards, in which author and character confess to a common nightmare from which only the character is absolved. By the time he wrote the story, Fitzgerald had succumbed to the Babylonian excesses Charlie Wales overcomes, and the story is his admission that he knew it. Later in the 1930s there were few stories of quality, and few of those were unmarred by wretched recriminations.

So apparent was this failing that even Hemingway addressed it—by writing his friend into "The Snows of Kilimanjaro." In the initial version of that story, published in *Esquire,* Hemingway wrote that "Poor Scott Fitzgerald" was ruinously in awe of the very rich: "He thought they were a special glamourous race and when he found they weren't it wrecked him just as much as any other thing that wrecked him." To that public libel, Fitzgerald replied in a letter that implicitly confirmed both Hemingway's judgment and his own fictional self-assessment. "If I choose to write de profundis sometimes," he wrote to Hemingway, "it doesn't mean I want friends praying aloud over my corpse."

"The Snows of Kilimanjaro" is one of Hemingway's best, if not one of his kindest stories, and it too is autobiographical and self-assessive: like Charlie Wales, Harry laments his wasted youth, but he claims for himself as a writer a place near the summit of the House of God. Hemingway was often his own hero, however peripherally, and often he projected his own insecurities on his characters.

A recurrent example is the relationship of fathers and sons. Dr. Hemingway disapproved of his son's life-style and his writing, and Hemingway thought his father too often unmanly. In a letter to his father in 1927, Ernest said of himself, "I am a rotten correspondent and it is almost *impossible* for me to write about my private affairs"; in the same letter he explained, "I *know* that I am not disgracing you in my writing but rather doing something that some day you will be proud of." Dr. Hemingway may be excused if he was less than proud of "Indian Camp" or "The Doctor and the Doctor's Wife," in both of which a doctor is disgraced before his son; but the disillusionments that the young Nick Adams suffers in those stories are of a kind with the private pains that inspired Hemingway to write them. A more overt example is the 1933 story "Fathers and Sons" in which Hemingway tried to put his father's life and death into perspective in fiction. Nick and his father are the "fathers" of the story's title, Nick and his son the "sons." In the story Nick is caught up in memories of his youth and his father, including some painful ones from earlier Hemingway stories in which Dr. Adams figures. When Nick's son interrupts his reverie to ask why they have not prayed at the tomb of his grandfather, present imperatives overcome past disappointments, and Nick can begin to reconcile himself not only to his father's failings but to his surpassing strengths. He sees that in order to be a father to his son he must be a true son to his father; and he understands that he must write what he remembers, knowing that "if he wrote it he could get rid of it. He had gotten rid of many things by writing them." In a story so autobiographically based, this is doubly salutary since some of the very personal business Nick now deems it appropriate to write had been written already by Hemingway. "Fathers and Sons" is a full retrospect in this sense: it links the author to his character and approves both the stories they have written and have yet to write. Moreover, "Fathers and Sons" is the final story of

Hemingway's last collection, *Winner Take Nothing,* as of *The First Forty-Nine:* as such it casts the light of final self-approval on all that goes before it in those volumes, including, in *The First Forty-Nine,* even the few great stories written after it.

Such stories as these by the previous decade's most prominent writers mark prominent endings in the contours and climate of the short story in the 1930s. They are counterbalanced in the history of the period by other stories already being written, beginnings of significant careers already underway.

• • •

The first, indisputable fact about William Faulkner's career as a writer of short stories is that he was first a novelist. No perspective on his short fiction would be complete without recognizing that his stories exist as part of a body of fiction in which the broadest outlines and deepest significance are defined by his nineteen novels. But no perspective would be complete, either, without the fact that the novels are intimately related, often indebted, to short stories. Sometimes Faulkner used short stories as preliminary sketches for ideas, characters, and techniques he later appropriated for his novels: the germinal materials from which *Absalom, Absalom!* (1936) grew are an unpublished story, "Evangeline," and a published one, "Wash." At other times he used stories as separate episodes or chapters in extended fictions: *The Hamlet* (1940) incorporates revised versions of five stories published in the 1930s, and *The Unvanquished* (1938) and *Go Down, Moses* (1942) are novels made up entirely of short story chapters, most of them revised from separate publications. *Notes on a Horsethief* (1951), published as a separate book, is a story extracted from a work in progress, the novel *A Fable* (1954). And, of course, Faulkner wrote stories that were stories in their own right, autonomous fictions designed and crafted to stand alone, and the best of these are among the best short stories ever written: "A Rose for Emily" and "Red Leaves" and "Dry September," to name a few. Probably it is true that many of them were written to earn the money Faulkner needed for uninterrupted work on his novels, but there are very few stories of second quality in the canon. Indeed, if they were written for money, they were less successful for that than they were aesthetically. Given the intricacy and experimental qualities that characterize Faulkner's short stories as well as his novels, it is surprising that some of the stories were published at all.

Properly speaking, Faulkner's short story career began in 1919 at the University of Mississippi where he published the story "Landing in Luck" in the college newspaper, the *Mississippian.* Based on his actual and imagined experiences with the Royal Air Force in Toronto the previous year, the story is about a cadet who crashes his trainer on his first solo flight. This story and the short sketch, "The Hill," published in the *Mississippian* in 1922, represent Faulkner's published fictional output until the mid-1920s. He thought of himself as a poet, and it was to peotry that he turned his early efforts and attention. In 1925, in New Orleans, he met Sherwood Anderson and began to write—and almost immediately to publish—prose fiction. A collection of eleven brief vignettes entitled "New Orleans" appeared in the *Double Dealer* for January-February 1925, and the *Times-Picayune* published a series of sixteen prose portraits of New Orleans characters that ran irregularly in the *Sunday Magazine Section* from 8 February to 27 September 1925. The final pieces were mailed from, and possibly written aboard, the steamer *West Ivis* on which Faulkner had taken passage for Europe. He was twenty-eight years old when the final one appeared. By the time he published his next story in April 1930, he had published four novels: *Soldiers' Pay* (1926), *Mosquitoes* (1927), *Sartoris* (1929), and *The Sound and the Fury* (1929). A fifth, the unrevised text of *Sanctuary,* was in manuscript, and a sixth, *As I Lay Dying,* would appear in October.

In Paris in the autumn of 1925, after a brief walking tour on the Continent, Faulkner settled down to serious work on his fiction. In October, he heard from Boni & Liveright that *Soldier's Pay* was to be published, but by then he was well into another novel, called "Elmer," that would become the long, unpublished story "A Portrait of Elmer." That story is more important for its autobiographical portrayal of the artist than as a self-contained story. More significant are the European stories that date from this time, in inception if not in finished form. "Mistral" and "Divorce in Naples" derive from events from Faulkner's walking tour; the war stories—"The Leg," "Victory," and "Crevasse"—are based on impressions of wounded war veterans Faulkner saw in England. None of these was separately published, but they were brought together in the first book of stories, *These 13* (1931), and in *Collected Stories of William Faulkner* (1950). When he returned from Europe, his work on novels intensified, and by 1927–28, he had begun writing and sending short stories to national magazines on a regular basis. His correspondence with *Scribner's Magazine* for those years and his announced plan in 1927 to put together "a collection of short stories of my townspeople" suggest that he was actively working with stories and had stockpiled some numbers of them by the time *Forum* published "A Rose for Emily" in April 1930. With that event, the career was truly begun.

The canon today consists of a hundred-odd stories, seventy of which were published in the period 1930–45. The majority of those appeared first in magazines, some in the big commercial slicks at which Faulkner aimed for the money they paid, others in more discriminating national magazines, such as *Scribner's Magazine* and *American Mercury,* which were dedicated to publishing first-class fiction, and a few in distinguished little magazines like *Story.* In effect, his magazine stories supported him in the early years of the Depression before he went to Hollywood as a screenwriter, but the magazines were a capricious and unreliable source of income. *Scribner's Magazine* is typical: although *Scribner's* eventually published nine Faulkner stories, many early ones were rejected on the grounds that they were not sufficiently "straightforward." As one editor put it, "The trouble with your writing, it seems to me, is that you get mostly the overtones and seem to avoid the real core of the story. It would seem that in the attempt to avoid the obvious you have manufactured the vague."

Certainly Faulkner's stories were not formula stories of the kind Sherwood Anderson had complained of. They were in-turning and inclusive and dealt already with the conflicts of the heart. They had the compression and unbounded interrelatedness of symbolist poems. And they were hard to place. Faulkner acknowledged his difficulty with magazines in a 1929 letter to *Scribner's* Managing Editor Alfred Dashiell. Admitting that his story, "Miss Zilphia Gant," might be too "diffuse" for *Scribner's,* he went on to tell Dashiell, "I am quite sure that I have no feeling for short stories; that I shall never be able to write them, yet for some strange reason I continue to do so, and to try them on Scribners' [*sic*] with unflagging optimism." In his rejection letter, Dashiell said, "you may be right in that you are like a distance runner trying short sprints." In June 1931, *Scribner's* published "Spotted Horses," the first of the Snopes stories. Thereafter, Dashiell laid claim to Faulkner's Snopeses, and *Scribner's* published most of those stories, but the money was never good. Although Dashiell paid $400 for "Spotted Horses," he was willing to pay only $300 in 1934 for "Mule in the Yard." The market at *American Mercury* was tighter still. H. L. Mencken published four Faulkner stories in 1930–32, including "That Evening Sun" and the Snopes story "Centaur in Brass," but Mencken seldom paid well either. And often he insisted on revisions in line with his humorless sense of public taste and decency. In a 1932 letter to his friend and sometime agent, Ben Wasson, Faulkner urged him to shop a story around. "If Harper's do not want it," he wrote, "try elsewhere. It has only been to Scribner's, and I need the money. Don't try it on Mencken save as a last resort; he only pays me $150 for stories." His correspondence is filled with querulous references like this one, reminders that fiction was his livelihood as well as his life. Living by his writing as well as for it, he was sometimes forced to revise stories to meet editorial strictures,

as he did "That Evening Sun" for Mencken—but when the story was collected in *These 13* later in 1931, it had been revised again and the offending
passages restored.

Understandably, Faulkner's preference in magazines in the 1930s was the
Saturday Evening Post, which had the widest readership and paid the most
money. And, remarkably, the *Post* did publish Faulkner's stories, twenty-one
of them, including the very early, undistinguished "Thrift" and major stories:
"Red Leaves" and "Mountain Victory," the first five stories from *The Unvanquished,* and in 1942 a text of "The Bear," the great central chapter of *Go
Down, Moses.* But even the *Post* was less generous with Faulkner than with
more popular writers. Perhaps, as Henry James once said of Americans (and
Sherwood Anderson said of the *Post*), the magazine was suspicious of anything that hinted of Art, as if Art was somehow vaguely, dangerously inju-
rious to a general readership. Perhaps it was only that Faulkner was not a
known name at the *Post.* In 1930 Fitzgerald was paid $3,600 for the master-
piece, "Babylon Revisited," and the sentimental melodrama, "A Nice Quiet
Place." In the same year, "Thrift" brought Faulkner $500 and "Red Leaves"
only $750. Four years later, the *Post* paid $900 for the comic story, "A Bear
Hunt," and by 1942 Faulkner was regularly earning $1,000 for the stories
the *Post* was willing to publish.

But by 1942 the great period in Faulkner's career as a writer of short
stories was at an end. He won the O. Henry Prize for "Barn Burning" in
1939 and again in 1949 for "A Courtship," and *Collected Stories* won the National Book Award for Fiction in 1950, but no new stories not connected to
novels were published thereafter except "Race at Morning" in the 1955 collection *Big Woods.* Looking back in 1957, the by then Nobel Laureate told a
questioner at the University of Virginia that, yes, novels were easier to write
than short stories:

> You can be more careless [in a novel], you can put more trash in it and be excused
> for it. In a short story that's next to the poem, almost every word has got to be
> almost exactly right. In the novel you can be careless but in the short story you
> can't. I mean by that the good short stories like Chekhov wrote. That's why I rate
> that second—it's because it demands a nearer absolute exactitude. You have less
> room to be slovenly and careless. There's less room in it for trash. In poetry, of
> course, there's no room at all for trash. It's got to be absolutely impeccable, abso-
> lutely perfect.

Was the novelist who described himself as a "failed poet" a failed short story
writer as well? He was not. His own earliest judgment is suggested by a passage

in a letter written to his mother from Paris in 1925. "I have just written such a beautiful thing that I am about to bust," he told Maud Faulkner; "2,000 words about the Luxembourg gardens and death. It has a thin thread of plot, about a young woman, and it is poetry though written in prose form. I have worked on it for two whole days and every word is perfect."

That sounds a little like the young Hemingway describing the vignettes he wrote in Paris for *In Our Time,* and Faulkner's piece, which was to become the concluding scene of *Sanctuary,* is like those prose poems. But the similarity ends there. It was Hemingway's dictum, set forth in his *Death in the Afternoon,* that the short story writer must "put down what really happened in action; what the actual things were which produced the emotion that you experienced." That simply does not describe a story like "A Rose for Emily," where half a century of communal observation and speculation are reposited with a narrator confronting the present fact that most of it is terribly, terrifyingly wrong. Faulkner himself was not much concerned with facts: he said they didn't cast shadows. Instead, it was the tellers in the tale, and their tellings, that captured his imagination. His stories and novels commonly portray the reactions to what may or may not have really happened from a variety of points of view which produce, in their totality, the emotional impact of single events. And since Faulkner's own impulse as author was to muse upon those musing characters—"with the same horror and the same astonishment," Cash Bundren says in *As I Lay Dying*—Faulkner's voice is often one dimension of the several in any story. Hemingway's much admired objectivity, in Faulkner, is subjectivity; what Hemingway cut, Faulkner compressed for inclusion. This may help to explain why Faulkner's short stories often seem novelistic in scope while Hemingway's novels, by contrast, are extended short stories—*The Old Man and the Sea* being only the most obvious example. In "A Rose for Emily," to cite only one of several distinguishing characteristics, there are seven named and specified characters, plus the narrator, plus significant townspeople who affect the action—aldermen, doctors, a Baptist minister, two female cousins, a druggist, and Confederate war veterans. In the 139 pages of *The Old Man and the Sea,* there are two, not counting Joe DiMaggio and the fish, and some random fishermen, two American tourists, and a writer.

There are at least two important results of such configurations in Faulkner's short fiction, both of which were immediately apparent. First, as we have seen, the magazines that paid high prices for stories could not be counted on to publish his because of the way they were made. Partly because of that, very early in the thirties, Faulkner began gathering unpublishable stories with published ones into short story collections, *These 13* in 1931 and *Doctor Martino and Other Stories* in 1934. Second, because those stories were made as they were, of stories within stories and times within the present time, they effectuated a complex, contrapuntal unity in the extended narratives where they served as separate but interrelated units of structure. Their adaptability to these still larger stories is due to a synecdochic assumption that underlies much of Faulkner's work, short stories and story collections as well as novels. Hugh Kenner explains it this way in his book, *A Homemade World*:

Faulkner's root need was not to symbolize (a condensing device) but to expand, expand: to commence with the merest glimpse and by way of wringing out its significance arrange voices and viewpoints, interpolate past chronicles, account for just this passion in just this ancillary passion, and tie the persons together, for the sake of intimacy, intensity, plausibility, with ties of blood and community and heritage.

As the impulse to expand forced him beyond the limits of a single story set at a single place and time, Faulkner's own place, the still closed society of the South, provided him a subject and a way of telling. Kenner says, "What the Old South gave him, what is inseparable from his preferred way of working, making possible in fiction what is essentially a method for poetry, was a society of which he could plausibly postulate that everything in it affects everyone." Thus the opening sentence of "A Rose for Emily": "When Miss Emily Grierson died, our whole town went to her funeral"; and of "Dry September": "Through the bloody September twilight, aftermath of sixty-two rainless days, it had gone like a fire in dry grass—the rumor, the story, whatever it was"; and of "That Evening Sun": "Monday is no different from any other weekday in Jefferson now," with that "now" echoing once in the next sentence and once more in the opening paragraph before Quentin turns to "then," fifteen years in the past, and the differences *then* that prompt his story *now.*

Stories like these are born of the legend maker's art, not the journalist's. Yoknapatawpha County, it is well to remember, is a region of the imagination, and its history, if it can be said to have a factual history, exists exclusively in the fictions where it is made and remade by characters directly, subjectively involved with the history they create. "A Justice," for example, is in one sense a document in the history of old Indian times in Yoknapatawpha County, the story of a contest between an Indian and a Negro slave for the slave's wife and of Chief Ikkemotubbe's belated intercession on behalf of the slave. Sam Fathers, the old half-Indian, half-Negro offspring of that contest, tells the story to Quentin as he heard it from his father's friend, Herman Basket. "This is how Herman Basket told it," he begins, "when I was big enough to hear talk." All three tellers are legend makers: Herman who told the tale, Sam who is the product of the tale he tells of Herman's telling, and Quentin who tells the story of Sam and his tale. The past interpenetrates the present in this fictional configuration in the form of an oral text, conserved by its tellers, and of a living artifact, the old man Quentin describes as "definite, immobile, and complete, like something looked upon after a long time in a preservative bath in a museum." That Quentin is too young to understand the tale he hears and retells is a favorite strategy of Faulkner's for extending the implications of bare facts. Like communal memory, in "A Rose for Emily" and detective stories such as "Tomorrow" and "Knight's Gambit," the child narrator involves the reader at an extratextual level of the story as assumed rememberer, deducer, theorizer. The great example of the technique is Benjamin Compson's chapter of The Sound and the Fury, the "short story" from which Faulkner said the novel developed. There Benjy "tells" what he can neither articulate nor comprehend, and the reader pieces a mosaic from the fragments. Modifications of the same inform the stories. At the end of "A Justice," for example, Quentin flees the facts of Sam's story in confusion, leaving the reader to confront what Sam knows but never says— that no court of appeal holds jurisdiction over lovers, that there is no "justice" in the conflicts of the heart.

"A Justice" was submitted to magazines five times without luck before Faulkner published it in These 13. But "A Justice," and stories like it that employ two or more dimensions of time and levels of understanding, proved uniquely suited to the short story collections Faulkner was constructing. Although there is disagreement about the theme of These 13, there is no disagreement that the stories work together to approximate the unity of extended narrative. The book is composed of three groups of stories: the four World War I stories, the six set at various times in Jefferson and Yoknapatawpha County, and three final ones set abroad. In this arrangement, the Yoknapatawpha stories at the core of the book serve as a keystone that draws strength from the framing stories it draws together. In his fine book The Achievement of William Faulkner, Michael Millgate says that "The experience of reading the central section according to Faulkner's scheme is one of continual recognition and awareness of reverberation: the recurrence of characters, setting, situations, and themes provokes the recollection and hence the continuing coexistence of the earlier story or stories and produces a total effect of progressive enrichment." Millgate finds in that progression Faulkner's constant reiteration of the power and presence of death. I have argued that the subtle transformations from war stories of Part I, through the Yoknapatawpha stories, to the stories of love and imagination in Part III reaffirm the regenerative motion of life and that the climax of that progression is in the transcendent imaginative vision of the final story, the poetic coda "Carcassonne."[3] In "Carcassonne," the nameless poet of Rincon, longing *to perform something bold and tragical and austere,*" soars outward in imagination, "a dying star upon the immensity of darkness and of silence within which, steadfast, fading, deepbreasted and grave of flank, muses the dark and tragic figure of the Earth, his mother." Whatever their themes, Faulkner was speaking of just such books when he wrote to Malcolm Cowley in 1948 about his plan for *Collected Stories of William Faulkner*. He said there that "even to a collection of short stories, form, integration, is as important as to a novel—an entity of its own, single, set for one pitch, contrapuntal in integration, toward one end, one finale." That principle describes the form of stories such as "A Rose for Emily" and "A Justice" as well as the books in which they are collected. It is a reminder of what Faulkner took to be the insufficiency of bare facts, simple causes, and single contexts.

The principle of counterpoint proved a source of some confusion, however, when stories like those in Faulkner's short story collections were elevated to chapters in novels composed of stories. Faulkner told Random House editor Robert Haas in 1948 that he wanted *Collected Stories* to have "an integrated form of its own, like the Moses book if possible, or at least These 13." But *Go Down, Moses* had been published in 1942 as a collection, subtitled "and Other Stories," not as a novel. Writing to Haas in 1949 about reissuing the book, Faulkner insisted that the new edition conform to his first intention. The letter documents the scope and significance of short story structures in Faulkner's longer fictions.

Moses is indeed a novel. I would not eliminate the story or section titles. Do you think it necessary to number these stories like chapters? Why not reprint exactly, but change the title from GO DOWN, MOSES and other stories, to simply: GO DOWN MOSES, with whatever change is necessary in the jacket description. We did THE UNVANQUISHED [1938] in this manner, without either confusion or anticipation of such; and, for that matter, THE WILD PALMS [1939] had two completely unrelated stories in it. Yet nobody thought it should be titled THE WILD PALMS and another story. Indeed, if you will permit me to say so at this late date, nobody but Random House seemed to labor under the impression that GO DOWN, MOSES should be titled "and other stories." I remember the shock (mild) I got when I saw the printed page. I say, reprint it, call it simply GO DOWN, MOSES, which was the way I sent it in to you 8 years ago.

In the second printing and subsequent reissues, Faulkner's title was restored.

Go Down, Moses is a multiple narrative, composed of seven story-chapters that tell the history of the McCaslin family in Yoknapatawpha County from the early 1800s to 1942. Each chapter is a self-contained story connected to the other stories by common setting, situations, and the characters' ties of common blood. In "Was," for example, Buck McCaslin is the white half-brother of his father's slave, Turl; Isaac McCaslin and Lucas Beauchamp, the protagonists of the novel, are Buck's and Turl's sons. Like their biblical analogues, Isaac and Ishmael, Isaac and Lucas are far from equal inheritors of the patriarch's largess, and accordingly their separate stories are told in separate, if often parallel and overlapping, narrative units. The counterpointed story-chapters allow for the omission of details from one character's tale by the remembrance of it in another, and the interposition of collective memory, and hence of legend, casts the McCaslins in a progressive structure of telling, hearing, and retelling. The book opens with this remarkable sentence from "Was":

Isaac McCaslin, "Uncle Ike", past seventy and nearer eighty than he ever corroborated any more, a widower now and uncle to half a county and father to no one
    this was not something participated in or even seen by himself, but by his elder cousin, McCaslin Edmonds, grandson of Isaac's father's sister and so descended by the distaff, yet notwithstanding the inheritor, and in his time the bequestor, of that which some had thought then and some still thought should have been Isaac's, since his was the name in which the title to the land had first been granted from the Indian patent and which some of the descendents of his father's slaves still bore in the land.

The interrupted chronology in the arrangement of the stories complements the alternating narrative focus of the book and reinforces repetitions that dramatize the past as a force of motion in the present—Isaac's reading of the McCaslin ledgers in "The Bear," for example, and the recurrence of miscegenatic love from generation to generation. In Go Down, Moses, as in the spiritual from which it takes its title, all the characters, white and black, feel the pull of their one blood and appeal to Pharaoh to "let my people go." By these means, the single but collective stories of the McCaslins and their "people" are carried forward. Representative moments in their history and represented lives gradually reveal the patterns and sequences that form parts of a larger, causal progression encompassing all time in this space—mythic and real, past and present, and even future.

    Such effects, and Faulkner's stated intention to produce them, define the kind of stories he wrote. The uses to which he put those stories demonstrate their considerable contribution to the making of that rival world he called a "cosmos of my own." His modernism, refined from sources as various as the symbolist poets and James Joyce at one extreme and Herman Melville and

Sherwood Anderson at the other, had long posited the book as a world in the world, and Yoknapatawpha County is, in fact, a world made in books. Committed to the integral relation of meaning to fictional form, he found in the cosmos he created a way of telling by which, as he said, he might arrest the motion of life "by artificial means and hold it fixed so that 100 years later when a stranger looks at it, it moves again since it is life." Short stories were essential to that aesthetic, first, because the multiple perspectives of separate stories approximate the fullness of a world and, second, because by their interaction together in a significant form they establish and sustain the lifelike motionlike conditions of the fictional cosmos.

Faulkner worked consciously to shape such a world from the stories that became *Go Down, Moses*. He made "The Fire and the Hearth" from three existing stories and wrote the 1935 story "Lion" into "The Bear," which he published in the *Post* without Part IV, claiming that Isaac's renunciation of his McCaslin heritage belonged to the novel and had no part in the short story. These changes and additions provide narrative balance, consistency, and connections between the story-chapters. They caulk the seams of the book. But there are changes of another kind in the transition from story-as-story to story-as-chapter in *Go Down, Moses*. In the slow float of shifting light and shadow, separate stories like separate lives are transformed by the force of context alone, without strategic revision. The stories alter the new environment and are altered by it. Expressive in themselves of Faulkner's need to expand, they are the stuff of larger expansions, building blocks of the fictional world he called "a kind of keystone in the Universe."

The title story, "Go Down, Moses," is one such, and it illustrates the wonderful elasticity of Faulkner's short fiction. "Go Down, Moses" was published in *Collier's* in January 1941, and that text, with some stylistic revisions, was incorporated as the final chapter of the novel. It is the story of how Mollie Beauchamp appealed to the county attorney, Gavin Stevens, to arrange the funeral of her grandson, Butch Beauchamp, "sold . . . into Egypt" by Roth Edmonds for local crimes and executed in Chicago for murder. To portray Jefferson, Faulkner uses the devices and strategies that give his short stories their characteristic scope and depth. Names without faces evoke imagined memories, peopling the town with characters and events from the actual present and an imaginary past—Roth Edmonds and Hamp Worsham, a storekeeper named Rounciwell and the Negro murderer who fathered Butch on Mollie's eldest daughter, long since dead. Facts, modified in combination, are gleaned from disparate sources—a Chicago census taker, a Memphis newspaper, and old Miss Worsham, whose grandfather owned Hamp's and Mollie's parents. In the story-as-story, Stevens is the protagonist in whose consciousness the past is gradually called forth, fragmentary and incomplete, suggesting by implication a depth of experience never detailed. In this broad, artifical context, he is the benevolent, indulgent representative of white southern paternalism. Mollie herself is portrayed in stereotypical terms that accord with his preconceptions about "darkies." To him she is "a little old negro woman with a shrunken, incredibly old face beneath a white headcloth and a black straw hat which would have fitted a child." He is concerned with Law and all the associated formulas of social order. She is the instrument of his partial and delayed understanding that social rites and forms are expressions of human feeling. Only when Butch Beauchamp's body has been returned, the newspaper obituary prepared, and the cortege has wound through the town square toward the McCaslin burying ground does Stevens realize that *"she doesn't care how he died. She just wanted him to come home, but she wanted him to come home right. She wanted that casket and those flowers and the hearse and she wanted to ride through town behind it in a car."*

This makes a good story—the kind of story, in fact, that Faulkner soon would write in *Intruder in the Dust*— and *Collier's* paid $1,000 for it. But it is not precisely the same story we read as the concluding chapter of *Go Down, Moses*, where Beauchamp and Edmonds are by now familiar names and Stevens's partially remembered facts are fragments to be measured against a fuller history. Stevens appears in the book only in "Go Down, Moses," in context one of several minor functionaries, usually white, always peripheral, the repositories of conventional understandings and communal misconceptions. The puzzled Deputy who tries to retell Rider's story at the end of "Pantaloon in Black" is another. In the story-as-chapter, Stevens is the near-stereotype, not Mollie: he represents the Law, but she is history's own living artifact, "child" of nothing less than her massed and portentous past. Beyond Stevens's understanding of her as "darkie," beyond even the heroic resignation he finally accords her, Mollie's appeal to him places her in that richer, legendary context.

"It was Roth Edmonds sold him" she said. "Sold him in Egypt. I dont know whar he is. I just knows Pharaoh got him. And you know the Law. I wants to find my boy."

Go Down, Moses is a multiple narrative, and it is a tragic one, where lives are so intertwined in time and place and blood that the most ennobling acts are self-defeating, the commonest gestures noble. Mollie's "my boy" echoes "my people" and God's injunction to Moses. Stevens is instrument of Mollie's will, agent of her re-enactment of other appeals in the novel and hence of other lives. As protagonist of the final story-chapter, Mollie Beauchamp is coessential with Buck and Buddy McCaslin, who freed hers and their own people from slavery in 1837 but could not free them from themselves, and with their long line of McCaslin and Beauchamp people similarly bound. Faulkner dedicated the novel to "Mammy Caroline Barr, Mississippi, 1840–1940, Who was born in slavery and who gave to my family a fidelity without stint or calculation of recompense and to my childhood an immeasurable devotion and love." Mollie is her analogue, and although the story "Go Down, Moses" ends with Gavin Stevens's well-meant tribute, the novel *Go Down, Moses* ends with her as it began.

Faulkner published nine books afer *Go Down, Moses,* three of them short story collections. *Knight's Gambit* (1949) is a gathering of detective stories from the 1930s and 1940s in which Gavin Stevens is prominently featured. After using Gavin as a minor character in *Light in August* (1934) and *Go Down, Moses,* Faulkner made him a major character in *Intruder in the Dust* (1948) and the protagonist of the Snopes wars in *The Town* (1957) and *The Mansion* (1959). But Stevens does not provide *Knight's Gambit* anything like the unity the McCaslin family gives *Go Down, Moses,* and the stories appear to be arranged in the order in which they were published rather than in a functional structure. The only new piece is the long title story, "Knight's Gambit," from which Faulkner drew Stevens's marriage to Melisandre Backus Harriss for *The Mansion.* In the following year, 1950, *Collected Stories of William Faulkner* was published, combining forty-two previously published stories from magazines and the two collections of the 1930s, *These 13* and *Doctor Martino and Other Stories.* This time Faulkner worked hard for formal integrity, arranging the counterpointed stories into six counterpointed subsections that juxtapose past and present, Yoknapatawpha and the world outside. The book contains all his finest stories, and their arrangement often produces reciprocal revelations as the peripheral issues of one story are emphasized by major imperatives in another. But the nine-hundred-page book is too large and too diverse to achieve the rich internal unity of *Go Down, Moses* or even of *These 13.* None of the stories was revised from its most recent previous publication. For *Big Woods,* five years later, he gathered together his hunting stories in a final collection that draws on material as old as "A Bear Hunt" (1934), as recent as "Race at Morning" (1955), and as autobiographical as the essay-story, "Mississippi," that appeared in *Holiday* in 1954. The book is deeply indebted to *Go Down, Moses*—it reprints "The Old People," "The Bear," Parts I, II, III, and V, and draws heavily on "Delta Autumn"—but *Big Woods* is a retrospective book, more a "reminiscence" even than *The Reivers* (1962), which bears that subtitle. The hunting stories and the poetic idylls that introduce them are fine enough, but static.

The very best of Faulkner's short fiction—stories and collections and novels made of stories—moves through its forms to the motion of life. In one of the best of those, in Part V of "The Bear" when Isaac returns to Sam Fathers's and Lion's graves, he re-experiences the myriad life of the wilderness,

which was no abode of the dead because there was no death, not Lion and not Sam: not held fast in earth but free in earth and not in earth but of earth, myriad yet undiffused of every myriad part, leaf and twig and particle, air and sun and rain and dew and night, acorn oak and leaf and acorn again, dark and dawn and dark and dawn again in their immutable progression and, being myriad, one.

That last phrase strikes to the heart of Faulkner's short stories and the stories he made from them, all of which are, "being myriad, one."

• • •

Flannery O'Connor might have been speaking for a whole generation of writers once removed from Faulkner's when she said in 1960 that "the presence alone of Faulkner in our midst makes a great difference in what the writer can and cannot permit himself to do. Nobody wants his mule and wagon stalled on the same track the Dixie Limited is roaring down." In that essay, "Some Aspects of the Grotesque in Southern Fiction,"[4] Miss O'Connor recognized in Faulkner—as Eliot had recognized in Joyce—a profoundly compelling and seductive writer whose specific discoveries she might fruitfully pursue but never imitate in her own fiction. He represented the highest achievement of the immediate tradition in which she wrote.

Today, sixty years after he began writing, his work constitutes a singularly instructive context for defining the careers even of his immediate contemporaries. He so dominated American fiction from the mid-1920s to his death in 1962 that he made that his era, and the achievements of other fine writers of the period are defined by his presence. This is true of Thomas Wolfe, whose first novel was published in the same year as *The Sound and the Fury;* of Katherine Anne Porter, whose short story career coincides almost exactly with his own; and of Eudora Welty, like him a Mississippian, whose short stories began to appear at the height of the Faulkner era. Their stories are not imitations of Faulkner's, nor are they derivative—being nearly concurrent with his, how could they be? They do share elements and approaches, in particular the deep-rooted concern with the themes of home and the past that have been called southern but are in fact American. Reflected in the steady light of his achievement, their various stories on these themes place them prominently in the native American tradition from Hawthorne forward, a tradition they both served and shaped.

Like Hawthorne, who remembered his own earliest ancestor in "The Custom House" as a figure bearing both a Bible and the persecutor's sword, Faulkner held attitudes toward his home that were too complex to be unambiguous. Drawn to the romance of his region and its past, he maintained the detachment to see it whole and made from it an alternate world, more unified and more universally significant than the real. In *The Portable Faulkner,* where many of Faulkner's stories were made widely available for the first time, Malcolm Cowley wrote, in his introduction, that Faulkner's work could stand "as a parable or legend of all the Deep South," and he added in the 1967 edition, "it was the South that aroused his apprehensions, that deeply engaged his loyalties." His detachment is nowhere more clearly evidenced than in the semiautobiographical, semifictional story-essay "Mississippi," published in April 1954 in *Holiday* magazine. At the conclusion of that piece, Faulkner described his protagonist as "loving all of it even while he had to hate some of it because he knows now that you don't love because: you love despite; not for virtues, but despite the faults." The distinction is crucial to the mixture of nostalgic longing and principled rejection in our stories of the remembered past, and crucial too to the sense they project of the story writer's "lonely voice." Frank O'Connor used that phrase, in his book *The Lonely Voice,* to suggest what he saw as the "intense awareness of human loneliness" in the short story, and to account for the short story writer's attraction to "submerged population groups, whatever these may be at any given time—tramps, artists, lonely idealists, dreamers, and spoiled priests." For such writers—Faulkner and his contemporaries among them— *home* is the first referent in the dialectic of alienation. Faulkner put the matter succinctly to his Mississippi friend Phil Mullen in a 1955 letter now in the private collection of Louis Daniel Brodsky. Writing from his home in Oxford, the Nobel Laureate told Mullen, "I fear that some of my fellow Mississippians will never forgive that 30,000$ [*sic*] that durn foreign country gave me for just sitting on my ass and writing stuff that makes my own state ashamed to own me."

Little wonder, in this context, that Thomas Wolfe's short stories are essentially homeless; for Wolfe, who possessed Faulkner's lyrical intensity in such abundance, finally lacked the artistic detachment to accommodate his lonely visions to any fictional home, real or imagined. Louis Rubin makes the important point, in his book *The Faraway County: Writers of the Modern South,* that after *Look Homeward, Angel* in 1929, "the narrowness of Wolfe's viewpoint, the subjectivity with which he viewed his experience, was a crippling disability, for he could not describe a man living among other men in a convincing fashion. There are only fragments, moments of illumination." *Look Homeward, Angel* contains one of the most fully drawn families in American literature, but at the end of that book Eugene Gant leaves Altamont to seek a truer, spiritual home "in the city of myself, upon the continent of my soul." Thereafter, what Thomas Wolfe wrote was only what Thomas Wolfe saw: he could not create a detached persona nor distance his own perceptions. During the 1930s, inspired partly by a generous prize offered by *Scribner's Magazine*, he wrote seven short novels, two of which and part of another are collected with eleven short stories in the 1935 book *From Death to Morning*. Like Eugene Gant, and like Wolfe himself, the heroes of these pieces search endlessly through their own inner distances for a door to community that, for them, does not exist. They are the children of Wolfe's vast, unstructured home in "dark time": the lonely man, in "No Door," drowning in "a sea of blind, dateless, and immemorable time"; the wanderer, in "Only the Dead Know Brooklyn," whose map of Brooklyn is all that keeps him afloat in the dark city of his subjectivity. Each such character is one with those Wolfe describes in "The Face of the War," engulfed in "the huge abyss and thronging chaos of America, the immense, the cruel, the indifferent and magic land, where all of us have lived and walked as strangers."

As strangers—pastless, alone, longing for the indefinite home Wolfe portrayed only by such effusions—the characters in *From Death to Morning* only occasionally recognize in each other the shared experience of a specific past or common home. In the third vignette of "The Face of the War," a nameless boy waits in line among strangers for his turn with a whore in an army gang shack at Newport News. She recognizes him, calls him "Georgia," and he recognizes that "He had known her the first moment he had looked at her. She was a girl from the litle town where the state university, at which he was a student, was situated, a member of a family of humble decent people, well known in the town." For a moment they share the "unconscious tenderness of people in a world of strangers who suddenly meet someone they know from home," and for that moment Wolfe's rhetoric of loss and alienation leaps into focus. The girl cannot send a message home with the boy; no more could he deliver it. They have in common the town of Hopewell, Georgia, but recognizing that only intensifies their loneliness. Whether inured to lost innocence or intent upon it, home is the context of regret. Their formulas of recognition evoke a specific and locatable but unreclaimable past that Wolfe uses to define the extent of present alienation.

"And I'm mad at you, 'Georgia,'" she said with a kind of mocking reproachfulness, "I'm mad at you for not telling me you were here. . . . The next time you come here you'd better ask for me—or I'll be mad! . . . We homefolks have got to stick together. . . . So you ask for Margaret—or I'll be mad at you—do you hear?"

The success of the contrastive contexts in "The Face of the War" is a reminder of Wolfe's failure to compose such constructs for his theme in other stories, where insistence on loneliness suffices for form. His short stories are fragments of a massive, progressive manuscript he never finished. Like Whitman, and with some of Whitman's visionary energy, he conceived of an America larger than the sum of its several parts, no one of which, as he recorded them, needed to be autonomous. Perhaps this is why he chose the epigraph for his collection from Whitman's *Drum-Taps*: "Vigil strange I kept on the field one night." In a sense, Wolfe's stories are records of strange night vigils. His antecedents lie elsewhere in the nineteenth century than Faulkner's, not in Hawthorne's tales but Whitman's songs of self, where "All goes onward and outward, nothing collapses, / And to die is different from what any one supposed, and luckier."

The difference between Wolfe's sense of the short story and that of representative modernist contemporaries is summed up in a remark of Katherine Anne Porter's in 1939 in "The Situation of American Writing."[5] Asked to judge the relative merits of Whitman and Henry James as models for her own writing, she said: "For myself I choose James, holding as I do with the conscious, disciplined artist, the serious expert against the expansive, indiscriminately 'cosmic' sort. James, I believe, was the better workman, the more advanced craftsman, a better thinker, a man with a heavier load to carry than Whitman." Craftsmanship is the hallmark of Miss Porter's stories, and counterpoint is her principal strategy of form.

In "Flowering Judas," from her first collection *Flowering Judas and Other Stories* (1930, 1935), she created a totally rootless character, an American expatriate in Mexico with no ties to the past or the future: "Uninvited she has promised herself to this place; she can no longer imagine herself as living in another country, and there is no pleasure in remembering her life before she came here." Laura is the Judas of the title: lovely without love, Catholic without faith, a socialist without ideals, she is caught in limbo between the world and her fear of it, and her present is a nightmare of self-alienation. In "Flowering Judas," Laura's exterior and interior selves are the terms in the dialectic of loneliness that gives the story its form. The collections that follow add the past and family as defining contexts of the individual present, and introduce Miss Porter's more autobiographical heroine, Miranda Rhea.

Two long Miranda stories, "Old Mortality" and "Pale Horse, Pale Rider," appeared in the second collection, Pale Horse, Pale Rider, in 1939; six others were included in the 1944 book The Leaning Tower and Other Stories; and two more were added to The Collected Stories of Katherine Anne Porter (1965) to make the section subtitled "The Old Order." Unlike the fragments in Wolfe's American mosaic, each of these is an autonomous story that makes part of the collective story of Miranda's childhood and young adulthood.

The basic elements and the outlines of Miranda's story were already in place in "Old Mortality" by the time Miss Porter turned to the stories of her childhood that make up "The Old Order." Divided into three sections of narrative, set in 1883–1902, 1904, and 1912, "Old Mortality" traces Miranda's developing sense of herself in relation to her family. The story sets forth the legend of Aunt Amy, whose elopement and untimely death at the end of the nineteenth century are at the heart of the remembered past; the disillusioning reality of Uncle Gabriel, Amy's widower, whom Miranda and her sister meet as children at the races in 1904; and the alternative, "realistic" version of the past that Miranda hears from cynical Aunt Eva in 1912 and recognizes to be every bit as romantic as Amy's hoopskirted legend. The recreated past of the Rhea family is the frame of reference for Miranda's rebellion against its fixed forms and legendary standards:

"It is I who have no place," thought Miranda. "Where are my own people and my own time?" She resented, slowly and deeply and in profound silence, the presence of these aliens who lectured and admonished her, who loved her with bitterness and denied her the right to look at the world with her own eyes, who demanded that she accept their version of life and yet could not tell her the truth, not in the smallest thing. "I hate them both," her most inner and secret mind said plainly, "I will be free of them, I shall not even remember them."

But Miss Porter knew the impossibility of not even remembering, and Miranda's promise to herself is made in "her hopefulness, her ignorance." "Flowering Judas" depicts the danger of absolute self-reliance, and "Pale Horse, Pale Rider" takes Miranda to the brink of Laura's nightmare before returning her to life in a world where she must find meaning for herself: "No more war, no more plague, only the dazed silence that follows the ceasing of the heavy guns; noiseless houses with the shades drawn, empty streets, the dead cold light of tomorrow. Now there would be time for everything."

In a 1940 introduction for an edition of Flowering Judas, Miss Porter described the stories she wrote between the world wars as "fragments of a much larger plan which I am still engaged in carrying out, and they are what I was then able to achieve in the way of order and form and statement in a period of grotesque dislocations in a whole society when the world was heaving in the sickness of millennial change" (Collected Essays and Occasional Writings). Her answer to that sickness, as a writer, was to return to her historical and family sources in stories such as "The Source" and "The Journey" and "The Grave" which she wrote for The Leaning Tower (1944) and later called "The Old Order." And there Miranda discovers her own "sources," symbolized in her grandmother, Miss Sophia Jane, whose strength of purpose, shaped by grotesque dislocations in her own life and time and brought decisively forward into the lives of her grandchildren, is the context of Miranda's discovery of herself as a self. In "The Source" she journeys with her grandmother each spring from the city to the country and back to the city home in a cycle of "home-comings" that binds the present and past into a seamless whole. In "The Journey" the grandmother's own sources are traced from her childhood through marriage and widowhood to her present position as matriarch of a far-spread family. At the end of "The Journey," the grandmother dies, but her influence does not. At the end of the final Miranda story, "The Grave," the past time that grandmother represents—that encompasses love and death and what Miranda calls "mingled sweetness and corruption"—rises in Miranda's memory "in a strange city of a strange country, . . . plain and clear in its true colors as if she looked through a frame upon a scene that had not stirred nor changed since the moment it happened." Time is the frame for such depth of experience in Miss Porter's stories, where home is a source of life and order, and homecoming, even in memory, is a restorative rite of self-recognition.

For Miss Porter, as for Faulkner, home is simultaneously a place and a way to tell stories. In her essay on "Place in Fiction,"[6] Eudora Welty calls it a location that the writer must discover, meaning by "discovery," not "that the place is new, only that we are." Revolt, she further says, "is a reference and tribute to the potency of what is left behind," and that quite precisely describes Miranda's rebellion and the power with which home returns to her in memory There are few such rebels in Miss Welty's own stories, where the discovered home is often a present and familiar place, fully imagined and fully, imaginatively alive. Home she inevitably associates with a family or village or region, where the past is forever and inescapably present in communal rites of renewal and time-bound conventions. In this she too is like Faulkner, although in form her stories are deceptively simple compared to his. There is little, too, of the tormented telling and retelling that captured Faulkner's imagination, still less of Wolfe's lyrical encomiums on loneliness, or of Miss Porter's idealistic assertions of independence. Miss Welty praised her friend for repudiating what is false, but for herself she is content to affirm what she discovers to be true. What is true for her is home, which encompasses the gentle and comic, the fantastic, and even the monstrous— though what is monstrous in her stories is more often a matter of what ordinary people do to one another or themselves than of actual monsters. Her artistic detachment, paradoxically, is a function of her so fully belonging to the community she portrays. Like a stranger within the gates of her village worlds, she sees the resources and the risks of shared community more clearly than those who have gone away.

The stories in her first collections, *A Curtain of Green and Other Stories* (1941) and *The Wide Net and Other Stories* (1943), are set in real Mississippi places like Jackson or Natchez, and in imaginary ones with names like Victory, China Grove, and Farr's Gin. In *The Golden Apples* (1949), she set the fictional town of Morgana in a fictional Mississippi county. But each of these towns is a fictional form as well as a place: each is a region of the imagination, a shaped place-in-time where time and place are shaping forces in the lives of characters as various as Lily Daw and Phoenix Jackson and old Mr. Marblehall, who leads a double life (or imagines that he does). In *The Eye of the Story,* Miss Welty says of Chekhov that "no life is too brief or too inconsequential for him to be inattentive to its own reality," and that meaning in his stories, deriving from character, "took form from within." This clear praise reflects her own practice. In her preface to *The Collected Stories of Eudora Welty,* she says they are "stories written from within. They come from living here—they were *part* of living here, of my long familiarity with the thoughts and feelings of those around me, in their many shadings and variations and contradictions."

The opening paragraph of the first story in *A Curtain of Green* sets the tone of this manner of telling, for both "Lily Daw and the Three Ladies" and the collection of stories it introduces.

> Mrs. Watts and Mrs. Carson were both in the post office in Victory when the letter came from the Ellisville Institute for the Feeble-Minded of Mississippi. Aimee Slocum, with her hand still full of mail, ran out in front and handed it straight to Mrs. Watts, and they all three read it together. Mrs. Watts held it taut between her pink hands, and Mrs. Carson underscored each line slowly with her thimbled finger. Everybody else in the post office wondered what was up now.

This is pure Eudora Welty, from Mrs. Carson's thimbled finger to the jarring Ellisville Institute, and it establishes the contrast between individual and institution that defines the boundaries of home. For a time the ladies appear to be on the side of institutions. They are a widow, a postmistress, and a Baptist preacher's wife, the self-appointed patronesses of lovely Lily Daw, whom they have joined together to protect from herself according to their ladylike notion of feminine propriety. Feebleminded though she is, "Lily has gotten so she is very mature for her age," as Mrs. Watts delicately puts it. "And that's how come we are sending her to Ellisville." But Lily is in love with the xylophone player from a traveling tent show and plans to marry. The conflict is joined when Mrs. Watts asks, "Did he—did he do anything to you?" and Lily answers, "Oh, yes'm." The opposing sides in this story are not drastically or inflexibly opposed: as Mrs. Carson says, Lily "can be a lady—she can be. . . . That's just what breaks your heart," and for their part the ladies can understand love. Often in Miss Welty's stories, as in this one, the community itself is the subject: we are less concerned with Lily Daw and her unusual lover than with the ladies, who likewise love her and have found a safe haven for her at the Ellisville Institute for the Feeble-Minded. They sway her to go there instead of marrying and then are themselves swayed by the xylophone player. And the fact that they are so readily moved by love is a victory for Victory, a community that permits and sustains shadings, variations, and contradictions in its people, including even the self-contradictions of Mrs. Watts, Mrs. Carson, and Aimee Slocum. The story reveals the community by its relationship to Lily and celebrates it: "The band went on playing. Some of the people thought Lily was on the train, and some swore she wasn't. Everybody cheered, though, and a straw hat was thrown into the telephone wires."

Given the cynical tenor of much short fiction of the Depression in America, this seems hopelessly romantic. But Miss Welty knows, as she says in *The Eye of the Story* that Katherine Anne Porter knew, that "some romantic things happen also to be true." Besides, whatever sustenance home and family offer her characters, not all her stories end like "Lily Daw." The Petrified Man is sold into prison for a $500 reward by ladies who are unlovely and unloving freaks; neither Keela, the Outcast Indian Maiden, nor very many others in Cane Springs mind that he was abducted for a circus geek; and Old Mr. Marblehall's is an unlived and barren life whether he lives with an ugly old wife in his marble hall or in a suburban Natchez bungalow or in both (or only imagines that he does). In "Why I Live at the P. O.," a family clenches against the neurotic eccentricities of the narrator; in "A Curtain of Green," Mrs. Larkin hides herself in a wild garden to hide her loneliness from the town of Larkin's Hill. And these essentially romantic things happen also to be true.

Lily Daw dwells in and leaves in love a "home" like that in which these characters flounder and are lost. But home is always present—in Mrs. Fletcher's reluctant acquiescence to Leota in "Petrified Man," for example, and in Steve's attempt to expiate his guilt to Little Lee Roy in "Keela, the Outcast Indian Maiden." In the concluding story of *A Curtain of Green,* it is lodged firmly in the protagonist herself. "A Worn Path" is the story of an old, old Negro woman named Phoenix Jackson making one of her periodic trips into Natchez for medicine for her grandson. In it, Miss Welty pits the old woman's faith and love against the community's grudging "Charity." Phoenix Jackson's road is a long, worn path, and there are allegorical overtones in the journey and the dangers it entails: a thorny bush that catches her dress, a ghostly scarecrow, a black dog who upsets her, and a queer, unpredictable white man with a gun. These are fantastic elements more than "real" ones, but Phoenix Jackson is a fantastic herself, completely at home with her perils and her perilous visions in a world that otherwise would debase her. Home is the center of life from which she ventures out on errands of love. At the charity clinic in Natchez, she reaffirms that faith:

> "My little grandson, he sit up there in the house all wrapped up, waiting by himself," Phoenix went on. "We is the only two left in the world. He suffer and it don't seem to put him back at all. He got a sweet look. He going to last. He wear a little patch quilt and peep out holding his mouth open like a little bird. I remembers so plain now. I not going to forget him again, no, the whole enduring time. I could tell him from all the others in creation."

In a short essay that she called "Is Phoenix Jackson's Grandson Really Dead?"[7] Miss Welty defended Phoenix against the charge that really she is a forlorn and senile old lady engaged in a mock ritual of love. Phoenix Jackson's grandson, she said, categorically is not dead. As the grandmother claims, "He going to last." And so will the virtues in her that sustain him. "What I hoped would come clear," Miss Welty said in her essay, "was that in the whole surround of this story, the world it threads through, the only certain thing at all is the worn path. The habit of love cuts through confusion and stumbles or contrives its way out of difficulty, it remembers the way even when it forgets, for a dumbfounded moment, its reason for being. The path is the only thing that matters." The theme is a well-worn path in her own fiction—as it is, also, in the most beautiful and the most terrible short stories of her American contemporaries.

James G. Watson

The University of Tulsa

THE QUESTION
OF REGIONALISM:
LIMITATION AND
TRANSCENDENCE

Apparently critics and scholars need to categorize, to arrange like alongside of like, and thus bring into control unruly, because numerous, fictional pieces that may or may not easily lend themselves to matched groupings. As far as the short story is concerned, what we have is a corpus of short prose fiction saved from fire or shredding machine, and we want to shuffle out stories and authors like a deck of cards: this for local color, that for the grotesque, this for regionalism. That, we say, is realistic; this sentimental. Here's a plot story; there's a character story; and this one is surely a story of setting. And sometimes the shuffling seems to work. It apparently worked toward the end of the last century with a group of writers whose major interest in short fiction appeared to be limited to their concern for common-place scenes and surface characteristics of particular localities. These were the local colorists—Bret Harte, George Washington Cable, Joel Chandler Harris, Sara Orne Jewett, Mary E. Wilkins Freeman. These authors make up a group, we say, who stress background, atmosphere, environment, setting, more than any other device of fiction. Robert Rhode, in *Setting in the American Short Story of Local Color: 1865–1900*, says: "To the extent that the elements of fiction are mutually inclusive, local color has to do with character and plot, but its chief business is with setting, in relation to which it stands either as an auxiliary or as a component part. If successfully used, local color strengthens the setting by adding to the impression of actuality, and by so doing adds to the total effect of the story. . . . The degree of emphasis which it can sustain depends largely on the functions it has in the story, or the type of story in which it is used. Generally only a story of setting can bear a major use of local color."

But though, as critics, we note the accurate reporting of specific details of the region, we also point out that local color writers were content to remain on surfaces, to be more concerned with verisimilitude of detail than with larger truths. We fault them also for digression, sentimentality, lack of perspective, superficiality, overdecoration, weakness of characterization. The nineteenth-century local color movement was a form of regionalism, we say, though not so mature or complex as twentieth-century regionalism.

Regionalism we define as fidelity to a particular geographical section carefully and truthfully depicting the region and the manners and morals of the people living there. We speak of the need for authentic voice and firm texture and call upon Henry James for the phrase "solidity of specification," thus placing regionalism in the realistic mode. Sometimes we try to distinguish local color from regionalism by saying that local colorists were mainly concerned with presenting the eccentric—that is, dealing with differences between regions—whereas regionalists are more concerned with commonalities that exist in spite of regional differences. But, if commonalities are what we're looking for, then what happens to the stricture that if one is to have regionalism, local conditions must be seen to shape people and the way they live and think?

To confuse the issue even more, two important works appeared in the 1930s. Donald Davidson defines regionalism as a "self-conscious expression of the life of a region" which exploits local detail thus recovering a region's usable past.[1] This kind of definition makes of nearly all literature a regionalist expression, a concept that Allen Tate in an article apparently agrees with. Tate speaks of regionalism as "only the immediate, organic sense of life in which a fine artist works."[2]

Well and good. All literature, then, if it has a recognizable physical locale, and if that locale is functional in the overall scheme, is regional. But a definition that embraces all sets is hardly useful in categorizing, especially when the category is either virtually ignored or applied haphazardly.

Mark Twain, for example, is sometimes called a local colorist—not for his major novels, but rather for his relatively inconsequential and aesthetically flawed short stories. William Faulkner, a regionalist in the broadest sense if there ever was one, is seldom so classified. Rather, we say, he transcends regionalism, and then we argue over whether he is basically realist or romanticist.

In *The American Short Story: A Critical Survey,* Arthur Voss places Bret Harte and Mark Twain in the category of local color and western humor, and he groups Jewett, Freeman, Cable, Harris, and Garland under the rubric of regionalism. Voss creates a category called "The Short Story in Transition" for

Crane, London, Wharton, Cather, and Dreiser and puts Caldwell, along with such writers as Steinbeck, Farrell, and O'Hara, under the grouping "Social Protest and Other Themes."

In *The American Short Story: Continuity and Change 1940–1975,* William Peden points out how absurd the term *regionalism* is and then mentions some one hundred writers whose works are regional in some respect or other. Peden uses some new categories imaginatively named: "Metropolis, Village, and Suburbia," "A Mad World, My Masters," "Oh These Jews . . .!" "The Black Explosion."

One can clearly see what Peden is doing and what writers would likely go in each category, but in making these categories, do we not diminish? Is someone just a Jewish writer or a black writer? If the world is mad, is it less real?

Basically, there are only three clearly distinguishable categories: the great is at one end of the scale and the bad (including the failed and the clichéd) is at the other end. Everybody else falls at various degrees in the enormous-in-between. Now it's the enormous-in-between that causes us the most trouble, because it's in here that we really seem to need the subcategories: local color, naturalism, regionalism, transition, black explosion. Categorizing the enormous in-between serves to create reference points. We can talk about skilled naturalists, and great local colorists, and fine humorists. We can say to our friends over dinner, "Say, I'm just rereading Suckow, and what a true sense she has of the small Iowa town." Another thing we do for the authors in the enormous-in-between is give them historical significance. Fifty or more years ago, most literary historians were putting everybody, whatever their category or subcategory, on some route to the great town of "reality." Now most of us seem to be charting the path to "surreality," in one of its various forms. We all do the best we can, however; and this chapter gathers together a group of writers who have, for one reason or another, been called regionalist. Some are, but a lot aren't. Two fall in the category of great; perhaps one in the category of bad.

• • •

Ruth Suckow's collection of stories, *Iowa Interiors* (1926), better illustrates the regionalist mode than many another volume. Author of more than forty short stories and critical essays, three novelettes, and six novels, Suckow was born in a small town in northwestern Iowa and lived in parts of Iowa most of her life. In all her fiction, she made use of her knowledge of Iowa's small communities and their people, showing by careful detail how local conditions color and shape characters and the way they live. *Iowa Interiors* is a collection of sixteen stories and, though nowhere near as intricate in design or complex in treatment as Anderson's rendering of *Winesburg, Ohio,* Suckow's stories are put together with admirable craft and meticulous detail, resulting in that firm texture and "air of reality" so valued by regionalists.

The title itself is significant, for the Iowa interiors are counterpoints of Iowa exteriors which reflect or harmonize with or against inner lives. As a place described by Suckow, Iowa is remote from the shores, inland, removed from the forefront of knowledge or the greater affairs of government, as the people of Iowa are removed, isolated, and landbound. The stories are scenes or views—pictorial, more static than dramatic.

"Four Generations," the best story in the collection, uses a photograph as objective correlative, holding in suspension four generations of a family grown apart, scattered, both physically and culturally. The story begins in medias res as a photographer tells the representatives of the four generations to move closer together and to put the little girl nearer to the center so as to make a more effective picture. The people posing for the photograph are great-grandfather, grandfather, mother, and daughter. The great-grandfather, originally from Germany, is an unlikely looking patriarch, small and bent, and still foreign looking, sitting in a homemade chair of willow, with his gnarled farmer's hands held between his knees. Charlie, his son, one generation removed, is plump and soft, a small-town banker of Midwest small-town prosperity. Charlie is the son who made good, the one who moved to town and became successful, the one who wanted to see that his daughter, Katherine, had more than he had and more than her cousins who were sunburned and wiry and, though without music and drawing lessons and a college education, still live close to home. Katherine, slim and fastidious, has never liked the farm; even as a child, her curled underlip expressed her disdain. She married into a New England family and believes that it is from the "refinement" and "culture" of her husband's family that she should have derived, not from this horde of male and female relations with whom she shares no interest and with whom she cannot talk. Katherine is determined that her daughter, Phyllis, will be even further removed. Treating Phyllis like a hothouse flower, Katherine will not let her accept gifts from her grandparents because they might be harmful, and the mother has even undertaken to teach the child at home.

In the photograph the tensions of these people are caught, while around them, out of the frame of the camera lens, are the relatives—the other sons, Chris and Gus, and their wives and children. This group, heavy and stolid, stands against the white wall of the farmhouse, which is framed by the green grove beyond and by the orchard and the spreading cornfields. These relatives form another picture, as do other scenes where dichotomies are established between town and country, German and New England background, East and Midwest, generation and generation. One view presents Grandpa and Charlie trying to talk, both wanting to communicate but unable to, because the real ties are broken and they cannot be re-established. Another view shows Katherine sitting with the "womenfolks," who are planted in their chairs, rocking and yawning, and telling stories of births and deaths and funerals and sicknesses. But Katherine suffers from what she considers the women's vulgarities and cannot see anything in the birth of Phyllis that she could share with common people. Still she is polite and sits courteous and ladylike, a dutiful smile on her lips.

The last scene in the story is of Grandpa and Phyllis. The old man has been left alone, and he sits now in the doorway of his room, rocking and puffing on his pipe. His eyes gaze out beyond the orchard and the cornfields, the river and the town, the wide western country, to the ocean. Behind him is his room with patchwork quilt and dresser and chest of drawers. On one wall hangs his watch, ticking slowly. Suddenly he notices Phyllis standing before him. The child in her pristine beauty, fragile, shining, and unused, contrasts with the man, etched by age, with his thin silvery beard and the marks and "netted" lines on his face. She is like a yellow bird; his hands flutter like a butterfly as he beckons her nearer. He sings her a song: "Du, du, liegst mir im Herzen," the words expressing his pain and his love. The song quavers on the summer air; the child listens and nods; a pleased smile curves her lips; for a moment, she understands. Then, like a bird with a delicate but frightened move, she "flits away," back to her mother.

Using the third-person omniscient viewpoint and patterned sequences of events rather than a fully developed plot line, Suckow presents the situation and stops, but leaves place and people frozen in space and time.

"A Rural Community" has more of a plot though certainly nothing spectacular or, in itself, interesting. Ralph Chapin comes home after fifteen years to Walnut, Iowa, to visit his foster parents, stays for a day, and leaves. Ralph is a writer for large newspapers and magazines, a world traveler involved in international politics and problems. His life is a series of journeys, what he thinks of as an "animated weekly." Unmarried, he is a man without a home. But after visiting far away countries and after an illness he had in Prague, he realizes that the people he called father and mother, Luke Hockaday and his wife, would not live forever, and he determines to visit them. Ralph enters the town by train at 10:10 in the morning and plans to leave that evening by the 11:30 train. On his way, by foot, to the Hockadays, Ralph notices the changes in the town, changes he had come prepared to see. But he is not

152   THE AMERICAN SHORT STORY 1900–1945: A CRITICAL HISTORY

prepared for that which remains the same. As he walks, Ralph feels himself going back, dreamlike, into his past. The lay of the land stirs his deepest feelings—the hills and woods and pasture land. It is autumn. The trees are russet or yellow with lyric beauty. On the porch of the Hockaday house are seed corn hung to dry, hickory nuts and walnuts spread out, and pumpkins set out to ripen. All around him is that which is abiding and eternal.

Ralph is welcomed exultantly by the Hockadays, hugged and patted, like one of their own. As the day proceeds, the character and pattern of the Hockaday life is revealed: the flavor still of rural England in their speech, though they are one generation removed from England; Mother Hockaday, aged, but still lovely and a little vain; Father Hockaday still profoundly simple and devout, though given to uttering platitudes. For Ralph, they will kill the fatted calf. The father goes to the store, the mother to the kitchen; she is horrified when Ralph offers to help, since no man has ever invaded her kitchen.

Midday dinner is an image of plenitude: fried chicken, mashed potatoes, gravy, homemade bread, with pickles and jellies and relishes. Afterwards, they invite the "real" Hockaday children to come, and while waiting, Ralph and the Hockadays spend the afternoon in conversation. As they talk, Ralph becomes conscious of a void in the center of his being; he realizes that his foster parents would like to see him settled like his "brothers," and he begins to feel a dissatisfaction with himself. Later he accompanies Mother Hockaday to the cemetery and realizes how in this quiet land one generation after another takes its place beneath the soil not far from the houses in which they lived.

After supper the relatives arrive—Ralph's "brothers," prosperous but tied to the land in the old ways. They are slow of speech, have calm eyes, and wear clumsy shoes. At first, conversation is slow and awkward, but soon Ralph is able to sit back and listen, and he begins to be glad of the slow voices and rustic air of his "relatives."

When it is time for Ralph to leave, he will not allow anyone to accompany him to the train station. He walks by himself slowly, deeply conscious of where he is and has been for a day. He feels steadied and satisfied, and though the train carries him quickly through the night, he remains aware of the country outside and its abiding presence.

Though not as subtle as "Four Generations," "A Rural Community" works with similar themes. An outsider from the beginning, Ralph never loses sight of the differences between himself and his "family," and though he yearns for the simpler pleasures and pains, he knows that for him, like the great-grandfather of "Four Generations" "Ach, ja, ja, ja . . . dot was all so long ago." There is in these stories an elegiac strain, of a past better than the present, more alive, more satisfying, but lost forever.

Not all of Suckow's stories, however, lament the passing of a better world. For some of Suckow's characters, the world is not good, and there is no hope of a better tomorrow. "A Start in Life" is about the child of a servant who is initiated into a knowledge of despair. While still a child, Daisy Switzer is going to her first employment in the home of a young couple with a small baby. Daisy's mother is a laundress and the family, mother and three children, live in two rooms. Here there is no plenitude, no order, no living attuned to natural rhythms, no beautiful children. Daisy is homely, skinny, with pale eyes set too close together and stringy red hair, but she does not know it. She feels important in her small world, and she is proud to be starting to work. Mrs. Switzer knows that she should tell Daisy something of what to expect, but she does not know how to tell her. Daisy will learn, the mother thinks: "She had so many things to learn."

Daisy starts learning the moment Elmer Kruse picks her up, for he puts her in the back seat of the new Buick and, by not responding to Daisy's naive questions, seems to be practicing his new role of employer of a household servant. Edna Kruse, also, needs to make the point that Daisy is a servant, not their own child, though Daisy, little more than a baby herself, identifies with the toddler and is puzzled by the fact that she is isolated and ignored. When the family go out for a ride in the big new car, Daisy expects to be taken along, but she is not invited; and then she knows that she is alone in what is for her a big world, and henceforth, there will be no one to comfort or care for her. Her future will be a replica of her present, ugly as she will find herself to be, and her mouth contorts into a "grimace of silent weeping."

Again, in "Uprooted," an elderly couple are surrounded by family, but circumstances are different from those in "A Rural Community." The children have all moved away and, except for one daughter, Hat, have seldom visited their parents over the years. Now, the parents are too elderly to stay another winter in their own home, and the family have gathered to make some satisfactory disposition of a troublesome situation. One son, Sam, takes the lead because he is the one willing to pay the most to solve the problem and because his parents will listen to him better than they will listen to anyone else, even Hat, who has visited and cared for them though she is the least able to afford it.

The line, "It's a good thing they have children to look after them," acts as an ironic refrain throughout the story as it becomes apparent that the children simply want to be rid of an unwelcome burden. Sam finally solves the problem by telling his parents that they have to move and that they can move in with Hat and take along all their belongings. This means he will have to build a room on to Hat's house (and tell Hat), but these are details easily and quickly settled, in fact, so quickly settled that Sam thinks he will be able to take the evening train home.

"Uprooted" is one of the lesser stories in the collection, not only because it is direct, proceeding mainly by means of simple ironic reversals, but also because the characters lack the complexity to be interesting. The children are unremittingly selfish; the parents simply weak and pathetic. Thus the story tends more to the maudlin than to the aesthetically articulate.

But some of the stories in *Iowa Interiors* are impressive and certainly deserve more attention than they have received since the stir over regionalism occurred in the 1930s. Suckow is today an almost forgotten short story writer, though it could be argued that her stories, as stories, are at least as important, if not more so, than those of such better known writers as Sinclair Lewis or Langston Hughes.

• • •

Another writer clearly in the regionalist tradition is Jesse Stuart, who does for the culture of the Appalachian region of eastern Kentucky what Ruth Suckow did for rural Iowa. One of our country's most prolific writers, Stuart wrote more than 350 short stories, many of which appeared in seven collections dating from 1936 to 1966. In addition to short stories, he has published seven autobiographical volumes, hundreds of poems, seven novels, five juvenile books, and scores of articles and lectures. Born in an isolated log cabin in Kentucky, Stuart appears to have lived a life fast passing into mythology, where boys roamed the hills shooting squirrels and, grown into men, continued male pleasures of fighting, handling guns, and shooting them whenever there was a chance; where the women were likely to be more educated, having attended a couple of years of school; where there was in the house one book, a Bible; and where, in spite of the paucity of reading material (or maybe a Bible is enough), education is sometimes valued, as Stuart came to value it along with firmly held democratic ideals.

Stuart is an optimist, an affirmer, in love with his people and his region, and though his stories sometimes tend to broad comedy and even black humor where grotesquerie is dominant, the world he presents is for the most part realistic, three-dimensional and characterized by solidity and depth. Stuart's hill and mountain people are strongly passionate, fiercely religious, loyal within families, and hardworking. And as hard as they work is as hard as they play. Buttressed by moonshine, they give themselves over to relaxations—courtships, basket dinners, fox hunting, and always fights. But the simple verities prevail, and, in this, Stuart is a cultural primitivist, blending in his stories of W-Hollow a romantic exuberance with realistic detail and an ear for idiom that cause the people and the region to come alive. The cumulative effect of the stories is of the presentation of authentic mountain folk, come alive by vigorous force. Also characteristic are the oral character of the narrative (mainly first person and present tense) and the abundance of visual and auditory images. For the most part, the stories are plotless, primarily incidents recording a response to an action. They are also simple and direct, so that a person used to and valuing the complexities of the modern short story must find Stuart's value as a writer of short stories in accumulated detail rather than in story valued as story.

Tales from the Plum Grove Hills is typical Stuart. Most of the stories are told in the first person by a boy (adolescent or a young man, depending on the story) named Shan who is Stuart's persona. The stories range from character sketch to incident to story with well-developed plot, and from the serious to the playful and humorous to the farcical and absurd.

"Another April," the first story in the collection, characterizes Grandpa, who is ninety-one and did not retire from cutting timber and farming until he was eighty. Grandpa is Shan's mother's father, and as the story opens, the mother is carefully putting layer after layer of clothes on the old man to prepare him for his first walk in the spring after the long winter. During his walk, Grandpa stops frequently to look at things in a careful manner, apparently making contact with life around him. When he returns, instead of coming in through the front door, he toddles around toward the back. Before long it becomes apparent that Grandpa is having a conversation with an old terrapin that is, at the least, ninety-five years old.

The boy wonders about who cut the date in the terrapin's back and about whether and how long that person lived in Plum Grove and whether that person, also, like Grandpa in the spring, enjoyed the April and his walks, and looked at the blossoming trees, and talked to the terrapin. At the end of the story, in order to make the identification clear, Stuart has the boy say, "Gee, Grandpa looks like the terrapin." In the identification of Grandpa and terrapin and in boy and grandfather and in boy and grandfather with the person who carved the date in the terrapin's shell, Stuart comments on processes where birth and death are no more than part of a natural order.

"My Father Is an Educated Man" makes clear a relationship between father and son and explains why the son of his father went to school and got educated and became a "book-writer." The scene is a town, the center of the father's universe, four miles from his home, where he meets a group of men on the courthouse square; they talk and tell stories and chew tobacco and whittle. The situation concerns the narrator's overhearing a schoolteacher talking to another group of men, telling them that the father never amounted to anything and never would. The narrator wants to walk over to the schoolteacher and tell him a few things—how his father could read his name and, if he wanted to, piece together letter sounds to make words, how his father came from a heroic race, tillers of the earth who brought plows to rocky mountain slopes, who helped to build the railroads and provide the coal, who helped to build the cities and the highways and the churchhouses. What use to them was book learning? But they were educated, Shan would insist. The father's tragedy was that he was educated in a time when that kind of education was not valued as much as sitting behind a desk and wearing a neat suit and tie. But the father knows enough to encourage his son's education; he knows also that an "educated" son can no longer kill his enemies, since the son will be caught in abstractions of the kind the father will never understand, for the father's life is based in the real, the solid, and the durable.

In "Thanksgiving Hunter," Stuart recounts how Shan could not kill doves, though his Uncle Walt had carefully taught him how to shoot and care for his gun and hunt. The occasion is a dove hunt, but the boy has two memories that interfere with his desire to join in the kill and please his uncle. The first is of live doves, singing their mournful songs, carrying straws to build their nest, flying in pairs, carrying food, and feeding the young. The other is of a time when he was younger and killed a groundhog with a sassafras stick because the groundhog was eating a blister-ear of corn; he remembers hitting the groundhog over and over again for no good reason. The boy waits for the hunting party, sunning himself on a rock and noting the death around him as the season changes to winter. Everything, he thinks, is dead but a few birds and rabbits: the gun, for him, means death, too.

But the hunters know nothing of these thoughts as they hunt doves for Thanksgiving dinner. Still, the boy, hearing them, believes that he has let his uncle down, and he hopes that he can overcome his feelings and kill one dove before the hunting party returns. So he whistles his dove calls, and he is answered. As the dove comes closer to him he lifts his gun; then seeing that the dove appears unafraid, the boy thinks that the dove is a pet and lowers the gun. The dove comes closer, and the boy sees that the dove is blind in one eye, caused by a hunter's bullet. The dove turns its head, and the boy sees that both eyes have been blinded. Nevertheless, though blind, the dove calls to its mate, and soon its mate answers, its whistle becoming a beckoning voice.

These kinds of stories, told from the perspective of a sensitive boy, are different from ones in which the narrator participates as part of a ritual experience. Apparently now a feisty young man in "Death Has Two Good Eyes," Shan and his cousin, Finn, have been summoned by other cousins who live at Blanton on the Big Sandy River. Shan and Finn are met at the station by their cousin Frank, who tells them there is trouble at home with "bloodkin" whom they respect enough to put aside pistols and knives to fight with fists, clubs, and rocks. The problem has been precipitated by their Uncle Melvin, who, it appears, has seven boys by a legal wife and seven boys and two girls by another woman. The knowledge that her husband has gone to live for good with another and younger woman is driving Aunt Mallie to her grave. Since seven brothers have been pitted against seven brothers, the fight has been in stalemate; therefore, Cousin Frank has sent for reinforcements with whom he intends to win the battle. So brothers fight brothers with a couple of cousins thrown in, and, indeed, the cousins do make the difference. The fight is stopped, mighty as it is, when the other woman, wringing her bony hands and pushing her coarse black hair back from her face comes crying, "My true love is dead."

It seems Uncle Melvin complained of a pain in his heart and then died in the outhouse. But dead or alive, Uncle Melvin is carried back to his lawful wedded wife while the unlawful wedded wife screams out her despair.

More like a tall tale in the local color tradition celebrating the rites of manhood than the kind of account celebrating kinship knowledge experienced by Shan in "Death Has Two Good Eyes," the story ends on the comment that Finn, who is a mighty fighter, must take after the father's side of the family, while Shan, who is not so good in a fight, undoubtedly takes after his mother's people.

At an even greater distance from the Shan of "Death Has Two Good Eyes" is the narrator of "Another Hanging." He speaks in a dialect, is overjoyed at the prospect of a hanging, joins crowds of drunken people on the way to the site, picks up a girl to watch the hanging with, and "loves her all the way home." The man who is being hanged is a murderer who has been too free with a razor and has finally slit someone's throat from ear to ear. The drunken crowd of people on their way to the hanging includes young men with pistols and girls. One is tempted to tie together these image patterns and those in "Death Has Two Good Eyes" and see in them grotesqueries of the male psyche, at least the male psyche in W-Hollow. Given, however, that Stuart's life experiences as presented in his autobiographical writing seem to deny such a meaning, and given that the story has been called an example of Stuart's "exuberant lyricism," a "wild and delirious ride" through the night proceeding with "joyous abandon," it might be better just to agree with Ruel Foster in his book on Jesse Stuart that the story is one of Stuart's "most potent and economical" and leave it at that. The narrator, Eif, is not Shan, and one can say that the callous views expressed are his and his neighbors', friends', and parents', not Stuart's. "Comic gusto," Foster goes on to tell us, "is a very American brand of humor."

• • •

Langston Hughes is not so clearly in the regionalist mode, though a case can be made, if not for specific literary geography, then perhaps for an inner space, a spiritual world. The settings of Hughes's stories range from the South to the Midwest, from Florida to New England, from Harlem to Paris. But wherever his black people are in present space and time, they are all a transported people and carry within themselves a common knowledge of both pleasure and pain. They are aware, if sometimes only dimly, of a folk culture that is theirs, a heritage of rhythm and warmth, of humor born from the incongruous, of ironic laughter mixed with weeping, of dignity, of durability, of strength. The realistic surfaces of Hughes's stories expose racism, social conditions, spiritual malaise; but beneath it all is the interior space of the black people themselves, Hughes's "soul world."

Hughes is as prolific as Jesse Stuart, but where Stuart is best known for his short stories, Hughes is distinguished most for his poetry. *The Ways of White Folks,* his first collection of short stories, was published in 1934, and though Hughes continued to write stories for magazines and journals, another collection was not to follow until 1952. The title comes from a story in the collection, "Berry," whose protagonist, Milberry, "a nice black boy, big, good natured and strong," says to himself: ". . . the ways of white folks, I mean some white folks, is too much for me. I reckon they must be a few good ones, but most of 'em ain't good—leastwise they don't treat me good. And Lawd knows, I ain't never done nothin' to 'em, nothin' a-tall."

All the stories in the collection are bitterly ironic and concern a relationship between whites and blacks; and though Hughes later in his career was able to characterize people, whether white or black, as participating first in a common humanity and second as individuals distorted by prejudice or fear, in these early stories, whites are mainly one-dimensional and stereotyped. The only exceptions are Mrs. Dora Ellsworth, a white patron of the arts who appears in "The Blues I'm Playing," and Miss Briggs, a lonely white spinster who is the protagonist in the story "Little Dog."

"The Blues I'm Playing" is one of the better stories in the collection. Beginning in medias res and ending in an epiphany, the story lends itself to multiple interpretations. It could be argued that the protagonist is Oceola, a young black girl and a genius on the piano, who accepts Mrs. Ellsworth as patron, but who is strong enough to hold on to that which is black within her and not allow herself to be seduced or dominated by Mrs. Ellsworth's middle-class values, the attractions of Paris, or art for art's sake. At the end of the stay, after Oceola has decided to marry because she sees no reason to live solely for her art, she is playing, perhaps for the last time, for Mrs. Ellsworth, and she begins to play the blues "that deepened and grew into rollicking jazz, then into earth throbbing rhythm before sinking back into the slow and singing blues." She hears Mrs. Ellsworth ask if this is what her money bought. "No," Oceola answers, "this is mine." In the blues, Oceola believes, is the perfect merging of antitheses—sad and gay, blue and happy, laughing and crying, white and black, man and woman, without which she would not be complete.

On the other hand, one could argue that Mrs. Ellsworth is the protagonist, and that the epiphany at the end is her revelation that her values would never mesh with Oceola's because the white woman identifies herself with the stars while Oceola defines herself in terms of the throbbing earth. Going one step further makes, perhaps, better sense. If Mrs. Ellsworth and Oceola could be identified as two sides of a single coin representing the earth and the stars, then it could be said that the two together make a single protagonist as two parts of a single psyche and that the plot of the story is a symbolic representation of the tension existing between the two parts. But, however the story is read, it is clear that it is considerably more complex in design than others in the volume and serves the sake of art better than the sake of propaganda.

"Little Dog" tells the story of a middle-aged white spinster who buys a dog because she is lonely. Soon her life revolves around the animal and his care and feeding. From its beginning, images and juxtapositions in the story form meaningful patterns. The white woman "upstairs" with the "fuzzy white dog" is contrasted with the black man "downstairs" and his pretty "brown-black children." The black man begins to service Miss Briggs's needs for meat for the dog, and soon the lonely spinster finds herself hurrying home. She, of course, never realizes that she rushes home not for the dog but for the nightly visits of the janitor. One day, inadvertently, she reveals her subconscious wishes. The dog is looking for food; the janitor has left to go home; and the woman says to her dog: "Oh, Flips . . . I'm so hungry."

The accumulation of references to bones, meat, services provides for the reader, if not for Miss Briggs, a moment of simple epiphany: "He almost keeps me broke buying bones," Miss Briggs says, and the janitor answers, "True."

More typical of stories in the collection, however, are such pieces as "Cora Unashamed," "Slave on the Block," and "Father and Son." Dripping with irony, they are propaganda pieces designed to show the shallowness, ignorance, hypocrisy, fear, brutality, self-satisfaction, arrogance, and lack of love of white people in their treatment of blacks.

"Cora Unashamed" is set in Melton, which is described by Hughes as a "miserable in between little place." Cora Jenkins has lived in Melton for forty years and has worked all her life for the Studevants, a white family, who, we are told, treat her like a dog. Once Cora takes a lover and bears a child. In the face of the child she is both "humble" and "shameless." The child is hers, and she believes it is a living bridge between the black world and the white world. Before long, however, Cora's child dies of whooping cough, and Cora finds herself not humble before death as she had been humble before the fact of the child. She screams and curses the God who took her child away from her. Soon, however, she goes back to work at the Studevants and becomes "gentle" and "humble" in the face of life.

Now giving her love to the Studevant child, Jessie, she becomes the girl's substitute mother, hearing from her accounts of her activities. Once Jessie tells Cora she is pregnant. Cora smiles at the news, but Jessie's mother is exceedingly angry. She falls into hysterics and pays no attention to Cora who tells her there is no trouble having a baby. The mother packs Jessie away to Kansas City for an abortion.

When Jessie comes home, she is sick and crying; she refuses food until she dies. Cora, present at the funeral, is, in the white folks' eyes, a part of the scenery, but at the end of the funeral, she makes her presence known. Once again she is not "humble" in the face of death, and she screams out to the Studevants that they killed the child. The white people are paralyzed and sit open-mouthed. Cora cries out: "They preaches you a pretty sermon and they don't say nothin', they sings you a song, and they don't say nothin'. But Cora's here, honey, and she's gone tell'm what they done to you." Cora is rushed out of the funeral, but in a few moments she gathers herself together, goes into the Studevants' house, picks up the few things that belong to her, and returns to her parents. Now on the "edge of Melton the Jenkins niggers, Pa and Ma and Cora, somehow manage," Langston Hughes says, "to get along."

In "Slave on the Block" we are introduced to Michael and Anne Carraway, a young white couple who "go in for the art of Negroes" and love the "darky spirit." They own Robeson records and all of Bessie Smith. They go to plays written about Negroes and by Negroes, and they read books written about and by Negroes, and they spend a lot of time in Harlem. But, in spite of the fact that the Carraways love blacks, blacks do not love the Carraways, for the Carraways rob the black people of their dignity, treating them like toys, denying them the reality of a sense of self.

"Father and Son" is the most violent story in the collection. It concerns a white man who has brought into his plantation home a black woman and has fathered five children by her. The man, however, will not acknowledge the children as his own. He does provide for their education and cares for them, but insists on a distance between them. Of course, a confrontation occurs, and when the father threatens the son with a pistol, the son strangles him. A lynch mob comes, and rather than being taken alive, the boy kills himself. The white men, however, assault the dead body and, not satisfied with that, they seek Bert's brother so they can lynch a man who is alive. The story ends with a newspaper account of the murder and the mob lynching, skewed to white psychology and making the comment: "The dead man left no heirs."

• • •

No propagandist was Jean Toomer, whose book, *Cane,* must be called not only the most significant fiction produced by a member of the Harlem renaissance, but also a collection of stories whose literary value, as far as the history of the short story in the United States is concerned, can be compared only with Anderson's *Winesburg.* Toomer is Langston Hughes's black artist supreme, representing that meshing of dualities that Hughes wrote about in "The Blues I'm Playing," but never himself achieved in the short story genre. When thinking about *Cane,* published in 1923, it is necessary for us to remember as Arna Bontemps points out in his introduction to the Perennial Classic edition of *Cane* that "DuBose Heyword's *Porgy* was still two years away. William Faulkner's first novel was three years away. His Mississippi novels were six or more years in the future. . . . Tennessee Williams was just nine years old."

In a way *Cane* fits more easily into the regionalist mode than Hughes's pieces do, since there are in *Cane* physical settings that Toomer manipulates in such a way that setting mirrors character and holds in itself essential thematic tensions. Nevertheless, if the structure of the book is considered, one could find oneself floundering among categories. The book is a collection of

sketches, stories, poems, the genres spilling over into each other and creating, finally, something of the effect of a story cycle. Nor is it clear that the
book falls in the tradition of realism, a category embraced by regionalists, for
mystery abounds and the seeking after something that cannot be defined by
reference to the experiential. Indeed, Toomer's search for a kind of cosmic
consciousness continues past the writing of Cane. In the same year as its
publication, Toomer began to explore the teachings of Georges Gurdjieff and
a year later joined the Gurdjieff Institute at Fontainbleau.[3]

The opening "sketch" is "Karintha," an exercise in poetic prose so dense
that one wishes to quote it all and then refer to lines and words in lines. But
since it is prose or, at least, is printed as such, perhaps the tone and style of
it can be grasped from the first two sentences: "Men had always wanted her,
this Karintha, even as a child, Karintha carrying beauty, perfect as dusk
when the sun goes down. Old men rode her hobby horse upon their knees."
How can anyone stop there? The mind continues: "Young men . . ."

Karintha is as both earth woman and earth goddess. As earth woman, she
matures too soon and is brought into sexual activity earlier than is good for
her. Because the men can see her only as sex object, she is contemptuous of
them and moves from one man to another. As a child of twelve she had been
a "wild flash" defining what it means to live, not earth bound with feet
"flopping" but running like a whir, mischievous and, even to the priest, "in-
nocently lovely." But occasions stimulated her sexually, not only the old men
jiggling her on their knees and the young men constantly looking at her, but
also the example of her parents whom she had perhaps seen or heard in the
second room of a two-room house. Karintha finds a "small boy" "not afraid
to do her bidding," and that starts the whole thing. No longer does she ride
the old men's knees, but she indulges them, when she is in the mood; she
accepts whatever money the young men can find; and within eight years she
is no longer child but woman, her sexuality and contempt smoldering like
the pyramidal sawdust pile. Once she is made pregnant, and she carries the
child to term, when it falls "out of her womb into a bed of pine-needles in
the forest."

No explicit mention is made of what happens to the child, but juxtaposed
images suggest that she put the infant on the burning sawdust pile whose
smoke spreads itself out over the village and is so pervasive that it can be
tasted in the water. In a sense it could be said to impregnate the village, and
it causes someone to write a song: "Smoke is on the hills, Rise up. / . . . And
take my soul to Jesus."

The morality of Karintha's actions is not an overriding concern. Considering her as a human being, we accept that she was "ripened" too soon, for

no reason other than her beauty; but she is, also, more than human. She is a primitive goddess figure identified with the earth and sun and moon, and of her actions no mortal person can make judgments. The child falls from her as easily as pine needles from trees as they go through the cycle of life and death, and Karintha has full power of life and death, as she has, finally full power of acceptance or rejection of the men who desire but never understand her.

"Esther" has more of a plot. At least it has a pattern of events arranged in cause-and-effect sequence, but if plot is what a reader needs in order to be firmly based in a reality of both expectation and the experiential, then fictional expectations are in this story shattered and "reality" nullified. The story ends: "There is no air, no street, and the town has completely disappeared."

Where Karintha is the image of perfectly realized and vital dark beauty, Esther is the image of the colorless, the flat, the pallid, and the dead. Half white and half black, she lives in a purgatory of unreality, unable to commit herself in any direction.

The story is told in four sections: when Esther is nine, sixteen, twenty-two, and twenty-seven. At nine, she witnesses King Barlo, a magnificent, huge black man, go into a religious trance and recount a vision: "I saw a man arise an' he was big and black an' powerful—" With spectators responding in rhythmic chants, Barlo creates an image of a strong, powerful, black Christ who will return to set his people free; and when Barlo rises to his full height to preach his gospel, he is immense and himself assumes the outlines of the envisioned Christ. Whether miracles occur that night or are only hearsay, stories circulate that demons and angels paraded the streets, that Barlo left town riding a black bull with gold rings in his nose, that Old Limp Underwood (what a wonderfully suggestive name in this story for a white man who hates blacks) woke up to find he held a black man in his arms. But whatever did or did not occur, it is certain that a "sanctified" black woman drew a portrait of a black madonna on the courthouse wall and that Barlo left town.

Barlo leaves behind his image "printed indelibly" on the mind of Esther, and his image becomes the only "life" she knows.

When she is sixteen, Esther has a vision of a fire and a rescued infant which she has "come by." She thinks of the infant "immaculately," thus herself assuming the role of madonna with Barlo as both God and (as infant) child: a baby, black, "singed, wooley, tobacco juice baby—ugly as sin." Esther's "dream," clearly of repressed sexuality and, by ordinary standards, heretical, is another "life" experience.

At twenty-two, Esther is more lifeless in appearance, her hair thinning and her face the color of gray dust. Barlo's image now gives her only a "slightly stale thrill," but she decides that she loves him and she determines to tell him so the next time he comes to town. At twenty-seven, Esther is listless, lean, beaten, weary with being. But suddenly Barlo is back, and Esther becomes as animate as possible with "pale flame." She has not forgotten her purpose. It is all that defines her life. So she seeks him out, but what she finds is not her black God but a drunken man hideous and repulsive; now all her life and all her reality disappear.

As the stories in the first part of *Cane* have women as protagonists, women who mirror for Toomer both the pleasure and pain of the southern experience, the stories in the second half of the book have men as protagonists, men who have left the rural South seeking life and opportunity in the city streets of the North. "Box Seat" tells the story of Dan Moore, who, like Barlo, envisions himself a savior.

Showing himself skillful with just about every variety of plot structure in *Cane,* Toomer uses in "Box Seat" a traditional plot rising to climax and then falling to resolution. His choice of plot line here is felicitous, since Dan's own sexual potency rises and falls with the movement of the plot, an orgastic movement not always consistent with the nineteenth-century plot line— unless one believes that the word *climax* necessarily refers to a similar experience in both literature and sex. However, whatever the answer to that conundrum, we can say that Toomer uses the nineteenth-century plot line with all the skill that went into its use by the great short story writers of that period, like Hawthorne, Poe, and Melville. In "Box Seat" plot is a symbolic embodiment of the conflict of the protagonist and, moreover, provides a surface structure on which Toomer hangs image patterns and symbols that provide the undergirding so necessary to the short story if it is to achieve complexity.

• • •

Throughout her career, Ellen Glasgow objected to being called a regionalist, pointing out that a work of art could not be both regionalist and art. She was not writing about Virginia life, she insisted, but about people who lived in Virginia. Her emphasis, she said, was not on the mores of Virginia but on the conventions of the civilized world; not on southern nature but on human nature; not on southern characteristics but on human conduct and a common heritage. She did accept the term *realistic* as describing her work but argued that the term must embrace the interior world as well as external appearances, because "documentary realism" produces only surface impressions. Indeed, technique could be, she believed, the most important factor in the production of a work of art, because the arrangement of material and the right focus or perspective is essential to bring life to a landscape, figure, or situation. Accuracy of detail and external verisimilitude are important, she said, but they are nothing unless illuminated by the imagination.

Glasgow's forte was the novel. She wrote few short stories, over the years producing some for publication in magazines and bringing together seven stories in the collection *The Shadowy Third and Other Stories* in 1923, the same year Toomer published *Cane* and four years after the publication of *Winesburg, Ohio*. Hardly exhibiting the vigor of new form, Glasgow's stories make use of a traditional plot line, apparently carefully crafted from exposition through resolution, with a concern for the perspective on which credibility hangs. But what is striking about the stories in *The Shadowy Third* is that most of them are ghost stories and very good ghost stories, indeed. In fact, Glasgow may have used this form to express her real interest in mysticism and idealist philosophy sparked by her reading in Oriental religions as well as in Kant, Fichte, and others.

"The Shadowy Third," the title story of the collection, is told in the first person by a nurse who recalls an event that took place ten years before, when she was working in a New York hospital. The nurse is from Virginia, and this is her first job in New York. Cheerful, competent, sympathetic, intelligent, she is, of course, the perfect focal point from which to tell a story that could strain credibility. Indeed, since the story is told ten years after the event and knowledge of it has not diminished the nurse but perhaps added to her capabilities (she is, in present time, a superintendent of nurses), credibility is strengthened even further.

The young nurse enters the employ of Doctor Maradick, the finest surgeon at the hospital, who is, at the same time, dark, handsome, mature, and the idol of all the nurses, including the narrator who conceives of him as more than a hero and "almost a god." It is, of course, appropriate that he be married to a woman so beautiful as to look like an angel. But she is ill and the narrator is employed to care for her. Like the narrator, Mrs. Maradick's heritage is also southern, and she has in her employ an old black man who ushers the narrator into a dark room muttering (in dialect) that he isn't going to turn on the lights until the child is finished playing. The room is lit only by a fire and, as the nurse stands waiting, two things occur. First, she is dazzled by the glare of headlights shining through the windows; second, she sees a child's red ball which she vainly tried to catch to return it to a small girl, dressed in Scotch plaid, who is standing before her.

The next time the nurse sees the child, she is coming from her mother's bedroom, this time carrying a doll. Mrs. Maradick is supposed to be suffering from hallucination but no one has told the nurse what the hallucination is. It turns out, of course, that the child is the hallucination, having died months before of pneumonia, though, her mother says, "she was never sick a day in her life." Having found out that the nurse, also, has seen the child, Mrs. Maradick trusts her and tells her that Dr. Maradick has murdered the child for her money, because it will go to him when both child and mother are dead. A reader now knows what will happen—what *has* to happen—but there are intricacies that make the story worth rereading.

The god figure becomes devil figure, though still tremendously seductive, so that the nurse is torn between two opposing forces—husband and wife—in battle not only for the narrator's soul but also for her intelligence; for if one is to believe in a supernatural presence, one's metaphysics must account for it, and this Glasgow certainly knows. The good and the innocent see the presence; the evil and the biased do not. One person who does not see the child is the alienist, Dr. Brandon, presented as half a man, seeing only half of the life that is before him. After one scene when the child appears to the mother and the nurse, though not to Dr. Brandon and another servant, the nurse says: "Only my vision—and I have asked myself since if the power of sympathy enabled me to penetrate the web of material fact and see the spiritual form of the child—only my vision was not blinded by the clay through which I looked."

At the beginning of the story, the nurse is told by her superior in the hospital that she has too much sympathy for a nurse and perhaps should have been a novelist. It is fascinating to speculate that Glasgow used the form of the short story imaginatively to embody the metaphysics that she herself held and tried to express when she insisted that surfaces are not enough and that realism must include interiors as well as exteriors. In "Dare's Gift," another story in the collection, Glasgow makes the point another way when she has a character say, "We nibble at the edges of the mystery, and the great Reality—the Incomprehensible—is still untouched, undiscovered."

As good a ghost story as "The Shadowy Third" is, however, "Whispering Leaves" is better. Here Glasgow makes use of some of the same devices that we find in all her ghost stories: a narrator whose credentials make him or her trustworthy, a vision seen by some but not by others (this time an old black woman needed to care for an isolated and lonely child), a carefully worked out plot structure designed to create and hold suspense, and an insistence upon a metaphysical reality. To this, Glasgow adds a more sophisticated blend of dream and reality, using lights and shadows and colors and shapes in conjunction with setting to create a mysterious penumbra and a rhythmic pattern of images resulting in a linkage of motifs from which meaning emerges.

Besides the ghost stories, *The Shadowy Third* contains several pieces that could be called problems in morality, or moral puzzles. The best of these is "The Difference," a story of Margaret, who, having learned that her husband is having an affair, fantasizes a highly romantic and noble love for which she is willing to be a martyr. She finds out, however, that for her husband the affair is simply a convenient recreation and not something worth her concern. "She felt like an actress who had endowed a comic part with the gesture of high tragedy." The fact both banishes Margaret's illusions and destroys her ego, for she finds she has lost more than love and happiness. She has lost her belief in life, and losing that, she loses herself. In this story, Glasgow shifts from her usual first person to third person focused through the protagonist, because this perspective is needed for the author to move in and out of the character's mind. Margaret's dignity must be maintained if the moral dilemma is to be presented with the high seriousness the theme deserves.

• • •

By virtue of his treatment of the Midwest, one would think that Sinclair Lewis should be called regionalist, as well as James T. Farrell, because he portrayed South Side Chicago, Erskine Caldwell for his rendering of the rural South, John O'Hara for his depiction of small towns in Pennsylvania, and John Steinbeck for telling us about life in the Salinas Valley. But, in fact, despite what they do or do not do in their novels, as short story writers, they are not regionalists.

Sinclair Lewis's examination of the small-town, midwestern, middle-class American society was so impressive that he not only coined terms still used and defined Americans to themselves in such a way that generations have tried to prove that they're not what they so often are, but also won a Nobel Prize, apparently because his definition of American society agreed with the Swedish Academy's own. All this for a writer dismissed by many critics as at least second or third rate and by some critics as one of the worst writers in our literature. Clearly the distinction being made here is between what is said and how it is said. The "what" catches the imagination and has held it for half a century; the "how" simply embarrasses most critics, who are, after all, a small part of the reading public.

Lewis's first collection, *Selected Short Stories,* was published in 1935 and contained stories written as early as 1917. All had been previously published in magazines like the *Saturday Evening Post, Cosmopolitan, Redbook,* and *Nation.* In his short introduction, Lewis speaks of the distant days before the war, when people were optimistic and full of hope and courage, and he wonders whether his own stories are still relevant, still authentic parts of American life. He concludes that hope, courage, and optimism are indigenous to Americans and that, in spite of his satiric thrusts and realistic mode, he must be seen as "a romantic medievalist of the most incurable sort."

The fact is that all Lewis's writings show this dichotomy. He was American to his toes—half believing both in Puritan virtues and in the myth of Horatio Alger. He wasn't criticizing the Midwest from an eastern perspective or from a European one, since he found nothing better anywhere else. The Midwest, at least, had the excuse of being young, and being young, it still could be the land of hope and opportunity.

"Let's Play King," a story Lewis singles out for special commendation, is over ninety pages in length. Set in Mechanicville, New York, another example of Lewis's Small Town, USA, the story opens in front of a gas station run by Mr. Rabbitt (echoes of Babbitt) who was christened Thomas Tate. Mr. Tate is married to a woman named Bessie, and they have a son Terry, a beautiful child with golden hair and white skin. The Tates are stereotypical lower middle class, coarse, and vulgar.

Complications are introduced when an old lady, who is said to be so rich and old that she had to be virtuous, comes by Tate's gas pump. When she sees the beautiful boy, she insists that the parents take him to St. Jukes in Albany because, unless they do something about getting him into some church school, he is likely to be drawn into the movies as a child star, and that, the old lady says, is the most frightful thing that one can think of. This comment gives Bessie Tate an idea, and she determines that she will get Terry into the movies. Bessie admits no possibility of failure.

Without transition, the story moves to Poppy Peaks, California, and a Spanish mansion owned by Mr. Abraham Hamilton Granville, president of a film corporation which includes Tate as one of its members. As in the first pages of the story, Lewis presents exposition by way of the language and syntax of the characters, a device that helps to set scene, characterize, maintain credibility, and allow the satiric comments that are the base of the narrative. In the gathering are Mr. Granville, Mr. Tate, now called T. Benescoten Tate, Mrs. Tate, Terry Tate, and a writer named Lugg, a woman who apparently has written all the screen plays on which Terry Tate's movies have been based. As the scene opens, Lugg is trying out various story ideas, finally hitting upon a story idea about a boy king that everybody seems to like but Terry.

As the story continues, the characters learn that, ironically, a real boy king is going to be in Paris. This turn of the plot makes possible a number of farcical attempts by Bessie, the queen mother of a Hollywood boy king, to force her way into the presence of a real royal mother and her son. When the boys do meet, they play various kinds of games and talk together Finally despairing of the roles that they must play, Terry as king of the movies and Max as king of Slovaria, they decide to run away and become pirates.

With the two boys away, the queen of Slovaria and Bessie finally do meet. Comforting each other in their despair, they turn out to be exactly the same kind of people, except that the queen of Slovaria is not so brusque or vulgar in her speech and actions. After some adventuring, the two kings walk into a newspaper office and declare who they are. Meanwhile, both mothers are more concerned with their own private needs than the wishes of the children. The story ends with both families back in place and the movie being made with Terry starring.

In this story satire is directed not only against the Tates but against the people in the Hollywood film community, against royalty, even against the people in Paris. Only the children emerge as having any positive values. In this, however, there is a problem with credibility. Terry Tate is too kind and understanding a boy to have been brought up in the kind of environment Lewis pictures, and the king of Slovaria retains an essential innocence which hardly seems appropriate, given his circumstances.

Although filled with sentimentality and replete with the happy ending one associates with overly romanticized motion pictures, a story called "Moths in the Arc Light" exhibits Lewis using a different style and presenting as part of the theme a dichotomy between Manhattan and the country, so that an antithesis between town and country is set up.

The story concerns a man named Bates, who at thirty-five has become the very model of an American businessman. His office is in the middle of Manhattan, twelve stories above New York pavements. His world is composed of reinforced concrete. "Continents and striding seas," Lewis says, are "office partitions and ink wells." Bates has not been in the country to see "storm clouds across the hills" or "moths that flutter over dusky meadows" in five years. While high above the New York pavements at night, when trolleys are still and the noise of new building is hushed, Bates can look down on a line of lights arching over the bridge. In this description, Lewis's style soars with Bates's spirit as the author describes the "splendid, aspiring, naked blue, in which the stars hung golden."

Bates has not taken the time to marry or to cultivate any interests other than his work. He finds that he can sleep in the office, as well as work there all day. He spends a good amount of time looking out of his office windows to a building opposite his own which he considers to be the very model of a business building since it is made of concrete and glass. One day while looking across the street he notices a new secretary, and her manner and bearing catch his eye. He finds himself spending more and more time watching her as she works.

In July, Bates goes on a vacation, not to the formal seaside motel where he usually spent three weeks, but rather to the Lebanon Valley, which for him is the valley of peace. There he discovers yellow cream and wild blackberries and cowslips and that the "art of walking without panting still exists." He wears soft shirts and becomes tanned. Part of his time he spends dreaming about taking a vacation with the girl across the way, and though he tries to be strong minded and practical, as soon as he gets back to his office, he rushes to the window, takes his hat off, and bows to her. Before long they build up a long-distance relationship, although they are just across the street from each other.

He realizes that he must meet her in spite of his fears and that she will turn out to be different from his imaginings; after several abortive attempts, he dashes up to her in the street. She listens to him and is honest and nice, not what he feared at all, but she tells him she is not just a woman, but a business woman, and she is not looking for courtship and marriage. She is, rather, she implies, a female counterpart to him. She asks him to help her find a better job. He does, but without her, he is miserable. Finally she calls him and over dinner tells him that she has discovered she is a woman, after all; he asks her to marry him, and without much coaxing, she appears to accept. He is ecstatic: "Mine, then! Mine! Think, dear—it's incredible, but the city didn't quite get us. We're still a man and a woman."

Beyond surface irony, there is little to a Lewis story. What he wanted to do, apparently, was to say things plainly; he disliked what, for him, was indirect and thus obscure. He was not a self-conscious stylist and apparently never considered complex substructures of any kind important in fiction.

• • •

Best known for his *Studs Lonigan* trilogy, James T. Farrell writes of the failure of institutions to provide moral sanctions sufficient to maintain spiritual values that define civilization at its best. The disease that takes over when a moral vacuum exists is both personal and social, manifesting itself in the disintegration of character. Farrell's popularity in recent years has diminished, although at one time he was considered to be one of this country's important writers.

As a short story writer, Farrell is better than Lewis, though Farrell, too, often gets no further than surfaces; still, his range is greater and his tone more varied. "The Power of Literature," is, for example, more subtly ironic than overtly satiric. Hardly complex, this very short story concerns itself with the essential loneliness of people in a big city. Told in the third person and focused through Samuel Lord, the protagonist, the story is based in an ironic reversal. Lord is the author of a first novel having to do with alcoholism and delirium tremens. Having himself been an alcoholic, Lord is able to write the novel with such force that it has become a best-seller and is discussed widely in the press and on the radio. The publishers decide to take advantage of its success by having a large party in recognition of the author. The focal situation is the party where hundreds of people mill around drinking the free liquor and staying until they are all very drunk. At the end of the story, Lord goes home alone, realizing that before he became famous he had been poor and an alcoholic, lonely and unhappy. Now he is rich and not an alcoholic, but he is still lonely and unhappy.

Farrell places a great deal of emphasis here on crowds of people who mill and jam and talk endlessly in excited voices. These crowds are compared with the isolation of the protagonist who soon is forgotten in their midst. At the end of the story, Samuel Lord sits in his penthouse looking down on the streets of New York, which are shrouded in mist. The lights appear to beckon him to life and romance. They appear to want to reveal to him the meaning and mystery of life. But the lights are an illusion. What they reveal is that everyone is alone in the crowd, destitute of values, and poisoned by blight.

With a little more direction by Farrell, "The Power of Literature" could have become more complex and thus more interesting. The protagonist's name is suggestive, as well as the fact that he is a creator, but there is no evidence in the story to suggest the mirroring that would be necessary to carry a substructure to completion. In the beginning was the word and the word has power, but, unfortunately, this story does not.

When reading stories written during the thirties, as many of Farrell's were, one must remember the force of the Depression and perhaps even speculate that social and economic conditions were such that Americans were faced, for the first time, with an image of failure powerful enough to become a backdrop against which was played everything they did or read. Thus ironies in a story would be strengthened not by the structure of the story but by the environment in which the story was read. "The Virginians Are Coming," for example, might have made a more lasting impression on Farrell's contemporaries than on readers of today (though, given another depression, who can tell?). The title of the story refers to a poem by Vachel Lindsey which says, among other things:

> Babbitt, your tribe is passing away,
> This is the end of your infamous day.
> The Virginians are coming again.

The protagonist of the story, Roland, and his friends are the next generation referred to in the poem, but they are making no impact. Roland is already graduated and the others soon will be, but there are no jobs for them, and for the few jobs that are available, they are overqualified. Before graduation Roland had always argued that there were not many Babbitts in the world, but after looking for work day after day and talking to businessmen, employment managers, department heads, and chief clerks, Roland has decided that they *are* Babbitts, giving gratuitous advice, eulogizing the value of time, boasting and bragging of their own rise in the world, lauding capitalism; all this, when Roland simply wants a job.

"John Hitchcock" has much the same theme. John wants to be a writer, but he is so busy writing reviews for a few dollars so that he and his wife can feed themselves, he is filled with frustration and fear: "He wished he were old, that he were at the end of his life. He thought how the old were the lucky ones. They had so little to go through. They didn't have to face this terrible future that he . . . had inherited." The story ends with John thinking: "Nothing! Nothing! Nothing!" It is, of course, hard to read the end of "John Hitchcock" without being reminded of the "Nada" that ends Hemingway's "A Clean Well-Lighted Place," but the stories are clearly different. Hemingway's is a microcosm and in it the *nada* is given cosmic force. Farrell's *nothing* is tied to a place and time.

"When Boyhood Dreams Come True" is a far better story because in it Farrell attempts not only to present a microcosm but also to use techniques and devices identified more with the twentieth-century experimental and avant garde than with nineteenth-century tradition. The protagonist, a soldier named Tom Finnegan, becomes an American Everyman, and insofar as American racism is identified with Nazi racism, Tom becomes a Western

European Everyman who suffers from anxiety and guilt, associated with a set of sins deriving from the distorted values by which he has lived and dreamed. These values have resulted in a nightmare world where people run mazes of every sort, either chasing or being chased, either hunting or being hunted, looking for ways out of the darkness by means of family, church, country, but always frustrated. Central among these perverted values is the kind of crazy ambiguity that makes it necessary for men at one and the same time to be macho and tender, domineering and submissive, soldier and poet, God and Christ; and for women to be loving mother, wife, and seductive whore/angel and witch/devil.

The dream Farrell skillfully presents is flawed only by his apparent belief that somewhere he had to explain that Tom is dreaming. Otherwise, the surrealistic juxtaposition of images crazily coalescing and dispersing to form different combinations forms a picture of a carnival/hell on earth where everyone is fast moving to an absurd judgment day. All life has led to the precipice on which Tom stands, when boyhood dreams are true. The past is dream, the future illusion, the present the space between ticks of the clock.

"When Boyhood Dreams Come True" is a superb short story, valuable in itself, intricate in design, and aesthetically pleasing. It is, however, not regional, and some people might even consider it to be more an example of surrealism than of realism.

• • •

In a critical foreward for a 1944 collection of stories by Erskine Caldwell, Henry Seidel Canby said that Caldwell at his most original, effective, and best "belongs in the distinguished list of American short-story writers who have made their place in world literature, beginning with Irving, Hawthorne, and Poe."[4] Just about three decades later, Arthur Voss, in his book *The American Short Story: A Critical Survey,* points out that Caldwell is "no longer regarded, as he once was in some quarters, as one of America's foremost writers of fiction, although he remains a widely read author. Canby speaks of Caldwell as a regionalist in the best sense, rooted in his native soil like Jewett and Faulkner but turning his knowledge and native experience of a particular part of the country into successful art of worldwide human significance. When Caldwell is not classified as a regionalist, he is labeled a social realist, whose major concern is with victims of social and economic injustice. Caldwell himself apparently didn't want to be bothered with categories or critics. In a 1946 collection, he says of his short stories: "The one and only thing they do is tell stories; if they do anything else, something is wrong somewhere."

Sometimes it's hard to tell what causes a writer to move in and out of critical favor. In this case, it is possible that critics have paid more attention to Caldwell's novels than to his short stories. It is also possible that Caldwell has been overshadowed by fellow southerners—O'Conner, Welty, Faulkner, among others. In the university, authors are kept alive by having their writing studied in the classroom or anthologized in the texts; when neither event occurs, a generation is long enough for a writer to be all but forgotten. It is true that Caldwell does not have the range of a Faulkner, since Caldwell's stories consistently treat the lower classes struggling for even a minimum of dignity; but it is also true that for sheer effect many of Caldwell's stories compare favorably with Faulkner's. As story, "Saturday Afternoon" is a gem; not as complex or as intricate as "Dry September," because the Caldwell story presents only one viewpoint. But Caldwell does deal with what Faulkner avoids in "Dry September"—direct feeling contact with the grossly insensitive and obscene, revealing the mentality that is the lynchers'.

Tom Denny is a white man and butcher, the only butcher in town; and he sells cow's meat, calling it pork or veal or whatever anyone asks for. Tom's butcher shop smells as though something has died within the walls and the odor gets worse year by year. Flies inhabit the shop, "fat and lazy and greasy flies." They fill up on fresh blood. When Tom gets tired in the middle of the day, he stretches out on the meatblock with a hunk of cool meat for a pillow and wiggles his toes. Tom's partner is Jim, who is the cashier, because his egg-shaped swollen belly is too big for him to work around the meatblock.

Like Faulkner in "Dry September," Caldwell avoids entering into the mind of the black man who is lynched, but the exterior details make the white men's motivations clear. The black man is a "yellow-face coon," a "gingerbread man" who works hard (harder than the white men), who lays by his provisions and makes money (more than the white men), who has three grown-up and married daughters and a healthy wife (Tom's wife has chills and fever all the time), who doesn't drink moonshine or take cocaine through iced Coca-Cola (the kind sold by the town's doctor to the men at the lynching party), and who doesn't carry a knife (Tom carries a cleaver).

Seventy-five (or "maybe a hundred and fifty" white men) show up for the lynching party at a spot already selected and prepared, as for a coming attraction. They burn the black man, and they shoot him, and they string him up, and then Tom and Jim rush back to service their afternoon customers. Everything is the same as it always is, except that Tom and Jim and some others have had a Saturday afternoon diversion.

Caldwell's ironic tone proceeds without inflection as the story unfolds, one detail carefully set next to another and all moving not to a startling climax but to understated and flat resolution. A reader needs to remember, as it is necessary to remember when reading "Dry September," that both these stories were written when society was still predominantly racist and long before people began to speak openly of inner motivations and mirrored reflections that drive white men to treat black men as a hunk of cow's meat.

In Caldwell's world, all white people don't lynch, but most are in desperate condition. "Man and Woman" tells the story of a husband and wife who are destitute and hungry and walking day and night, if they can find the strength. Moving, but apparently without motion, their feet mark their progress in scuffed-up dust. The woman bites her lip to force herself to keep moving; the man, having to throw one leg in front of another to keep moving, appears lifeless as though at any moment he might fall to the ground. What impels them to travel is a persistence beyond the bounds of reason, but also a loyalty and a love that are admirable.

Very short, "Man and Woman" is carried along by raw emotion as painful as the steps of the couple. There is no misplaced word and so few modifying phrases that pitch and coloration are entirely avoided; in fact, the sparseness of the language is itself a reflection of the gaunt and spare couple.

In speaking of this kind of depression, not only of the economics of the country, but also of the land and its people, Joseph Warren Beach *(American Fiction: 1920–1940)* speaks of the "almost universal state of hopeless misery prevailing throughout large regions" of the South: "The chief theme of Caldwell's writing," Beach points out, "is the agony of the impoverished land." But Caldwell's major interest is in what happens to people who steadily decline into moral degradation as material well-being vanishes, and they are left with little more than a constant craving for food.

• • •

Although some critics and scholars mention regionalism in association with John O'Hara, most prefer to classify him as a social realist, a historian, an interpreter of manners and morals. O'Hara's career as a short story writer breaks into two parts, the first, containing some 130 stories, published between 1935 and 1947, and the second, containing just under 100 stories, published after 1961. Many critics believe that the stories published in the second half of his short fiction career are better than those he published earlier since they have more substance and greater interests. In the later stories, O'Hara makes greater use of a Gibbsville, Pennsylvania, setting.

When O'Hara is called a regionalist, reference is made to his longer works set in Gibbsville, which he thought of as his Yoknapatawpha County. What he meant was that he took a real town's physical layout and made it conform to his own ideas, usually subordinating setting to character. And although a story like "The Doctor's Son" is set in Gibbsville, it really could take place in any small town.

O'Hara, himself the son of a doctor, apparently uses autobiographical material in "The Doctor's Son," notably the setting, his own experience as driver for his father during emergency calls, and his early intention to be a newspaper reporter. The story is told in the first person by the fifteen-year-old son, Jim, who recounts a series of incidents that take place in the fall of 1918, when Gibbsville is overrun by a flu epidemic. Jim is busy helping his father who is working to the point of near exhaustion.

The major portion of the story concerns what happens when a young senior medical student named Meiers comes to take over the practice of Jim's father, who is finally too exhausted to continue. Dr. Malloy gives orders to Jim to help the young "Doctor" Meiers, and so the boy is in a position to narrate the events that occur.

Much time is spent in characterization, which is skillfully achieved through a combination of event and comment from the narrator. For the most part, the characters are sympathetic, whatever their place on the social scale of the town. The narrator has little difficulty in understanding the male characters, but he appears to be greatly troubled by the females, especially the three most important women in the story: the foreign woman whose entire family dies, not from influenza, but from diphtheria; Mrs. Evans, the wife of a friend of the boy's father; and their daughter, Edith, Jim's girlfriend.

"Over the River and Through the Wood" is a much shorter story and consequently more typical of the kinds of stories that O'Hara wrote early in his career. It concerns Mr. Winfield, who is taking a trip with his granddaughter to the home of her mother, the home that used to be Mr. Winfield's. The granddaughter, Sheila, is traveling with two of her friends, Helen and Kay. The girls are using the comfortable back seat of the limousine, leaving Mr. Winfield to sit either on a small seat opposite them or outside with the driver. Since he is not dressed adequately, he is unable to sit outside, so he must remain in a cramped, uncomfortable position inside the car.

The epiphany is a revelation for the old man as well as for the reader. Winfield realizes that all he has left is time, and there is too much of that. He knows that before long he will begin to hate himself, and he believes that hate will soon turn into terror. The reader knows that Winfield has already been discarded, although he may not altogether realize it, and that he is already terrorized, though he doesn't realize that either.

Coming from the same volume and appearing early in O'Hara's career, this story is considerably better than the "The Doctor's Son." In fact with its in medias res beginning, sparse detail and truncated plot, it appears to be one of the models for most of O'Hara's successful stories.

"Do You Like It Here," which was published in O'Hara's second collection, is even shorter than "Over the River and Through the Wood." It does, however, make use of the same formula. Told in the third person focused through the mind of the protagonist, a boy name Roberts, the story concerns the kind of verbal assault that can be visited upon a boy by a superintendent or a principal of schools, exhibiting the kind of tactics that adults in authority often use with children who are too young to fight back. The boy knows that he has been assaulted and threatened, his dignity trampled on. All he can do, however, is sit on his bed and first violently, then weakly, curse the schoolmaster.

"The Decision" exhibits similar characteristics. It, too, is told in the third person through the consciousness of Francis Townsend. However, instead of ending in an epiphany, O'Hara uses delayed revelation. Through the course of the story, the reader follows Townsend as he gets up, has his first breakfast, dresses, greets his housekeeper, has his second breakfast, engages the postman in a friendly conversation, and takes his walk, which he has taken every day for the last forty years. On his walk he greets merchants and makes the first stop at the bank where the teller gives him a filled-in check. Townsend signs the check, gives it back to the teller, and receives three five-dollar bills. He then resumes his walk, heading for a bar. Townsend spends the whole morning in the bar, quietly drinking and keeping to himself. He then buys a bottle of rye whiskey and makes his way home. His housekeeper has prepared supper, and he eats and then sits to read a book. This, we now learn, is the way Francis Townsend has spent his time since he finished medical school. We learn that an uncle raised him, allowing him to go through medical school without telling him that he can neither marry nor practice medicine because there is insanity in the family. When Townsend asked his uncle how he was to spend the rest of his life, his uncle said that Townsend shouldn't worry, there was sufficient money so that he could take his time making up his mind. Townsend's first impulse is not to stay in the village. The story ends with the following sentence: "But that, it turned out, is what he did decide to do."

All of O'Hara's stories, whether they end with an epiphany or a delayed revelation, are ironic, focusing mainly on character; although setting is a component, it is not emphasized enough to place O'Hara in a regionalist mode. He provides few complexities and little depth, although because the stories proceed through indirection resulting from the use of the dramatic present, readers must deduce from the situation what the meaning of the ironies are. Otherwise there is very little by way of substructure of symbols that provide the complexity and intricacy we are accustomed to in stories by master craftsmen. What some readers appear to be referring to when they say O'Hara is a "master of the short story" is his use of the very short form that is free of excess verbiage and builds to epiphany or delayed revelation. A lack of sentimentality may also be a contributing factor in the judgment.

What needs to be said about O'Hara is that he did what he apparently wanted to do in his hundreds of short stories and many novels and plays. He used the literary form to present American manners and morals with insight and vivid detail.

• • •

John Steinbeck has been better known for his novels, especially *The Grapes of Wrath, Tortilla Flat,* and *Of Mice and Men,* than for his short stories. In the end, however, his reputation may rest on the short stories, not the novels. As a novelist he is competent; as a short story writer, he can be superb.

Critics disagree concerning *The Pastures of Heaven;* some consider it a collection of short stories less intricate than those collected in *The Long Valley;* others consider it a story cycle akin to *Winesburg, Ohio;* still others call it a novel. Warren French's argument in his *John Steinbeck* is persuasive; he insists the book should be called a novel and, moreover, one of Steinbeck's best. French argues that an overall design unites stories like chapters and that when viewed as a novel, *The Pastures of Heaven* can be seen to possess both complex design and profound theme. There is no doubt, however, concerning the stories collected in *The Long Valley,* which appeared in 1938 when Steinbeck was at the height of his career. Most of these compare favorably with the best in our language; and even if *The Red Pony,* originally intended to comprise three stories, but actually comprising four, is seen as story cycle, the stories stand by themselves and do not have to rely on a greater structure to give them aesthetic value. The four stories—"The Gift," "The Great Mountains," "The Promise," and "The Leader of the People"—together show the progressive maturing of a young boy, Jody, and his relationship with members of his extended family from the time that he receives the red pony until he learns to come to terms with disappointment and mortality.

Since its publication, *The Red Pony* has become a kind of minor American classic of a boy's life on a storybook ranch at the westerly edge of our country. But in Steinbeck's work, illusions seldom prevail. The red pony dies, and the one planned to take its place survives birth only because its mother is sacrificed. Jody's grandfather makes the point explicit at the end of "The

Leader of the People." Jody says, "Maybe I could lead the people some day."
The old man answers: "No place to go. . . . But that's not the worst. . . .
Westering has died out of the people. Westering isn't a hunger anymore."
The old man could live only by sustaining his dream; but Jody has to face the
reality and live in it.

Warren French speculates that the reason Steinbeck's stature diminishes
after the publication of *The Grapes of Wrath* is that the author moved away
from California and, in his fiction, moved away from places and people that
he knew intimately. Steinbeck was thirty-seven when he published *The
Grapes of Wrath*. The year was 1939. World War II was with us, and Steinbeck's career took a dramatic change. Whatever the cause of his decline, he
was at the height of his powers when he published *The Long Valley*, and many
of the stories in that collection are set in Salinas Valley. Whether this means
he should be classified as a regionalist is questionable, however. It is true that
often he uses setting as an important element of a story, but for Steinbeck
setting is never so strong an element that it diminishes any other part of the
story.

Perhaps what must be said is that a really good short story cannot be at
the same time both good and regionalist because all aspects of a short story
by definition must blend. Consequently, setting as a single component cannot be allowed too much emphasis. It should be neither more nor less important than any other component but should function as all the other parts
function in relationship to the whole.

The Salinas Valley is important in "The Chrysanthemums," for example;
but the details of description that Steinbeck uses to open the story are cho-
sen not simply to render setting visible but to operate symbolically by establishing image patterns that will recur throughout the story and establish
meaning. Elisa is, like the valley, isolated and waiting. Her body is as closed
off by her bulky man's costume as the valley is shut off by the weather and
the mountains; a "closed pot" is Steinbeck's image. Waiting, she is dormant,
eager, easy to be aroused; when open, she is as vulnerable as the "broad level
land bit deep by the plows." Her house and immediate surroundings are no
match for her energies. She has made everything inside clean and neat, and
now she uses her strong fingers to care for her chrysanthemum garden and
her scissors to indicate her anger. Her husband, Henry, is a kind man, himself
ordered and logical, but unaware of his wife's needs. In fact, as he congratu-
lates her on the immense size of her flowers, he says, "I wish you'd work out
in the orchard and raise some apples that big." She responds eagerly, telling
him that she could; but he has not been serious in the offer and cannot
comprehend that she is serious in her response. Nor does he understand that

she is bored with the narrowness and rigidity of her life and yearns to be more closely attuned to the natural, including the sexual rhythms of life.

The traveling repairman seems to be immediately aware of Elisa's personality and needs, and like a con man skilled in playing on people's vulnerabilities, he manipulates her until, unaware of what she is doing, she reveals her desires for change and urgent sexual stirrings. She thinks the man understands her, but his concern is only to practice his trade, and the reader knows that he will forget her as soon as he leaves.

The repairman goes, but he leaves Elisa glowing, and without really being aware of what she is doing, she transforms herself into her estimate of what a woman ought to be—clean and soft, and clothed in pretty things with her face painted and her hair carefully combed. When Henry comes in, she will not allow him to see her until she is finished dressing. But Henry is simply confused. He tries to compliment her, but she won't accept the compliment until finally he admits his lack of understanding: "You're playing some kind of game." Henry's lack of appropriate response foreshadows Elisa's knowledge that the dark speck she sees on the road is the chrysanthemum she gave to the repairman; he threw away the flower but kept the pot.

The anger and frustration Elisa feels is directed in two ways. She asks for wine at dinner and wonders whether they should go to the fights where men bloody themselves in violence. In this way she attempts to escape self and identify herself with the masculine world. In another sense, she wants to bring violence upon the men who use her for their purposes, never realizing who she is or what she needs. In the end, she rejects the fights, turning the violence in upon herself and acting the role of the one who is beaten. She turns up her coat collar so that Henry can't see that she is crying "weakly— like an old woman."

In "The White Quail," symbols carry meaning and frustration levels create problems that can be solved only through violence. The woman, Mary, is afraid of the unknown which is couched in terms of the natural world. She tries to hold back the brush by planting fuchsias. Mary is compared with her husband, Harry, whose own need for security causes him to engage in what for him is the morally ambiguous practice of making loans to people during hard times. Husband and wife never really understand each other or speak directly in terms both can understand. Mary identifies herself with a white quail and Harry deliberately kills the bird, thinking he shouldn't have but saying to himself, "I'm so lonely."

One of the most powerful stories in the collection is "The Snake." The story is said to be based on a factual incident (a woman watching a male snake eat a rat), which Steinbeck professed not to understand. But whatever the meaning of the fact, the fiction Steinbeck created makes very good sense. The problem in interpretation seems to lie in a persistent effort to identify the snake solely with the woman, an identification that apparently doesn't work on the level of "psychological sex symbols," as young Dr. Phillips is himself aware. But what Phillips is *not* aware of is the precise manner in which his own actions, having to do with caging, feeding, and killing animals, and germinating seeds of living things, mirror the action of the snake and the rat. The snake kills the rat with a movement as precise as that of the doctor's slitting the throat of a cat he had previously killed by poison gas. During most of the evening, the doctor busies himself by feeding his caged animals. He has also fed himself in his own apartment where he, too, is penned as surely as any of the creatures he collects. The doctor has carefully set up a series of actions where he first sets into motion the process of germination in starfish and then in ten-minute sequences kills the results. The snake kills the rat and then, the throat crawling up and down in "peristaltic" movements clearly expressive of sexual intercourse, engulfs the rat slowly until nothing is left but an inch of pink tail. The action is clearly a reversal of the birthing process, even to the reversal of head and tail.

The young doctor believes that his actions are correct, that he is morally secure in his behavior because his actions are for the sake of science and are, therefore, to be admired. He is irritated, even angered, when the woman shows no interest in his actions. Only her eyes reveal that she has responded to his caging, killing, feeding, and artificially germinating sperm and egg.

A struggle of wills ensues. He does not want to put the rat in the cage, although he has done it many times before. He identifies rats with people and feels sorry for the rat: "Such a feeling had never come to him before." He becomes angry and turns on the woman, trying to humble her, but she will not release him: "Put in a rat." The action that follows parallels the movements of snake and rat with the movement of man and woman. Her body crouches and stiffens; he feels blood moving in his body, his veins throb. He says: "It's the most beautiful thing in the world. . . . It's the most terrible thing in the world." But his ecstasy turns suddenly to repulsion as he sees her weaving with the movement of the snake. "Perfect," he cries as the snake strikes; the woman relaxes "sleepily." Parallel actions continue through the eating of the rat until, the act done, the woman leaves, telling him she will be back. However, she doesn't return, and for months he finds himself searching for her. "But he never saw her again—ever."

"The Snake" concerns a classic battle of the sexes, where roles are established and then reversed again and again. It is also a retelling of the Eden story with the woman allowing entrance to Lucifer and the man, therefore, losing his innocence and being humbled and confused. (Why the woman calls on Dr. Phillips is never overtly established; nor are her motives that cause her to want to watch a male snake kill and eat a rat. Rather her motives seem deeply buried, appearing as "givens," acts a priori, but making immediate sense in context.) The man had meant to teach her a lesson; instead she provides him with an essential act defining existence.

In any good story, such an essential act recurs in endless variation, and the motifs describing it are repeated in such a way that there develops a harmony so intricate that no one part can be disentangled from the whole without damaging the whole, and no one part can be added without destroying the balance. There is nothing new in this concept; it's what Poe argued many years ago. But it is a concept perhaps helpful in a discussion of regionalism and the short story. If regionalism is defined in terms of its attention to locale, then setting takes on extraordinary importance. Now setting, that aspect of short fiction that anchors it in time and place (or, as in much contemporary fiction, in no-time and no-place) is an essential ingredient of a short story—as are, for example, character, plot (or no-plot), point of view, tone, and mood. When one of these elements becomes so dominant that we have a "character story," or a "plot story," or a "story of setting," what we get, in actual practice, is a lesser story. This may be why Katherine Mansfield railed agains the "plotty story" and Sherwood Anderson complained about "poison plots," and, maybe, why Ellen Glasgow didn't want to be called a regionalist. This explanation could also help us understand why great writers escape categories and why many critics want to say there are only bad stories and good ones which defy limiting categories and insist on taking larger proportions.

Mary Rohrberger

Oklahoma State University

Notes and References

INTRODUCTION

1. Quoted in Harvey Swados, ed., *The American Writer and the Great Depression* (Indianapolis: Bobbs-Merrill, 1966), p. xii.

2. Sherwood Anderson, *A Story Teller's Story* (Cleveland, Ohio: Press of Case Western Reserve University, 1968), p. 262.

3. Alan Spiegel, *Fiction and the Camera Eye: Visual Consciousness and the Modern Novel* (Charlottesville: University of Virginia Press, 1976), p. 101.

4. Frederick S. Hoffman, *Freudianism and the Literary Mind* (Baton Rouge: Louisiana State University Press, 1945), p. 244.

5. Raymond Chandler, Introduction to *The Simple Art of Murder*, quoted in E. M. Beckman, "Raymond Chandler and an American Genre," *Massachusetts Review* 14 (Winter 1973):152.

THE "LESSER" RENAISSANCE:
THE AMERICAN SHORT STORY IN THE 1920s

1. This essay is dedicated to Sherwood Anderson who made an art of honesty and compassion; and to Edward J. O'Brien, Blanche Colton Williams, and Martha Foley who sifted for the "best" in the American short story.

2. F. Scott Fitzgerald suggests the influence of advertisers. In a 1926 letter, he confessed, "It's become a sort of chore to me to write a short story having had to cook up so [many] tasteless morsels under the whip of the national advertisers." See *The Letters of F. Scott Fitzgerald*, ed. Andrew Turnbull (New York: Charles Scribner's Sons, 1963), pp. 206–7.

3. *Ring Around Max: The Correspondence of Ring Lardner & Max Perkins*, ed. Clifford M. Caruthers (DeKalb: Northern Illinois University Press, 1973), p. 11. Perkins also arranged Hemingway's *Men without Women* (1927): "His general procedure was to space the strongest pieces at the beginning, middle, and end, varying the rest of the contents by alternating stories of different qualities back to back." See A. Scott Berg, *Max Perkins: Editor of Genius* (New York: E. P. Dutton, 1978), p. 109.

4. Ronald Primeau, *Beyond Spoon River: The Legacy of Edgar Lee Masters* (Austin: University of Texas Press, 1981), p. 168.

5. *New York Evening Post Literary Review,* 11 April 1925, p. 12. Others were critical of O'Brien's annual volume. Fitzgerald considered it a "trash-album"; see *Letters of Fitzgerald,* p. 176.

6. *New York Evening Post Literary Review,* 9 May 1925, p. 14.

7. *Ernest Hemingway: Selected Letters, 1917–1961,* ed. Carlos Baker (New York: Charles Scribner's Sons, 1981), pp. 122–23.

8. Ibid., p. 82.

9. *The Short Stories of Ernest Hemingway: Critical Essays,* ed. Jackson J. Benson (Durham, N.C.: Duke University Press, 1975), p. xiii.

10. Enrique Hank Lopez, *Conversations with Katherine Anne Porter: Refugee from Indian Creek* (Boston: Little, Brown & Co., 1981), p. 210.

11. Jean Toomer, *Cane,* introduction by Darwin T. Turner (New York: Liveright, 1975), p. xxii.

THE AMERICAN SHORT STORY: 1930–1945

1. Gordon Taylor, "Voices from the Veil: Black American Autobiography," *Georgia Review* 35, no. 2 (1981).

2. Herbert Schneidan, "Style and Sacrament in Modernist Writing," *Georgia Review* 31 (1977).

3. James G. Watson, "Faulkner's Short Stories and the Making of Yoknapatawpha County," in *Fifty Years of Yoknapatawpha,* ed. Doreen Fowler and Ann J. Abadie (Jackson: University Press of Mississippi, 1980).

4. Flannery O'Connor, "Some Aspects of the Grotesque in Southern Fiction," in *Flannery O'Connor: Mystery and Manners: Occasional Prose,* ed. Sally and Robert Fitzgerald (New York: Farrar, Straus & Giroux, 1961).

5. Katherine Anne Porter, "The Situation of American Writing," *The Collected Essays and Occasional Writings of Katherine Anne Porter* (New York: Delacorte, 1970).

6. Eudora Welty, "Place in Fiction," in *The Eye of the Story* (New York: Random House, 1978).

7. Welty, "Is Phoenix Jackson's Grandson Really Dead?," in ibid.

THE QUESTION OF REGIONALISM: LIMITATION AND TRANSCENDENCE

1. Donald Davidson, "Regionalism and Nationalism in American Literature," *American Review* 5 (April 1935).

2. Allen Tate, "Regionalism and Sectionalism," *New Republic* 69 (23 December 1931).

3. A year earlier, he would have met Katherine Mansfield, who died at the institute and whose stories along with Joyce's were as important to the history of the short story in England as were Anderson's and Toomer's in the United States. When I was a student at the university studying the short story, I never once heard the

name of Jean Toomer, which is not surprising, considering that *Cane* went through two small editions and then, apparently, dropped from sight. I can remember the first time I encountered a Toomer story. It was in the late sixties when publishers were frantically trying to set into print fiction by black writers, and I was frantically trying to learn about an area I had never encountered in my schooling. I read "Karintha" which I found in an anthology of black literature. And then, astounded, I read it again. I felt cheated, angered. And though I realize that my professors didn't tell me about Toomer because they didn't know about Toomer, I still feel cheated, because I came to *Cane* so late.

2. Henry Seidel Canby, introduction to *Stories by Erskine Caldwell* (New York: Duell, Sloan, and Pearce, 1944), p. vii.

Selective Bibliography of Books of General Interest

Aldridge, John W. *After the Lost Generation: A Critical Study of the Writers of Two Wars.* New York: McGraw-Hill, 1951.

Allen, Walter. *The Short Story in English.* New York: Oxford University Press, 1981.

Bates, H. E. *The Modern Short Story: A Critical Survey.* London: T. Nelson & Sons, 1948.

Beja, Morris. *Epiphany in the Modern Novel.* Seattle: University of Washington Press, 1971.

Bryer, Jackson R., ed. *Sixteen Modern American Authors: A Survey of Research and Criticism.* Durham, N.C.: Duke University Press, 1973.

Canby, Henry S. *The Short Story in English.* New York: Holt, 1901, reprinted 1932.

Cowley, Malcolm, ed. *After the Genteel Tradition: American Writers, 1918–1930.* Rev. ed. Carbondale: Southern Illinois University Press, 1964.

————. *Exile's Return: A Literary Odyssey of the 1920's.* New ed. New York: Viking, 1951.

Current-Garcia, Eugene, and Walton Patrick. *What Is the Short Story?* Rev. ed. Chicago: Scott, Foresman, 1973.

Grabo, Carl H. *The Art of the Short Story.* New York: Scribner's, 1913.

Hicks, Granville. *The Great Tradition: An Interpretation of American Literature Since the Civil War.* Rev. Ed. New York: Macmillan, 1968.

Hilfer, Anthony C. *The Revolt from the Village, 1915–1930.* Chapel Hill: University of North Carolina Press, 1969.

Hills, Rust. *Writing in General and the Short Story in Particular.* Boston: Houghton Mifflin, 1977.

Hoffman, Frederick J. *Freudianism and the Literary Mind.* Baton Rouge: Louisiana State University Press, 1945.

————. *The Twenties: American Writing in the Postwar Decade.* 3d ed. New York: Viking, 1965.

Ingram, Forrest L. *Representative Short Story Cycles of the Twentieth Century: Studies in a Literary Genre.* The Hague: Mouton, 1971.

Jones, Howard M., and Richard M. Ludwig. *Guidle to American Literature and Its Backgrounds Since 1890.* 4th ed. Cambridge, Mass.: Harvard University Press, 1973.

Kazin, Alfred. *On Native Grounds.* New York: Reynal & Hitchcock, 1942.

Kempton, Kenneth Payson. *The Short Story.* Cambridge, Mass.: Harvard University Press, 1947.

Malin, Irvin, ed. *Psychoanalysis and American Fiction.* New York: Dutton, 1965.

O'Connor, Frank. *The Lonely Voice: A Study of the Short Story.* Cleveland: World Publishing Co., 1963.

O'Faolain, Sean. *The Short Story.* New York: Devin Adair, 1951.

Pattee, Fred Lewis. *The Development of the American Short Story.* New York: Harper & Row, 1923.

Peden, William. *The American Short Story: Front Line in the National Defense of Literature.* Boston: Houghton Mifflin, 1964.

Reid, Ian. *The Short Story.* London: Methuen, 1977.

Ross, Danforth. *The American Short Story.* Minneapolis: University of Minnesota Press, 1961.

Summers, Hollis, Ed. *Discussions of the Short Story.* Boston: Heath, 1963.

Thorp, Willard. *American Writing in the Twentieth Century.* Cambridge, Mass.: Harvard University Press, 1960.

Thurston, Jarvis et al. *Short Fiction Criticism: A Checklist of Interpretations Since 1925 of Stories and Novelettes (American, British, Continental), 1800–1958.* Denver: Alan Swallow, 1960.

Voss, Arthur. *The American Short Story: A Critical Survey.* Norman: University of Oklahoma Press, 1973.

Weixlmann, Joe. *American Short Fiction Criticism and Scholarship, 1959–1977. A Checklist.* Chicago: Alan Swallow / Ohio University Press, 1982.

West, Ray B., Jr. *The Short Story in America: 1900–1950.* Chicago: Regnery, 1952.

Woodress, James. *American Fiction, 1900–1950. A Guide to Information Sources.* Detroit: Gale, 1974.

Wright, Austin. *The American Short Story in the Twenties.* Chicago: University of Chicago Press, 1961.

The two essential works on magazine publication are:

Hoffman, Frederick J., Charles Allen, and Carolyn F. Ulrich. *The Little Magazine: A History and a Bibliography.* Princeton: Princeton University Press, 1946.

Peterson, Theodore. *Magazines in the Twentieth Century.* Urbana: University of Illinois Press, 1964.

The bibliography on genre fiction, by now quite large, was for many years mostly superficial and cultish. In recent years, however, a substantial body of sophisticated criticism has appeared of which the following works are a sample. All primarily address themselves to fiction of novel length, but their concepts are easily transferable to the short story.

Cawelti, John G. *Adventure, Mystery, and Romance: Formula Stories as Art and Popular Culture.* Chicago: University of Chicago Press, 1976.

Gurian, Jay. *Western American Writing: Tradition and Promise.* Deland, Fla.: Everett Edwards, 1975.

Haycraft, Howard. *Murder for Pleasure: The Life and Times of the Detective Story.* New York: Appleton-Century, 1941.

LeGuin, Ursula. *The Language of the Night: Essays in Fantasy and Science Fiction.* New York: Putnam, 1979.

Madden, David, ed. *Tough-Guy Writers of the Thirties.* Carbondale: Southern Illinois University Press,

Oriard, Michael. *Dreaming of Heroes: American Sports Fiction, 1868–1980.* Chicago: Nelson-Hall, 1982.

Porter, Dennis. *The Pursuit of Crime: Art and Ideology in Detective Fiction.* New Haven: Yale University Press, 1981.

Ruehlmann, William. *Saint with a Gun: The Unlawful American Private Eye.* New York: New York University Press, 1974.

Scholes, Robert, and Eric S. Rabkin. *Science Fiction: History, Science, Vision.* New York: Oxford University Press, 1977.

Wolfe, Gary K. *The Known and the Unknown: The Iconography of Science Fiction.* Kent, Ohio: Kent State University Press, 1979.

Selective Bibliography of
Articles of General Interest

Aycock, Wendell. "The American Short Story into Film, Once Again." *Studies in Short Fiction* 18 (1981):324–26.

Bader, A. L. "The Structure of the Modern Short Story." *College English* 7 (November 1945):86–92.

Baker, Howard. "The Contemporary Short Story." *Southern Review* 3 (1938):576–96.

Baldeshwiler, Eileen. "The Lyric Short Story: The Sketch of a History." *Studies in Short Fiction* 6 (1969):443–53.

Beck, Warren. "Art and Formula in the Short Story." *College English* 5 (November 1943):55–62.

———. "Conception and Technique." *College English* 11 (March 1950):308–17.

Boynton, Percy H. "American Authors of Today: The Short Story." *English Journal* 12 (May 1923):325–33.

Brickell, Herschel. "The Contemporary Short Story." *University of Kansas City Review* 15 (1949):267–70.

———. "What Happened to the Short Story?" *Atlantic Monthly* 188 (September 1951):74–76.

Canby, Henry S. "Free Fiction." *Atlantic Monthly* 116 (July 1915):60–68.

———. "On the Short Story." *Dial* 31 (16 October 1901):272–73.

Clarke, John H. "Transition in the American Negro Short Story." *Phylon* 21 (1960):360–66.

Colum, Mary M. "The American Short Story." *Dial* 62 (19 April 1917):345–47.

Cory, Herbert Ellsworth. "The Senility of the Short Story." *Dial* 62 (3 May 1917):379–81.

Eastman, Richard M. "The Open Parable: Demonstration and Definition." *College English* 22 (October 1960):15–18.

Elliott, George P. "A Defense of Fiction." *Hudson Review* 16 (1963):9–48.

Fitz Gerald, Gregory. "The Satiric Short Story: A Definition." *Studies in Short Fiction* 5 (1968):349–54.

Friedman, Norman. "What Makes a Short Story Short?" *Modern Fiction Studies* 5 (1958):103–17.

192   THE AMERICAN SHORT STORY 1900–1945: A CRITICAL HISTORY

Gerould, Katherine Fullerton. "The American Short Story." *Yale Review* 13 (1924):642–63.

Gullason, Thomas A. "Revelation and Evolution: A Neglected Dimension of the Short Story." *Studies in Short Fiction* 10 (1973):347–56.

―――. "The Short Story: An Underrated Art." *Studies in Short Fiction* 2 (1964):13–31.

Hartley, L. P. "In Defense of the Short Story." In *The Novelist's Responsibility*. London: Hamish Hamilton, 1967, pp. 157–59.

Lawrence, James Cooper. "A Theory of the Short Story." *North American Review* 205 (February 1917):274–86.

Marcus, Mordecai. "What Is an Initiation Story?" *Journal of Aesthetics and Art Criticism* 14 (1960):221–27.

May, Charles E. "The Unique Effect of the Short Story: A Reconsideration and an Example." *Studies in Short Fiction* 13 (1976):289–97.

Moffett, James. "Telling Stories: Methods of Abstraction in Fiction." *ETC* 21 (1964):425–50.

Munson, Gorham. "The Recapture of the Storyable." *University Review* 10 (1943):37–44.

Pattee, Fred Lewis. "The Present Stage of the Short Story." *English Journal* 12 (September 1923):439–49.

Peden, William. "The American Short Story During the Twenties." *Studies in Short Fiction* 10 (1973):367–71.

―――. "Esthetics of the Short Story." *Saturday Review* 36 (11 April 1953):43–44.

Pinsker, Sanford. "Speaking about Short Fiction: An Interview with Joyce Carol Oates." *Studies in Short Fiction* 18 (1981):239–43.

Pritchett, V. S. "Short Stories." *Harper's Bazaar* 87 (July 1953):31, 113.

Saroyan, William. "What Is a Story?" *Saturday Review* 11 (5 January 1935):409.

Smith, Julian. "Short Fiction on Film: A Selected Bibliography." *Studies in Short Fiction* 18 (1981):239–43.

Sojka, Gregory S. "The American Short Story into Film." *Studies in Short Fiction* 15 (1978):203–4.

Suckow, Ruth. "The Short Story." *Saturday Review* 4 (19 November 1927):317–18.

Stroud, Theodore A. "A Critical Approach to the Short Story." *Journal of General Education* 9 (1956):91–100.

Welty, Eudora. "The Reading and Writing of Short Stories." *Atlantic Monthly* 183 (February and March 1949):54–58, 46–49.

West, Ray B. "The American Short Story." In *The Writer in the Room* Detroit: Michigan State University Press, 1968, pp. 185–204.

―――. "The Modern Short Story and the Highest Forms of Art." *English Journal* 46 (December 1957):531–39.

Wharton, Edith. "Telling a Short Story." In *The Writing of Fiction*. New York: Scribner's, 1925, pp. 33–58.

Articles and Books by and
Devoted to Specific Authors

Conrad Aiken

The Collected Short Stories of Conrad Aiken. Cleveland: World Publishing Co., 1960.

Martin, Jay. *Conrad Aiken: A Life of His Art.* Princeton: Princeton University Press, 1962.
Tabachnick, Stephen E. "The Great Circle Voyage of Conrad Aiken's *Mr. Arcularis.*" *American Literature* 45 (1974):590–607.
Waterman, Arthur. "The Short Stories of Conrad Aiken." *Studies in Short Fiction* 16 (1979):19–31.

Sherwood Anderson

Sherwood Anderson: Short Stories, ed. Maxwell Geismar. New York: Hill & Wang, 1962.
Winesburg, Ohio, ed. Malcolm Cowley. New York: Viking, 1958.

Anderson, David D., ed. *Critical Essays on Sherwood Anderson.* Boston: G. K. Hall, 1981.
————. *Sherwood Anderson: Dimensions of His Literary Art.* East Lansing: Michigan State University Press, 1976.
Baldeshwiler, Eileen. "Sherwood Anderson and the Lyric Story." In *The Twenties: Fiction, Poetry, Drama.* Edited by Warren French. Deland, Fla.: Everett Edwards, 1975, pp. 65–74.
Ciancio, Ralph. "'The Sweetness of Twisted Apples'" Unity of Vision in *Winesburg, Ohio.*" *PLMA* 87 (1972):994–1006
Howe, Irving. *Sherwood Anderson.* Stanford, Calif.: Stanford University Press, 1951.
Rideout, Walter B., ed. *Sherwood Anderson: A Collection of Critical Essays.* Twentieth Century Views. New York: Prentice Hall, 1974.
Sutton, William A. *The Road to Winesburg: A Mosaic of the Imaginative Life of Sherwood Anderson.* Metuchen, N.J.: Scarecrow Press, 1972.
White, Ray Lewis, ed. *The Achievement of Sherwood Anderson.* Chapel Hill: University of North Carolina Press, 1966.
————. *Sherwood Anderson: A Reference Guide.* Boston: G. K. Hall, 1977.

Kay Boyle
Thirty Stories. New York: Simon & Schuster, 1946.

Carpenter, Richard C. "Kay Boyle." *College English* 15 (November 1953):81–87.

Erskine Caldwell
Complete Stories. Boston: Little, Brown, 1953.

Devlin, James E. *Erskine Caldwell.* Boston: Twayne , 1984.
MacDonald, Scott. *Critical Essays on Erskine Caldwell.* Boston: G. K. Hall, 1981.

Willa Cather
Willa Cather's Collected Short Fiction, 1892–1912. Lincoln: University of Nebraska Press, 1965.
Uncle Valentine and Other Stories: Willa Cather's Uncollected Short Fiction, 1915–1929. Lincoln: University of Nebraska Press, 1973.

Bloom, Edward A., and Lillian D. Bloom *Willa Cather's Gift of Sympathy.* Carbondale: Southern Illinois University Press, 1962.
Daiches, David. *Willa Cather: A Critical Introduction.* Ithaca, N.Y.: Cornell University Press, 1951.
Randall, John H., III. *The Landscape and the Looking Glass: Willa Cather's Search for Value.* Boston: Houghton Mifflin, 1960.
Schroetter, James, ed. *Willa Cather and Her Critics.* Ithaca, N.Y.: Cornell University Press, 1967.
Slote, Bernice, and Virginia Faulkner, eds. *The Art of Willa Cather.* Lincoln: University of Nebraska Press, 1974.
Stouck, David. *Willa Cather's Imagination.* Lincoln: University of Nebraska Press, 1975.

Theodore Dreiser
Free and Other Stories. New York: Boni & Liveright, 1918.

Griffin, Joseph. "Dreiser's Short Stories and Dreams of Success." *Etudes Anglaises* 31 (July/December 1978):294–302.
Hakuntani, Youshinabu. "The Making of Dreiser's Early Short Stories: The Philosopher as Artist." *Studies in American Fiction* 6 (1978):47–64.
Pizer, Donald. *Critical Essays on Theodore Dreiser.* Boston: G. K. Hall, 1981.
Warren, Robert Penn. *Homage to Theodore Dreiser.* New York: Random House, 1971.

James T. Farrell
An Omnibus of Short Stories. New York: Vanguard, 1967.
The Short Stories of James T. Farrell. New York: Vanguard, 1937.
When Boyhood Dreams Comes True. New York: Vanguard, 1946.

Branch, Edgar M. *James T. Farrell.* New York: Twayne, 1971.

William Faulkner
Collected Stories of William Faulkner. New York: Random House, 1950.
Uncollected Stories of William Faulkner. ed. Joseph Blotner. New York: Random House, 1979.

Beck, Warren *Faulkner.* Madison: University of Wisconsin Press, 1976.
Howe, Irving. *William Faulkner: A Critical Study.* New York: Random House, 1952.
Kinney, Arthur F. *Faulkner's Narrative Poetics: Style as Vision.* Amherst: University of Massachusetts Press, 1978.
Meriwether, James B. "Faulkner's Correspondence with *Scribner's Magazine.*" *Proof* 3 (1973):253–82.
Milgate, Michael. *The Achievement of William Faulkner.* Minneapolis: University of Minnesota Press, 1954.
O'Connor, William Van. *The Tangled Fire of William Faulkner.* Minneapolis: University of Minnesota Press, 1954.
Skei, Hans. *William Faulkner: The Short Story Career.* New York: Columbia University Press, 1981.
Wagner, Linda Welshimer, ed. *William Faulkner: Four Decades of Criticism.* East Lansing: Michigan State University Press, 1973.
Watson, James G. "Faulkner's Short Stories and the Making of Yoknapatawpha County." In *Fifty Years of Yoknapatawpha.* Edited by Doreen Fowler and Ann J. Abadie. Jackson: University Press of Mississippi, 1980.

F. Scott Fitzgerald
All the Sad Young Men. New York: Scribner's, 1926.
Flappers and Philosophers. New York: Scribner's, 1920.
The Price Was High: The Last Uncollected Stories of F. Scott Fitzgerald. Edited by Matthew J. Bruccoli. New York: Harcourt Brace Jovanovich / Bruccoli Clark, 1979.
Six Tales of the Jazz Age and Other Stories. New York: Scribner's, 1960.

Higgins, John A. *F. Scott Fitzgerald: A Study of the Stories.* Jamaica, N.Y.: St. John's University Press, 1971.
Miller, James E. *F. Scott Fitzgerald: His Art and His Technique.* The Hague: Martinus Nijhoff, 1957.
Perosa, Sergio. *The Art of F. Scott Fitzgerald.* Ann Arbor: University of Michigan Press, 1965.
Piper, Henry Dan. *F. Scott Fitzgerald: A Critical Portrait.* New York: Holt, Rinehart & Winston, 1965.
Sklar, Robert. *F. Scott Fitzgerald: The Last Laocoon.* New York: Oxford University Press, 1967.

Ellen Glasgow
The Collected Stories of Ellen Glasgow. Edited by Richard K. Meeker. Baton Rouge: Louisiana State University Press, 1963.

Rouse, Blair. *Ellen Glasgow.* New York: Twayne, 1962.

Caroline Gordon
The Collected Stories of Caroline Gordon. Introduction by Robert Penn Warren. New York: Farrar, Straus and Giroux, 1981.
The Forest of the South. New York: Scribner, 1945.

Landess, Thomas H., ed. *The Short Fiction of Caroline Gordon: A Critical Symposium.* Dallas: University of Dallas Press, 1972.
Stuckey, William. *Caroline Gordon.* New York: Twayne, 1972.

Ernest Hemingway
In Our Time. New York: Scribner's, 1925.
Men without Women. New York: Scribner's, 1927.
The Short Stories of Ernest Hemingway. New York: Scribner's, 1954.
Winner Take Nothing. New York: Scribner's, 1933.

Baker, Carlos. *Ernest Hemingway: The Writer as Artist.* Princeton, N.J.: Princeton University Press, 1952.
Baker, Carlos, ed. *Hemingway and His Critics: An International Anthology.* New York: Hill & Wang, 1961.
Benson, Jackson J. *The Short Stories of Ernest Hemingway: Critical Essays.* Durham, N.C.: Duke University Press, 1975.
————. *Hemingway: The Writer's Art of Self-Defense.* Minneapolis: University of Minnesota Press, 1969.
De Falco, Joseph. *The Hero in Hemingway's Short Stories.* Pittsburgh: University of Pittsburgh Press, 1963.
Howell, John M., ed. *Hemingway's African Stories: The Stories, Their Sources, Their Critics.* New York: Scribner's, 1969.
Shelton, Frank W. "The Family in Hemingway's Nick Adams Stories." *Studies in Short Fiction* 11 (1974):303–5.
Smith, Julian. "Hemingway and the Thing Left Out." *Journal of Modern Literature* 1 (1970):169–82.
Stein, William Bysshe. "Love and Lust in Hemingway's Short Stories." *Texas Studies in Literature* 3 (1961):234–42.
Wagner, Linda W., ed. *Ernest Hemingway: Five Decades of Criticism.* East Lansing: Michigan State University Press, 1974.
Young, Philip. *Ernest Hemingway: A Reconsideration.* University Park, Pa.; Pennsylvania State University Press, 1966.

Langston Hughes
The Ways of White Folks. New York: Knopf, 1947.

Kearns, Francis E. "The Un-Angry Langston Hughes." *Yale Review* 60 (1970):154–60.
Emmanuel, James A. *Langston Hughes.* New York: Twayne, 1969.
Presley, James. "The American Dream of Langston Hughes." *Southwest Review* 48 (1963):380–86.

Henry James
The Complete Tales of Henry James. 12 vols. Edited by Leon Edel. Philadelphia: Lippincott, 1961–64.
The Art of the Novel: Critical Prefaces by Henry James. Edited by R. P. Blackmur. New York: Scribner's, 1934.

Dupee, F. W., ed. *The Question of Henry James.* New York: Holt, 1945.
Chatman, Seymour. *The Later Style of Henry James.* New York: Barnes & Noble, 1972.
Edel, Leon, ed. *Henry James: A Collection of Critical Essays.* Englewood Cliffs, N.J.: Prentice Hall, 1965.
Krook, Dorothea. *The Ordeal of Consciousness in Henry James.* New York: Cambridge University Press, 1962.
Putt, S. Gorley. *Henry James: A Reader's Guide.* Ithaca, N.Y.: Cornell University Press, 1966.
Stowell, H. Peter. *Literary Impressionism, James and Chekhov.* Athens: University of Georgia Press, 1980.
Ward, J. A. *The Search for Form: Studies in the Structure of James's Fiction.* Chapel Hill, N.C.: University of North Carolina Press, 1967.

Ring Lardner
How to Write Short Stories. New York: Scribner's, 1924.
The Love Nest and Other Stories. New York: Scribner's, 1926.
Round Up: The Stories of Ring W. Lardner. New York: Scribner's, 1929.

Hasley, Louis. "Ring Lardner: The Ashes of Idealism." *Arizona Quarterly* 26 (1970):219–32.
Ingram, Forrest L. "Fun at the Incineration Plant: Lardner's Wry Waste Land." In *The Twenties: Fiction, Poetry, Drama.* Edited by Warren French. Deland, Fla.: Everett Edwards, 1975, pp. 111–12.
Spatz, Jonas. "Ring Lardner: Not an Escape But a Reflection." In *The Twenties: Fiction, Poetry, Drama.* Edited by Warren French. Deland, Fla.: Everett Edwards, 1975, pp. 101–10.
Phelps, Donald. "Shut Up, He Explained." *Shenandoah* 29 (1978):84–100.
Webb, Howard. "The Development of a Style: The Lardner Idiom." *American Quarterly* 12 (1960):482–92.

Sinclair Lewis

Selected Short Stories. Garden City, N.Y.: Doubleday, Doran, 1935.

Dooley, D. J. *The Art of Sinclair Lewis.* Lincoln: University of Nebraska Press, 1967.

Jack London

Jack London's Tales of Adventure. Edited by Irving Shephard. Garden City, N.Y.: Hanover House, 1956.

Henricks, King. *Jack London: Master Craftsman of the Short Story.* Logan: Utah State University, 1966.
Labor, Earle. *Jack London.* New York: Twayne, 1974.
May, Charles E. "'To Build a Fire': Physical Fiction and Metaphysical Critics." *Studies in Short Fiction* 15 (1978):19–24.

William March

Trial Balance: The Collected Short Stories. New York: Harcourt Brace, 1945.

John O'Hara

Here's O'Hara. Cleveland: World Publishing Co., 1946.
The O'Hara Generation. New York: Random House, 1969.

Grebstein, Sheldon Norman. *John O'Hara.* New York: Twayne, 1966.

Dorothy Parker

Here Lies: The Collected Stories of Dorothy Parker. New York: Viking, 1939.
The Portable Dorothy Parker. New York: Viking, 1973

Gray, James. *On Second Thought.* Minneapolis: University of Minnesota Press, 1946.
Kinney, Arthur F. *Dorothy Parker.* New York: Twayne, 1978.
Labrie, Ross. "Dorothy Parker Revisited." *Canadian Review of American Studies* 7 (1976):48–56.

Katherine Anne Porter

The Collected Stories of Katherine Anne Porter. New York: Harcourt, Brace & World, 1965.
Essays and Occasional Writings. New York: Delacorte, 1970.

Emmons, Winifred S. *Katherine Anne Porter: The Regional Stories.* Austin, Texas: Steck-Vaughn Co., 1967.
Liberman, M. M. *Katherine Anne Porter's Fiction.* Detroit: Wayne State University Press, 1971.
Lopez, Enrique Hank. *Conversations with Katherine Anne Porter.* Boston: Little, Brown, 1981.
Nance, William L. *Katherine Anne Porter and the Art of Rejection.* Chapel Hill: University of North Carolina Press, 1964.

Poss, S. H. "Variations on a Theme in Four Stories of Katherine Anne Porter." *Twentieth Century Literature* 4 (April-July 1958):21–29.

Thompson, Barbara. "Katherine Anne Porter: An Interview." *Paris Review* 29 (Winter-Spring 1963):87–114.

Warren, Robert Penn., ed. *Katherine Anne Porter.* Englewood Cliffs, N.J.: Prentice-Hall, 1980.

William Saroyan

The Daring Young Man on the Flying Trapeze. New York: Modern Library, 1934.

Floan, Howard Russell. *William Saroyan.* New York: Twayne, 1966.

Wilbur Daniel Steele

The Man Who Saw through Heaven and Other Stories. New York: Harper, 1927.
The Best Stories of Wilbur Daniel Steele. Garden City, N.Y.: Doubleday, Doran, 1945.

Bucco, Martin. *Wilbur Daniel Steele.* New York: Twayne, 1972.

John Steinbeck

The Long Valley. Garden City, N.Y.: Sun Dial Press, 1941.

Davis, Robert Murray, ed. *Steinbeck: A Collection of Critical Essays.* Englewood Cliffs, N.J.: Prentice-Hall, 1972.

French, Warren. *John Steinbeck.* Boston: Twayne, 1975.

Fontenrose, Joseph. *John Steinbeck: An Introduction and Interpretation.* New York: Barnes & Noble, 1963.

Lisca, John. *Steinbeck: Nature and Myth.* New York: Crowell, 1978.

Watt, Frank W. *John Steinbeck.* New York: Grove Press, 1962.

Jesse Stuart

Tales from the Plum Grove Hills. New York: Dutton, 1946.
A Jesse Stuart Reader. New York: McGraw HIll, 1963.

Foster, Ruel E. *Jesse Stuart.* New York: Twayne, 1969.

Ruth Suckow

Iowa Interiors. New York: Knopf, 1926.

Kissane, Leadice McAnally. *Ruth Suckow.* New York: Twayne, 1969.

James Thurber

The Beast in Me and Other Animals. New York: Harcourt, Brace, 1948.

Elias, Robert. "James Thurber: The Primitive, the Innocent, and the Individual." *American Scholar* 27 (1958):361–62.

Holmes, Charles S. *The Clocks of Columbus: The Literary Career of James Thurber.* New York: Athenaeum, 1972.
Morsberger, Robert E. *James Thurber.* New York: Twayne, 1964.
Tobias, Richard C. *The Art of James Thurber.* Athens: Ohio University Press, 1970.

Jean Toomer
Cane. New York: Boni & Liveright, 1923.

Benson, Brian Joseph, and Mabel Mayle Dillard. *Jean Toomer.* Boston: Twayne, 1980.
Bone, Robert. *The Negro Novel in America.* 2d ed. New Haven: Yale University Press, 1965.
Jackson, Blyden. "Jean Toomer's *Cane:* An Issue of Genre." In *The Twenties: Fiction, Poetry, Drama.* Edited by Warren French. Deland, Fla: Everett Edwards, 1975, pp. 317–34.
Reilly, John M. "The Search for Black Redemption: Jean Toomer's *Cane.*" *Studies in the Novel* 2 (1970):312–24.

Eudora Welty
A Curtain of Green. Garden City, N.Y.: Doubleday, Doran, 1941.
The Wide Net and Other Stories. New York: Harcourt, Brace, 1943.
The Eye of the Story: Selected Essays and Reviews. New York: Random House, 1978.

Appel, Alfred. *A Season of Dreams: The Fiction of Eudora Welty.* Baton Rouge: Louisiana State University Press, 1965.
Prenshaw, Peggy Whitman. *Eudora Welty: Critical Essays.* Jackson: University Press of Mississippi, 1979.

Edith Wharton
The Collected Stories of Edith Wharton. 2 vols. Edited by R. W. B. Lewis. New York: Scribner's, 1968.

Howe, Irving. *Edith Wharton: A Collection of Critical Essays.* Englewood Cliffs, N.J.: Prentice-Hall, 1962.
Navius, Blake. *Edith Wharton.* Berkeley: University of California Press, 1953.
Wolff, Cynthia Griffin. *A Feast of Words: The Triumph of Edith Wharton.* New York: Oxford University Press, 1977.

William Carlos Williams
"A Beginning on the Short Story (Notes)." In *Selected Essays of William Carlos Williams.* New York: Random House, 1954.
The Knife of the Times. Ithaca, N.Y.: Dragon Press, 1932.
Life along the Passaic River. Norfolk, Conn.: New Directions, 1938.
Make It Light: Collected Stories: William Carlos Williams. New York: Random House, 1950.

Thomas Wolfe
From Death to Morning. New York: Scribner's, 1935.
The Hills Beyond. New York: Harper, 1941.

Kennedy, Richard S. *The Window of Memory: The Literary Career of Thomas Wolfe.* Chapel Hill: University of North Carolina Press, 1962.
McElderry, B. R. *Thomas Wolfe.* New York. Twayne, 1964.

Richard Wright
Uncle Tom's Children: Five Long Stories. New York: Harper, 1938.
Eight Men. Cleveland: World, 1961.

Bone, Robert A. *The Negro Novel in America.* 2d ed. New Haven: Yale University Press, 1965.
Brignano, Russell Carl. *Richard Wright: An Introduction to the Man and His Works.* Pittsburgh: University of Pittsburgh Press, 1970.
Burgum, Edwin Berry. "The Art of Richard Wright's Short Stories." *Quarterly Review of Literature* 1 (1944):198–211.
Hakutani, Yoshinobu. *Critical Essays on Richard Wright.* Boston: G. K. Hall, 1982.
Margolies, Edward. *The Art of Richard Wright.* Carbondale: Southern Illinois University Press, 1969.
Rubin, Steven J. "The Early Short Fiction of Richard Wright Reconsidered." *Studies in Short Fiction* 15 (1978):405–10.

Index